IREK
MUKHAMEDOV

IREK MUKHAMEDOV

THE AUTHORISED BIOGRAPHY

Jeffery Taylor

With a Foreword by
Dame Ninette de Valois, DBE

FOURTH ESTATE · *London*

First published in Great Britain in 1994 by
Fourth Estate Limited
289 Westbourne Grove
London W11 2QA

A catalogue record for this book is available from the British Library.

ISBN 1–85702–074–X

Typeset by York House Typographic Ltd
Printed in Great Britain by The Bath Press Ltd

Contents

List of Illustrations

Kazan: first steps
Matyanova's star pupil
First day at the Moscow Ballet School, 1970
Final-year barre work, 1978
Final-year barre work, 1978
Graduation examination, 1978
Class concert, 1977
Graduation performance, 1978
The class of '78 (courtesy Alexander Prokofiev)
Mukhamedov with Natalia Stavro in the 'Carnival in Venice' pas de deux
The Fourth Moscow International Competition, 1981: in the 'Diana and Acteon' pas de deux (copyright G. F. Soloviev)
First round: with Galina Krapivina in the *Le Corsaire* pas de deux
Third round: with Galina Krapivina in the *Don Quixote* pas de deux
Mukhamedov receives his prize from Yuri Grigorovich
Third round: in a variation from the *Don Quixote* pas de deux (copyright G. F. Soloviev)
Mukhamedov in his début in *Spartacus*, 1981 (courtesy Bolshoi Theatre Museum, copyright G. F. Soloviev)
With Natalia Bessmertnova in *Spartacus* (copyright Kristyna Kashvili)
Mukhamedov and Yuri Grigorovich (copyright A. Makarova)
Bessmertnova, Mukhamedov and Grigorovich rehearsing *The Golden Age*
First night of *The Golden Age*
As Boris in *The Golden Age*
With Ljudmilla Semenyaka in *Ivan the Terrible* (courtesy Bolshoi Theatre Museum)
Mukhamedov with Nadezhda Pavlova in his last performance of *Spartacus*, 1990 (copyright Kristyna Kashvili)
Masha and Mukhamedov with his family, Kazan, 1990 (copyright V. Zotova)
Mukhamedov with Darcey Bussell in the 'Farewell' pas de deux, 1990 (copyright Kristyna Kashvili)
Mukhamedov and Kenneth MacMillan (courtesy Tamara Finch)
Mukhamedov and friends at the Royal Opera House, 1991 (courtesy Tamara Finch)
Mukhamedov as Des Grieux in *Manon* (copyright Leslie Spatt)

Mukhamedov with Viviana Durante in *Manon* (copyright Kristyna Kashvili)

Mukhamedov, Masha and Sasha (courtesy Vanya Kewley)

Mukhamedov and Sasha at home (copyright Kristyna Kashvili)

Mukhamedov with Lesley Collier in *La Fille mal gardée*, 1991 (copyright Leslie Spatt)

Mukhamedov with Viviana Durante in *Giselle*, 1992 (copyright Leslie Spatt)

Mukhamedov as Albrecht in *Giselle* (copyright Robbie Jack)

Mukhamedov as the Foreman in *The Judas Tree*, 1992 (copyright Bill Cooper)

Mukhamedov in the 'Diana and Acteon' pas de deux, 1992 (copyright Kristyna Kashvili)

Mukhamedov as Rudolf in *Mayerling*, 1992 (copyright Leslie Spatt)

Mukhamedov and Masha after the death of Kenneth MacMillan (courtesy *Mail on Sunday*)

Mukhamedov in the title role of *Apollo*, 1993 (copyright Leslie Spatt)

Mukhamedov with Lesley Collier in *The Sleeping Beauty*, 1993 (copyright Leslie Spatt)

Mukhamedov in the title role of *The Prodigal Son*, 1993 (copyright Sasha Gusov)

En famille in London, 1992 (courtesy Keith Waldegrave/*Mail on Sunday*)

Foreword

IREK MUKHAMEDOV IS one of the great names in ballet today, a superb dancer and actor and a wonderful example of the great Russian technical tradition. I take it as the greatest compliment he could pay us when he left his native country and came to us, one of the smallest and newest ballet companies in Europe. He came not as a distinguished visitor; he came to learn.

His presence in the Royal Ballet is a marvellous tonic for the company, his different style and schooling an example to everyone, particularly the men. He is a charming man, quite unspoilt, with a natural, healthy humility, and makes no attempt to hide his need to learn. The Royal Ballet repertoire, with the richness and variety of its choreography, represented a challenge to Mukhamedov and he has enriched it with consummate skill and artistry and by so doing has broadened our perception of classicism.

I welcome this interchange between nations. Without it we all stultify.

Dame Ninette de Valois, DBE, founder of the Royal Ballet

Acknowledgements

FIRST OF ALL I must say what a pleasure it has been to work with Irek and Masha Mukhamedov, whose co-operation went far beyond the call of duty. Masha coped with Sasha, made endless pots of tea and unstintingly gave me the benefit of her almost encyclopedic memory. Irek entered into the spirit of the interviews with the gusto and humour that makes him one of the most likeable of men, and working with him was a delight.

May I also thank the following: artist Robert Heindel for his permission to use the sketch of Irek on the title page; Keith Waldegrave, staff photographer of the *Mail on Sunday*, for his generous help and first-class work; Adam Edwards, editor of the *ES Magazine*, for introducing me to Fourth Estate; Audrey Stubbs; Sharon Greening; the Bolshoi Theatre Museum; the Moscow Classical Ballet; the Royal Ballet Press Office; Gurmail Dhaliwal, of the *Mail on Sunday* systems department, for saving my computer, and my life, on at least two occasions; Paula Johnson, books editor of the *Mail on Sunday*, for words of encouragement when I most needed them; all the many kind people who have given so generously of their time to talk to me about Irek both in this country and in Russia; and Jane Carr, my editor at Fourth Estate, for her patience, understanding and remarkably incisive editing skills.

I regret that Mukhamedov's first wife, Ljudmilla Kudriavtseva, declined my invitation to contribute to this biography.

My particular gratitude goes to Julia Matheson, my researcher, who has transcribed hundreds of taped interviews with a rare accuracy and endured my incessant pestering as though she enjoyed it. Julia has cheerfully lifted innumerable loads from my shoulders and her knowledge and experience have made an invaluable contribution to this book.

Finally, my heartfelt thanks go to my wife, the teacher and former dancer Joanna Denise, without whose co-operation and support the project would have been impossible. Not only has she endured almost two years of domestic upheaval with the patience of a saint, but she has proofread, advised and counselled with common sense and impeccable taste. It was her love of ballet that inspired me as a dancer, and I hope some of that feeling has found its way on to these pages.

Introduction

RUMOURS COMING OUT of Russia in the early 1980s centred on a sensational young man with an unpronounceable name. Visitors to Moscow returned to London talking of the Bolshoi Ballet's latest phenomenon: a true successor to Vasiliev and Lavrovsky, they said, a natural inheritor of the title 'the world's greatest male dancer' after Nureyev and Baryshnikov.

Irek Mukhamedov danced in Britain for the first time in July 1986 and surpassed all expectations. His performances in *Ivan the Terrible, The Golden Age* and, particularly, in *Spartacus* were a revelation. London was at his feet. And still is. Mukhamedov is now the principal male dancer with Britain's Royal Ballet, his performances sell out before the advance postal booking period expires, he is as valuable an asset to the Royal Opera House as Rudolf Nureyev was in the 1960s and he is in demand, as was Nureyev, as a guest artist all over the world. But there the similarity with his fellow Tartar ends.

Mukhamedov is a permanent member of the Royal Ballet company, not an occasional, if spectacular, visitor. In Russia he epitomised the Soviet style of dancing, combining an athletic technique with an heroic panache that was breathtaking in its impact. But in the West he is not an exotic transplant, imposing the Bolshoi approach on the British style. Mukhamedov was determined to dance western choreography on its own terms, not his. A glimpse of the struggle that entailed was given in the BBC *Omnibus* programme, produced by Julia Matheson, in November 1991, when Mukhamedov was filmed rehearsing for his début in his first full-length western ballet in Britain, Kenneth MacMillan's *Manon*.

The leading male role of Des Grieux was created in 1974 for Anthony Dowell, now artistic director of the Royal Ballet, a dancer of remarkable gifts, with his high extensions, precise technique and flowing, lyrical *ports de bras*. Many experts in London felt that

1

Mukhamedov could never transfer his muscular and overtly masculine attack, not to mention his soaring jump, to MacMillan's tightly
crafted choreography. They were wrong. Indeed, Mukhamedov is
now acknowledged as one of the finest exponents of MacMillan's
work, having scored his greatest successes in *Manon, Mayerling* and
Romeo and Juliet, and given an extraordinarily powerful performance
as the Foreman in *The Judas Tree*, created for him in 1992, shortly
before MacMillan's death.

But it is in his personal life that the contrast between Mukhamedov
and Nureyev is the most compelling. Nureyev pursued a hectic,
hedonistic lifestyle across two continents and compensated for the
loss of his beloved Russia with an appetite for material possessions,
which included six homes, two private islands and a priceless
collection of artefacts. Mukhamedov now lives with his second wife,
Masha, and his daughter Sasha, born in August 1990, in a house in
west London. He is never happier than when he is preparing
breakfast for his daughter and driving her to nursery school before
his morning class. His favourite recreation is spending the evening at
home watching cartoon videos with Sasha or, better still, lying on
the sofa with a glass of wine watching his wife and daughter play. To
those who know him, Irek Mukhamedov appears perfectly at home
in a foreign culture, a devoted family man and a great and popular
artist – in other words, as complete a human being as anyone might
hope to be. But, like most success stories, it was not as easy as all that.

Until today only he and Masha know how perilously close they
came to losing it all, how the success of Mukhamedov the dancer
masked a personal conflict that nearly destroyed the man. Had it not
been for a pivotal crisis of conscience that he grappled with, and
overcame, at the peak of his career, supported by Masha's love, none
of it might have happened.

1

Kazan

Irek Djavdatovich Mukhamedov is both the victor and the victim of a political ideology. It is unlikely, had he been born in any other place, at any other time, that his innate and insatiable desire to succeed would have flourished quite so vigorously. The price he paid was an emotional atrophy that created a chasm between his professional achievements and personal maturity that all but ruined him.

He was born on 8 March 1960 in Kazan, capital of the Tatar Autonomous Soviet Socialist Republic, a town where, outsiders say, nothing ever happens, and where the only invitations for the local football team to play away come from the wastes of Siberia. Although the town has a thriving opera house, which supports both opera and ballet companies, as well as popular art galleries and museums, Kazan is given a wide berth by cultural and political leaders alike, and is generally dismissed as a cultural desert, a provincial backwater. According to Mukhamedov, this is a harsh point of view.

But Kazan was, in 1960, the archetype of Communist middle Russia. The city claims the doubtful honour of being among the first to embrace Communism in 1917. St Petersburg fell to the Bolsheviks on 17 October, Moscow on the 18th, Kazan on the 19th. And Communism worked in Kazan. Khrushchev was in power in Moscow – the world trembled in 1960 when he rattled his missiles for the first time in the May Day parade in Red Square – Lenin was still the Soviet saviour and the shops in Kazan had full shelves.

The Soviet economy was entering its final and fatal stages of stagnation, but the discovery earlier that year of vast Siberian gas reserves meant a boom time for Kazan, with its huge new port and already established road and rail links. Great concrete apartment blocks mushroomed throughout the city and, although a few essential foodstuffs were rationed, no one went without. Russian

3

living standards were reported by the United Nations to be rising, the Soviet Union ruled half the world and the trains and trams ran on time. The Communist myth was intact. Disarmament talks were in progress in Geneva, and Khrushchev felt secure enough, in response to Harold Macmillan's 'wind of change' speech, to announce arms reductions in the USSR; the savings were to go towards the nation's health. And there was no reason for honest, hard-working Soviet citizens to disbelieve him. There was no doubt that the likes of Irek Mukhamedov's parents had complete faith in their leader.

Rasheda and Djavdat Mukhamedov, who were both born in 1926, belonged to that middle generation of seventy-three years of Communist rule who knew of no other social structure. They were old enough to have experienced the 'Dunkirk Effect' of the Great Patriotic War that pulled together a staggering 250 million people of sixteen federated states and justified the Bolshevik chauvinistic dogma – and too young to know of life before Lenin. They accepted the stifling Communist propaganda machine without question. Rasheda and Djavdat were model Soviet citizens, lifelong party members, patriotic and industrious – in short, the bedrock of tyranny. And they reared their sons, Irek and his elder brother Nail Djavdatovich (born in March five years before Irek), to inherit what they saw as the only honourable way of life.

When Irek was twelve months old, the Mukhamedovs moved into Flat 57, 61 Gagarin Street, a self-contained, two-room apartment with the luxury of its own bathroom and kitchen, the only home Irek was to know until he left for the Moscow Ballet School nine years later. Djavdat Mukhamedov did his duty by his family and government as a state gas company supervisor, a conscientious worker who was as honest as they came; Rasheda, a primary school teacher, is still a well-known figure on the streets of Kazan.

There were no material shortages in Flat 57. Djavdat was a popular man with a famous sense of humour, and the customary gifts from his colleagues as he toured the area's gas installations were more than usually generous. The Russian custom of giving presents with the least excuse often smacks of bribery to western tastes, especially when the exchange is between an employee and his superior. But the custom is rooted in the innate generosity of the Russian character and, in the same way as the complexities of the Japanese bow cannot be fathomed by a foreigner, only a native can truly appreciate the social resonances of the Russian gift. So Djavdat secured a regular supply of fresh eggs, meat and fruit and vegetables and both his sons grew up with scarcely a day's illness between them. It was Rasheda who made sure that the family's morals were as healthy.

All human beings, particularly little boys, are born lazy, she reckoned, and prone to bad behaviour. Her remedy was simple: her boys would work hard, and play hard, leaving no time, or energy, for the devil's work. This time-honoured solution was, for the young Irek, a spectacular success, at least in early life. Luckily for him, and for us, the serious-minded Rasheda also loved classical music and served a relentless diet of it to her family.

The flat radio was usually tuned to the classical station, the television set switched on for concerts, and the record player stood in when necessary. Irek Mukhamedov has been described by British choreographer David Bintley as one of the most musical dancers he has ever worked with. Little did Rasheda imagine, as she tuned her Bakelite wireless in Gagarin Street, that her younger son would receive such a compliment thirty years later on the other side of the world.

Privacy is a luxury for a family of four in a two-room flat whose living-rooms double as bedrooms, and the cramped accommodation was soon to be stretched to the limit by the arrival of the boys' blind maternal grandmother. The brothers grew up in a communal atmosphere that bred confidence in the younger and sowed seeds of dissatisfaction in the elder. Irek found a life of mutual dependence a perfectly natural medium for growth. When Irek was five years old, Rasheda had him admitted to hospital with a stubborn bout of flu, his only serious childhood ailment. She returned the next morning to check on her son. 'Can you hear the noise upstairs?' she was asked by the nurses. 'That's how ill he is.' Rasheda discovered Irek on a first-floor landing, surrounded by a group of patients, dancing out his infant interpretation of a popular song.

From then on Irek scarcely stood a chance. He was enrolled into gymnastic and ice-skating classes. 'My mother had no clear intention of encouraging me to dance at that time,' he remembers. 'She knew, though, that she wanted me to share her love of music.' In the dance-oriented Soviet Union most physical disciplines started with a ballet warm-up, and at five Irek learned his first plié.

The Mukhamedov brothers were reared on the virtues of competition, discipline and consideration for others. Irek found no problem with this. As with many great artists, there is a simplistic streak in his nature, an unquestioning acceptance of the world around him. Some call it clear-sighted, others naïve. The world surrounding Irek in 1965 was Flat 57, Gagarin Street, and he naturally absorbed his parents' credo and grew intensely competit-ive, rigorously self-disciplined and considerate. These attributes served him well in the narrow, intense and short-lived world of a ballet dancer, but they left no room for natural curiosity or healthy rebellion. It was an inheritance that ultimately became a strait-jacket.

Irek Mukhamedov cannot recall a time in his life when winning was not the only point. If he competes, he must win, a maxim learned on his mother's knee. His childish tears were shed not only when his self-will was frustrated, but when he came second or, even worse, third in any of his sporting activities. There were quite a number of them – gymnastics, skiing, volleyball and football – but it was Irek's ice-skating, particularly ice-dancing, that persuaded Rasheda to involve her younger son in more esoteric pursuits.

Kazan's ice-rink is housed in the Lenin Stadium, built in the shape of a grotesque flying saucer to celebrate Soviet achievements in space. Three times a week Irek would travel, usually alone, the few stops on the trolley-bus between Gagarin Street and the stadium. First the children would be given a simple ballet warm-up, a few demi-pliés, tendus and some small jumps, then they went on to the ice. The technical challenges were satisfying enough, but that session took place in silence; what truly captured Irek's imagination was the free dancing, improvised to music.

Rasheda and the rest of the family were, by chance, present when Irek's group was being put through its paces. Each child demon-strated his or her mastery of the simple steps, then danced to a record played by the instructor. Irek finished his dance, on a long, last chord, holding a position that made him feel like a gliding bird; his arms were outstretched, his legs in the nearest he had yet come to an arabesque.

He launched himself across the ice, as adventurously as his young muscles allowed, lost in the thrill of his own daring. The music stopped. He had not finished, so he threw another of his by now regular tantrums. But they were not just tears of temper. Something else was lurking in the background. Surges of a power that he could neither understand nor control were confusing him. And it happened when he moved to music.

Rasheda saw it and recognised that Irek's involvement with music must go deeper. National folk-dancing clubs abounded in the USSR, supported and controlled by the Young Pioneer section of the Communist Party. They concentrated almost solely on Russian dances, and were an integral part of the Soviet drive for Russian hegemony. Irek already attended the best known of these in the town, run by an ex-dancer, Veronika Matyanova. When Rasheda discussed with her the affinity with music and movement Irek showed on the ice, Matyanova said that it was now time to choose between ice-dancing and the real thing, and in her opinion Irek should concentrate on ballet. Rasheda agreed and started him on a path that would transform the enthusiasm of a wobbly child teetering across the ice into high art.

Even today Mukhamedov feels guilty when his energies are not engaged in mental or physical endeavour. He absorbed with his mother's milk his parents' profound belief in the abstract concepts of Communism, never doubting that it was the individual's duty to work for the common good, that doing right by oneself, and others, was the way to fulfilment. Never rock the status quo, never question your elders and betters. But Rasheda and Djavdat failed to recognise – indeed, they were conditioned to ignore – an individualism in Irek that was fighting for survival and would lead to both unimaginable professional success and profound emotional trauma when he left behind their small-town philosophy and took on the real world.

So Irek grew up to be a good little Communist, an example to others, the physical embodiment of his parents' aspirations – an odious notion to a more sophisticated society, but it was the blinkered thinking that Communism demanded and he was to be rewarded handsomely for it. Even family games were no fun without competition. The Mukhamedovs loved cross-country skiing during Kazan's long, snowy winter, but it had to be done with arms behind the back – an excruciating exercise for young muscles. Even so, Irek soon left his brother and father trailing. 'If it is easy, it is not worth doing' was a basic family doctrine.

The annual hunt for the autumn crop of mushrooms and blackberries was certainly never easy for Irek, even though he was closer to the ground than his mother, but one day his obedient nature brought unexpected dividends. Bored and uncomfortable crawling through the undergrowth on the banks of the Kazanka river one October, Rasheda told Irek to sing a song to bolster his flagging determination. Autumn is the rutting season for deer, and an inquisitive and amorous bull elk (the world's largest deer), who found the ground-level warbling irresistible, nosed through the brambles to investigate, startling Irek. 'Keep singing,' hissed Rasheda. The libidinous animal clearly found what he had hoped to be an interesting variation on a mating call deeply disappointing and wandered away.

Irek happily collected the milk at six each morning, helped his mother in the kitchen in the evening and went to bed after gymnastics, or ice-skating or dancing, tired but content. He was a 'good boy', an epithet in the Mukhamedov household that was worth striving for, not a term of derision. When the family was at home together at weekends or evenings, they would sit round the table and talk, or listen to music, or political broadcasts. A solemn existence for a vigorous young boy, it developed discipline, but stifled initiative. The frown-line of concentration that divides Mukhamedov's forehead today was scored into his skin by the time he was six.

Roaming the streets with the gang of boys from his block of flats was a pastime that held little attraction. Smoking made him sick; eating the pigeons they snared, gutted and spit-roasted made him even sicker. Sledging with the gang on the icy, winter streets gave him his first scar. In spite of the strong physique he possessed even as a child, Irek failed to control his sledge on one reckless dash and cannoned into the apartment block's concrete steps. He cut his forehead, producing torrents of blood and consternation at home. But these aimless pursuits left him feeling guilty and ill at ease.

Even on holiday the boys swam hard, ran hard and helped around the house. The family spent the three summer months at Borovie Matushe, a government-run camp on the banks of the Volga, an hour's drive south of the city. Set in a primeval forest of pine and birch, the village straggles along the banks of the Volga, forest at the back, beaches in front – a boy's paradise. 'We never washed in the morning,' Mukhamedov remembers. 'We pulled on trunks and dived straight in the river.' Cycling and swimming the summer away, the brothers made little contact with other children in the village. They were fiercely loyal to each other and their family ethics.

Overlooking the confluence of the Kazanka and Volga rivers, at Kazan's heart, stands one of those monumental statues with which the Soviet authorities so dearly loved to ruin their environment. It commemorates a local figure, the Tartar poet Musa Dzhalil, who was killed in a German concentration camp. He proudly stands gazing into eternity, stripped to the waist and bound with barbed wire. Round its base are engraved two lines of a poem written just before his execution. 'My life is a song bringing hope to the people/ My death will be a clarion call for victory.' The Mukhamedovs revered Dzhalil and for the boy Irek he was a hero.

Returning home from Borovie Matushe one year, Irek travelled to Kazan alone with the family's luggage in a stranger's van and was unloaded early one morning, along with the suitcases, at the wrong address. He sat on the pavement all day, surrounded by his family's possessions, not just afraid of being abandoned, but determined to protect what was his. There is a direct link between the young Irek, grimly loyal, if tearful, on a strange street in Kazan emulating the determination of his idol, Dzhalil, and the role that eventually brought him world prominence, Spartacus.

His back was naturally strong and supple, his jump strong and his general musculature well developed, but Irek had few other natural balletic attributes. His feet did not point freely, a drawback with which he was to battle for the rest of his life, and he was tight in the hips. But Matyanova had rarely seen such single-minded determination – particularly in a five-year-old boy. If he could not instantly obey when asked to arch his feet more, or jump higher, or lift his legs, he cried – not from pique, but because he felt he was letting his teacher down. And the astonishing efforts Irek made to comply with her wishes made Matyanova realise that such a powerhouse of naked will was a talent worth infinitely more than a natural turn-out or pretty feet. Irek's improvement was rapid.

Another notable quality was his feeling for music. Irek did not then, nor would he ever, count the number of steps to the musical bars. He quite instinctively structured them to the melody. Then there was his ardent attention to his partners, an uncannily mature chivalry in a naturally boisterous male child, and his complete lack of self-consciousness, an essential characteristic for any stage career. And all this was in spite of never having seen a ballet in his short life. Matyanova gradually came to the conclusion that Irek must take proper ballet lessons.

Rasheda was not convinced, but was conscientious in her efforts to encourage Irek in an activity he took so very seriously. When Irek danced his first solo, a cat, in his first annual club show, they both spent hours watching the local feline population – not just studying the physical complexities of washing, stretching, jumping and hunting, but attempting to grasp a cat's essential mood and nature. This search for the truth in a role was to be a striking characteristic of Mukhamedov's future.

Djavdat had even more reservations than his wife about a career in ballet for his younger son. Attitudes in provincial Russia were only slightly more enlightened than in the West. The stigma of effeminacy clung to the word 'ballet', not so much because of fear of sexual deviation but because dancing was not considered man's work. More importantly for Djavdat, the theatre was dismissed as being unlikely to provide a manly income. On both counts, Irek was to prove Kazan's and his father's prejudices spectacularly wrong.

But Djavdat was reluctant to cross his wife, and if Irek enjoyed dancing, why not? The boy was, after all, only five years old. He started to photograph his son's progress, a practice he continued until Irek's early days with the Bolshoi Ballet, thereby providing a remarkable twenty-year record of outstanding professional success.

In 1967 there were big changes in Irek's life: he started school and lost Matyanova. The seven-year-old came back from the family holiday at Borovie Matushe in September and enrolled in State School 22, but naturally went first to re-establish contact with his dancing class. To his dismay, he was told that it had been disbanded.

Matyanova had been offered another, better, job, had closed down her club and moved on. He blamed himself for his loss, like any child facing rejection. Years later, when he won the Grand Prix at the Moscow Competition that launched his career with the Bolshoi Ballet, he received a note from Matyanova: 'Irek, I kiss you. You will always have this success. Thank you, you have not let me down. I do not have words to express how happy you make me. Veronika.' She died shortly after.

Starting school not only ended Irek's infancy, as he broke out of the cocoon of family life, but initiated a process of growth that inevitably took him out of Kazan. His twelve-year-old brother Nail, who also attended State School 22, was already showing signs of academic promise – an increasing amount of his spare time was spent studying – and the absorbing onset of Nail's puberty was creating a gulf between him and his younger brother of far more substance than their five-year age gap. The family still paid their occasional visits to the cinema together, went out to friends and sat and talked. But as the boys grew, their interests naturally diverged and their circle of friends inevitably separated.

At the time when he began his formal education Irek's overriding concern was to find another group in which to continue his dancing. Eventually, after much pressure from Irek, Rasheda put his name down with the Gaidar Pioneer Club. Irek found his new dancing club, run by Ivan Kruglov, presented even more of a challenge than Matyanova's had. There was greater emphasis on ballet, which he enjoyed more and more, and he felt comfortable having a male teacher at last. This added impetus increased the pressure on his parents to send him to ballet school, and that meant St Petersburg (then Leningrad) or Moscow. Irek's roots were loosening.

As Nail grew away from him and talk of St Petersburg promised wider horizons, Irek developed a modicum of companionship with a boy his own age. Vadim Pashinin had joined Matyanova's club at the same time as Irek, two years previously; having discovered that dancing held no appeal for him, he left almost immediately. Vadim and Irek found themselves sitting at adjacent desks on their first day at State School 22 and struck up a friendship that provided Irek with an essential bridge between childhood and the adolescent independence he later found in Moscow.

Needless to say, Irek was a model pupil at school. His grounding as a good young Communist meant that his was always the first hand in the air, his essays on local hero Musa Dzhalil were usually the longest and he soaked up the romance of the past like blotting-paper. The propaganda-drenched Soviet curriculum placed great emphasis on historic ideals of chivalry, and service and sacrifice for others. To Irek it was all perfectly natural. He volunteered for everything. If a class monitor was needed, Irek was it. He was captain of this, captain of that. On parents' days he was held up as an example to all as a natural leader, a bright hope for the future of the USSR. His inability to add two and two correctly was discreetly overlooked.

Irek was blissfully unaware that he must have been driving his less ideologically indoctrinated fellow pupils wild. Perhaps a healthy kick in the pants from an exasperated compatriot might have helped adjust his priorities. But no one, certainly not his parents, ever laid a finger on him. Djavdat still boasts that he never took a belt to either of his sons. The only complaint Irek voiced was about the bizarre haircut that his parents insisted he and his brother sport. The closely cropped skull and prominent tuft left on the forehead was traditionally thought to encourage growth. But he accepted even that imposition.

Irek had also been used as the exemplar in Matyanova's dancing group. 'See how Mukhamedov looks at his partner,' his probably irritated companions were told. 'Do it like Mukhamedov.' In his first ballet, *Rabushan*, with the Gaidar Club in May 1970 he was given two roles to dance, a Sunbeam and Bird. Already he showed physical promise. His back and legs were remarkably straight for a seven-year-old and his turn-out appeared unstrained.

But his greatest talent was his unquenchable desire to succeed. 'Work, work, work,' he remembers. 'If I couldn't do straightaway what I was asked, I worked until I could.' And with each achievement came more plaudits. Approval from his superiors became a drug without whose daily fix life was inconceivable.

By the time the decision was made to send him to the Moscow Ballet School a shutter was descending on Mukhamedov, then only ten years old. Society had already added a subtle twist to his vigorous desire to succeed – a need to please.

He took little, or no, personal pride in his achievements. All the power of his personality, considerable even at that age, went into being good for the sake of others: his parents, his schoolteachers, his dancing instructors. A damper was already in place over his personal needs and desires. It was only on-stage, finding the truth in a characterisation, that Mukhamedov felt in touch with himself.

It was the start of a dichotomy that was to bring Mukhamedov nothing but trouble.

2

The Audition

NO DRAMA SURROUNDED the Mukhamedovs' decision to send Irek to ballet school. By the age of nine he thought of little else and did not apply himself as diligently to any other pastime. There was no need for family conferences; money was no problem in the subsidised Soviet system and the will was clearly there. The only question was, had he the talent?

Ivan Kruglov thought so, but to make sure Rasheda and Djavdat took Irek to see the head of the resident ballet company at the Kazan Opera House, Yultieva Ninel Datovna, in February 1970, a month before his tenth birthday. She examined Irek in her office and checked his feet, which were still not particularly well pointed, his general stance, the looseness of his extension (in other words, how high his legs moved upwards) and his jump. 'All right, try,' she said.

Traditionally the Tartar nation, and Kazan in particular, sent its promising young dance talent to St Petersburg. Rudolf Nureyev, who came from Ufa in neighbouring Bashkirskaya, had graduated from the Vaganova Academy in St Petersburg in 1958. A letter of application was sent to the academy. The reply was not good. The boarding dormitories were full, so Irek would have to find his own accommodation, which might have overstretched the family budget. But the real obstacle was the required academic qualifications.

The Vaganova Academy expected straight As from its students, for example, good to excellent marks in mathematics, Russian language and literature, history and geography. They asked to see Irek's school records. It was pointless to pursue the matter further, for Irek's marks in mathematics were never better than poor. The Mukhamedovs forgot about St Petersburg; and they had no reply from the company school in Perm on the Russian side of the Ural Mountains to which they had also applied.

Luckily Rasheda's sister, Galina, had spotted an advertisement pasted on a Moscow street for auditions for the Moscow Ballet School, with no academic requirements specified. The auditions are the second week in May, she wrote; come and stay with me. They did. On 20 May 1970 Rasheda took Irek on the overnight train from Kazan to Moscow to join the throng of other young applicants at the ugly concrete and glass building on Second Frunzenskaya Street that housed the Moscow Ballet School.

The next ten days were a blur. Backwards and forwards between Galina's communal flat on Dubnensnaya Street and the ballet school, being prodded and poked by strangers, hours of waiting, days of idleness and the nerve-racking search for his name on lists that meant entry into the next round. Irek's introduction to the gruesome meat-market of the dancer's audition was on a grand scale: two thousand girls and one thousand boys applied for the handful of places that year.

On Monday, the first day of the ordeal, Rasheda and Irek had arrived with hundreds of other children and parents at 10 a.m. to audition for the eighty places annually filled at the school. They sat in the foyer and waited. Eventually Irek's name was called and he trooped upstairs with ten other boys, changed into trunks and singlet and waited. Then it was along the corridor and into a studio for his first encounter with the former Bolshoi ballerina and undisputed mistress of the Moscow Ballet School, Sophia Golovkina. She sat in the mirror-lined studio, a baize-covered table in front of her, teachers and assistants on either side, her blond hair rigidly arranged, rapidly filling page after page of her large notebook. Golovkina had taken over as director of the school in 1959 and was already earning a reputation as a woman of formidable power and influence. Irek was suitably intimidated.

The children sat in a silent row along the wall as, one by one, they were taken to the middle of the room. 'Irek Mukhamedov,' called the lady with the clipboard and the nervous boy with the embarrassing haircut joined the two young teachers in front of an unsmiling Golovkina. He was bent forward and backwards, his legs lifted, his feet inspected. They measured his limbs and back to calculate growth. He jumped, he turned. Then he sat down again, and waited.

Irek lost track of time. There were too many people, too many ladies with lists, too much waiting in harshly lit, empty rooms. Too many important, unfriendly faces. He and his mother finally left for Galina's flat at six that evening, drained and anxious and knowing nothing. The names of the successful entrants to go through to the next round of examinations would be posted on the foyer notice-board in the next few days, they were told.

Three days later they found the name Mukhamedov.

Now came the medical examination. Once again, hours sitting in the front hall, waiting for the clipboard carriers to bark out his name; another disorienting trip through the unfamiliar building before changing and then sitting and waiting to be tapped, pulled and scrutinised. Rasheda relaxed, confident in the robustness of her son's physical well-being.

The doctors found the scar on Irek's forehead deeply sinister and demanded an immediate explanation. How had he come by it? Was this dark-eyed, powerfully built boy a hoodlum, a potential troublemaker? Had the wound received proper treatment? Rasheda telephoned home and dispatched Djavdat to the local hospital. Two more anxious days passed in Moscow before the accommodating doctor wrote to the school authorities to say that Irek had not received the wound as the result of childish gang warfare, but had innocently collided with a tree and had indeed been promptly and properly stitched up by him, his family physician. Another hurdle cleared.

And so to the final and most crucial test: an assessment of his musicality and his basic potential to be a dancer.

Yet again, ten o'clock in the foyer and another hour's wait, then follow the clipboard up two flights of stairs and change into trunks and singlet with nine young colleagues. Out of the changing-room, along the passage and back into the brightly lit ballet studio to face Golovkina. This time the boys all knew their fates would be sealed before they bowed farewell to her.

Golovkina's secretary asked each one what they would dance, and which piece of music they would require the pianist to play. Irek had prepared a solo, 'Chapaevtsi', to a traditional tune and confidently told the secretary so. He could scarcely believe his ears when he was informed that the pianist could not play it. 'Can you manage without music?' he was asked. 'No,' he mumbled in reply. 'Then you will have to dance to one of the tunes we are going to play,' they said.

Irek sat and waited his turn in a sweat of fear. He knew he could do 'Chapaevtsi', and do it well; everyone had told him so. He had never improvised, certainly not in public, since his five-year-old capers in hospital. What would he do? What would happen when they called his name?

One by one the boys were called to the piano to clap, run and jump in time to different rhythms, then to dance their solos. Luckily for Irek, they nearly all chose to dance to the same piece of music, a folk-tune adapted by the composer Glière from his ballet *Red Poppy*, called 'Yablochko', the sailor's dance.

Now it came to Irek, still in a state of shock. For him keeping time to changing rhythms was instinctive, achieved through feeling, not thought. The solo, though, was another matter. The music started, so he had to do something. The panic-stricken boy somehow managed to string together the steps he had watched the other boys do, improvising sequences he had desperately memorised as he waited his turn.

He sat down white and shaking. His first and most crucial audition, he felt, had been a fiasco. Rasheda, when he finally made it back downstairs to tell her the news, agreed. What a disaster!

They hardly considered it worth returning the next day to study the list of successful entrants, but they did. Which was just as well, because Irek Mukhamedov had won one of the eighty places on offer and was therefore accepted as a pupil of the Moscow Ballet School and would start his studies in September.

Anatoly Yelagin, Irek's first teacher at the school, was a member of the auditioning commission, and picked him out almost at once. 'He was a little boy, not very tall. When he came into the audition, he sat quietly on the chair and almost against my will I found myself looking at him. He made a very clear visual impression on me. He was a quiet and very balanced little boy.

'It's not possible to say that he had very good feet, and his build was slightly stocky, but when we asked him to dance something, they played the music and he improvised, and he danced so well that we said, "Yes, he must study with us."'

17

Irek and Rasheda spent two more days in Moscow, waiting for the official letter of confirmation from the school authorities, and phoned the good news to Djavdat and Nail in Kazan. They went to the zoo and visited Children's World, that veritable paradise of childish dreams facing the Lubyanka Prison across Dzerzhinsky Square. They also made plans with Galina for Irek's stay in the capital. He would board in the Internat section of the school during the week, which would cost the Mukhamedovs 65 roubles a month, just under half of Djavdat's monthly salary of 140 roubles; everything else, including school uniform, practice clothes and exercise books, was provided by the Moscow Ballet School. His weekend accommodation at his aunt's would be free. Galina, who still has enough maternal instinct to mother every one of the six hundred pupils at the Moscow Ballet School, was delighted at the prospect of a surrogate child spending the weekends with her.

Mother and son eventually boarded the night train to Kazan, and slept on the bunks in the communal wagon-lit. As Irek journeyed back home, the process of severing his family ties, begun five years earlier when he started dancing with Veronika Matyanova, continued. Ballet, as far as his limited experience allowed, was already his life. It was a channel for his unquenchable energy and voracious appetite for work. And he must be doing the right thing, he felt, otherwise he would not have won the approval of the Moscow Ballet School. The situation was simple. Soon he would leave his parents, his brother, Vadim, Ivan Kruglov and Kazan and enter another world in Moscow – another world in which, if he worked hard enough and played by the right rules, he would earn his just rewards, though he had no way of knowing what they might be. It was a blinkered logic and one that the ten-year-old boy was worlds away from articulating. Mukhamedov remembers no sense of loss or sadness at the impending separation, just an acceptance of the fact. It was a lack of sentimentality that blunted his natural feelings, but without it he would not have survived in later life.

Back in Kazan, Irek finished the few weeks left of school term speculating with Vadim on life in Moscow. Even though his friend had no ambitions to escape to the capital, he was impressed by Irek's achievement and was eager to hear of his experiences. Rasheda, Irek and Nail spent some time on the banks of the Volga while Djavdat remained at work to earn some extra money for his younger son's education; then they returned home and began the round of goodbyes.

When it came time to make the journey to Moscow and start Irek in his new life, Rasheda was unable to take time off from her teaching duties, so Djavdat claimed his first holiday in two years to accompany Irek. The night before departure Rasheda packed her son's suitcase. It contained some bark from the local lime trees (which, when dried, was the Russian steam-bath equivalent of the loofah), pyjamas, a change of socks and shirt and nothing else – no photographs or any other memento of his family. It was the first of many landmark voyages embarked on by Irek with hardly any clutter of material possessions or sentimental souvenirs. On 27 August 1970 the Mukhamedov clan gathered at Kazan railway station to wish the boy well, aunts Madina and Raikhana, cousins Rashid, Renad and Farid and, of course, brother Nail and friend Vadim. Clutching farewell bunches of flowers, Djavdat settled his son down for the eleven-hour journey.

They took a trip together that, for Irek, has not yet ended.

3

Moscow

IREK AND HIS father disembarked from the overnight train at Moscow's Kazan Station and straightaway took the tram to Second Frunzenskaya Street. Djavdat has decided to call at the school on the way to Galina's flat, ostensibly to leave what little belongings Irek had brought from Kazan. But, in fact, he was anxious to get his first glimpse of the strange new world to which he was about to entrust his son. Irek was to board in the Internat section, which housed the non-Muscovite students, and they were met by Maria Stepanovna, the chemistry teacher acting as Irek's class mother, who showed them to the third-floor dormitory that Irek would share with three other boys. He deposited his socks, shirt and pyjamas in his locker and followed Maria Stepanovna to the Internat wardrobe. He returned to his room laden with more clothes than he had ever owned at one time – school uniform, practice clothes and ballet shoes – and they joined the sparse possessions in his locker. Irek and his father made their way to Galina's home. To while away the four days before the start of term Irek explored Moscow with his father and Aunt Galina. It was an unreal hiatus for the pragmatic little boy, who was eager to start what he now recalls as his 'separate life'.

Professional dance training began in earnest in Moscow in 1773 when the Italian dancing master Filippo Beccari was given permission to train inmates of the Moscow Orphanage, now the Dzerzhinsky Military Academy, a rambling yellow stone building on the north bank of the Moskva river where it arcs south in front of the Kremlin. To allay the fears of a doubtful Council of Trustees, Beccari waived his fees until the conclusion of the first three-year course of training, when the pupils were deemed capable of 'performing a figure with perfect precision'. It was worth the wait. Of the sixty-two students involved, twenty-two graduated as soloists, each earning Beccari 250 roubles, and the rest netted the astute dancing master 150 roubles apiece. His professional credo was simple. 'The children,' he is on record assaying, 'will jump without taking a rest for hours on end, even to the detriment of their health.' Little, some would say, has changed.

Beccari not only founded a great artistic heritage, but also initiated a tradition (which endured for the next century and a half) that the training was the exclusive monopoly of the citizens of Moscow. The dancers performed in the operas at the city's Petrovsky Theatre and the Znamensky Opera Theatre and at court entertainments. They gradually gained proficiency and popularity, until in 1780 the twenty-two leading orphanage dancers performed *The Magic School*, the Petrovsky Theatre's first full evening of ballet, choreographed by Leopold Paradis, who had succeeded Beccari two years earlier. And Moscow's first independent ballet company was thus established. In 1806, shortly after the Petrovsky Theatre was razed by fire, the Russian Imperial Theatres took over the company, which had, in effect, become an increasingly important branch of its own activities. French maestro Charles-Louis Didelot brought the Romantic movement to Moscow, where he indulged his passion for 'flying' his dancers across the stage on wires and put his ballerinas on pointe for the first time. His Russian protégé, Adam Gluszkovski, sought more adventurous and literary scenarios for his ballets, turning, naturally, to Pushkin, who described ballet as 'a dance executed by the human soul'. Royal patronage added to its prestige, and when the New Bolshoi Petrovsky Theatre was opened in 1825 (designed by architect Albert Cavos and known to this day simply as the Bolshoi), the company has grown to forty-seven dancers. In the late 1860s a magnificent mansion in Pushetchnaya Street, across Theatre Square from the Bolshoi, was made available for the school, and the course of training was extended to seven years. The Moscow Ballet School had come of age.

After the turmoil of the 1917 October Revolution Russian ballet was seriously under threat as a hated symbol of the *ancien régime*. But, luckily, when the Soviet government settled on Moscow as the Union's capital, it also realised the domestic and international propaganda value of one of the city's main cultural assets and poured vast resources into the Bolshoi company and its school. In 1920 the school was finally open to all the Soviet republics, but those who were born Muscovites still formed an élite, as Mukhamedov, a Tartar, was to discover fifty years later.

In 1959, Sophia Golovkina, the wife of an army colonel, retired from the Bolshoi Ballet, with whom she had earned a reputation for virtuosity and a brilliance of attack that in the 1940s and 1950s was, it seemed, the special prerogative of Soviet dancers. She was appointed director of the Moscow Academic Choreographic Institute, as the school was by then officially known, having herself graduated from it in 1933. She supervised the transfer to its purpose-built premises in Second Frunzenskaya Street in 1967.

The Moscow Ballet School occupies a whole city block and is built on the site of a wartime municipal refuse tip; it has separate entrances for Muscovites and those students resident outside the capital. On its completion the three-storey glass and concrete building was the largest in the world devoted exclusively to the training of classical ballet. There are twenty ballet studios, all raked to match the angle of the Bolshoi stage, in addition to the schoolrooms needed to educate six hundred pupils to university standard; when a student graduates from the Moscow Ballet School, it is with the equivalent of a university entrance qualification. The school also has an integral three-hundred-seat theatre, with a full Bolshoi-size stage equipped with the most modern technology, where the pupils are put through their yearly assessments and rehearse for the annual performance at the Bolshoi. There are dormitory facilities for three hundred boarders, a clinic, gymnasium and refectory. Out of a total of three hundred members of staff, sixty-seven are dance teachers, giving an enviable ratio of one teacher to every nine students.

The belief that ballet schools are a soft option for the preparation of a future career is never further from the truth than in Russia. The single-minded, almost tunnel-visioned dedication is tangible the moment you enter the building. The process is ruthless. The number of children selected is minute, compared with the size of the population, but they are made aware of their good fortune, not treated as an élite. Hard work and achievement are expected in return for privilege. The discipline and physical demands imposed on ten-year-olds, let alone adolescents, is testing in the extreme. At the end of each year difficult temperament, a lack of technical improvement or unsuitable physical development could lead to a tearful interview in the director's office and instant dismissal. This, then, was the harsh, often lonely dancer's life to which, unknowingly, Djavdat Mukhamedov delivered his younger son.

On the first day of term, 1 September 1970, Irek dressed at his aunt's apartment in his new uniform, the grey flannel worn in every school in the Soviet Union, and set off with his father to Second Frunzenskaya Street. They picked up a bunch of flowers from a street vendor on the way, the traditional first day of term gift for a Russian child's teacher, and were careful to use the Internat door at the side of the building. After the auditions the previous May, Irek was never again to use the main, Moscow entrance. They joined the crowd of nervous adults and excited children in the school's central courtyard in the customary gathering at the start of term; the older students impatiently pushed their way through to join their friends. Djavdat settled down to wait in the hall with the other parents while the new intake was marshalled upstairs for registration. 'All we had to do was to put up our hand and say, "Hello, yes, I'm here,"' Mukhamedov remembers. Then there was the annual ritual of receiving ballet shoes from the older boys. Each of the new boys and girls was given a pair of shoes on arrival by the graduate students, a gesture of welcome that was soon replaced by covert bullying by the seniors, as Mukhamedov was to discover. He and his father spent the afternoon sightseeing in Moscow before Djavdat said goodbye in the Internat foyer and left his son to his new life. The Moscow Ballet School was now Mukhamedov's family.

'I never felt homesick,' he says. 'Kazan was one life, Moscow Ballet School was another. I ate supper that night in the canteen with the boys I shared a room with and slept soundly.'

The three boys with whom Mukhamedov shared for his first year as a boarder were Igor Terentiev from Turkmenistan, Yevgeni Zaharchenko from Saratov in Russia and Sasha Sahknovsky, a Moscow boy who had to be accommodated in the Internat because his parents had suddenly moved from the capital. The first two, Terentiev, who recently retired from the Moscow Classical Ballet Company, and Zaharchenko, who joined the State Ballet Theatre in Perm, were Mukhamedov's room-mates throughout their eight years at the school.

The gifted Terentiev was to bring about the painful but inevitable transformation of the young Mukhamedov from big to little fish, a metamorphosis commonly experienced by provincial talent planning to take a capital city by storm. As he learned the following morning when the twenty new boys in the Internat took their first ballet class together.

The cream-washed studio, one of the four main rooms at each corner of the building's second floor where all the dance classes take place, was unnervingly huge to the boys of class 1V who filed in to meet their teacher. Anatoly Yelagin, a former dancer with the Bolshoi Ballet, has the special gifts of patience and thoroughness required to establish in young bodies the foundations of what is probably the most demanding physical discipline created by man. Russian children are virtually moulded by hand when they take their first steps in ballet; only in India do teachers physically manipulate their young charges in a similar way. Nature's imperfections in each pupil are straightened out or disguised from the moment they enter the studio. From the precisely angled heads to the carefully placed feet, a slow and meticulous process of living sculpture takes place. An exhausting method for the teacher, it demands enormous resources of concentration, but it provides a sound future for the pupil. Looking back today, Mukhamedov has nothing but praise and gratitude for the sense of discipline instilled into him as a ten-year-old by Yelagin.

Owing to the mirrors that covered one wall and the floor-to-ceiling windows that made up another, the studio, like most of those at the Moscow Ballet School, was particularly light and spacious. The practice barre ran round three walls, at two levels, one at waist height for the seniors, another set about 30 centimetres lower for the juniors. The piano and Yelagin's chair occupied the fourth wall; the watering-can used to dampen the floor to prevent the dancers' shoes from slipping stood in a convenient corner. When the boys entered, there was no casual jostling for the best view in the mirror or avoiding the awkward corner places where legs can clash and the floor always seems slippiest. They solemnly made their greeting, and Yelagin placed each boy in a strict pecking order that was to be altered only by hard work and merit. Mukhamedov was on the end of the first barre nearest the window and Terentiev was given the star position, the centre spot of the centre barre. 'He had everything from God,' Mukhamedov remembers, 'pointed feet, high extension – everything.' The role of model pupil and teacher's favourite that Irek had enjoyed in Kazan came to an abrupt end. For the next eight years Terentiev, the golden boy, maintained his pole position, while Mukhamedov, from his place on the sideline, had most to work for and, as it turned out, the furthest to go.

The class lasted for one hour and thirty-five minutes, the regular period for ballet classes at the school, and consisted of only barre work, taken very slowly and with lengthy corrections and instructions from Yelagin. It was the first time that Mukhamedov, because of his background in folk-dancing clubs, had seen ballet dancers at close quarters. Although many of the boys had less training than himself, there were those in the class, like Terentiev, whose natural attributes made Irek acutely aware of his own physical liabilities. His turn-out was not good, his ankles were stiff and would not allow his feet to arch freely and he found difficulty in lifting his legs to the front and side. Arabesques were always easy, however, as, thanks to his mother, his back was unusually supple. She had supervised his gymnastic exercises at home, laying him face down on the floor and lifting his legs to touch the back of his head with his feet.

Then there was his shape. Mukhamedov has fought a battle with his weight all his life. Meeting him in the street, the physical impression he gives is far from imposing. He appears shorter than his 1.77 metres (5 feet 11 inches) and, while there is a healthy burliness in his shoulders, like most dancers his frame is considerably more slender than that of the average man. But not slender enough to satisfy the harsh criteria of classical ballet. In later life this led to a strict dieting regime – it is a fallacy that constant exercise automatically results in a loss of body fat. Throughout his working life Mukhamedov has eaten nothing after 2 p.m. on the day of a performance.

The Mukhamedovs are a stocky family, and the broad shoulders and hips that Irek has inherited are the source of considerable strength, but also the cause of a categorisation of his talents that began in his first class at the Moscow Ballet School.

Most ballet dancers fall into two broad divisions, classical and demi-character – both difficult to define, based more on a feeling than on a job description. There is a particular configuration about those labelled classical dancers, a certain outline that suggests nobility and hints of eternity. The technique must be pure, of course, but the dancers seem to have a different understanding of their physical language from the rest of us. On the other hand, while possessing the most brilliant techniques, there is an irresistible earthiness about the demi-character dancer; he appeals directly to our emotions as a fellow human being rather than, or rather as well as, reflecting eternal truths. During his nine years as principal male dancer with the Bolshoi Ballet Mukhamedov earned a reputation as one of the greatest demi-character dancers of all time. It was only later in life, particularly after he met British choreographer Kenneth MacMillan, who extended his repertoire in unimaginable directions, that Mukhamedov saw this accolade as a limitation.

These subtle shades of definition closed round Mukhamedov at the age of ten, triggered by accident of birth. And his ethnic origins were as much against him as his inherited shape.

The Communist campaign to stamp out local loyalties in the republics had virtually reduced the Tartar nation, and many other ethnic groups, to the status of vagrants and nomads. Residency restrictions were strict and few ordinary citizens could freely choose where to live in the Soviet Union. One way to earn a permit to reside in Moscow was to take a manual job with the city council and to work as a street cleaner, construction worker or refuse collector for anything up to three years. The word 'Tartar' was thus synonymous with 'menial' in Moscow in 1970. Muscovites tend to have a higher opinion of themselves than the natives of most capital cities, and taunts of provincialism were common. Yet Djavdat had taught his sons to be proud of their race. Irek spoke the Tartar language at home – his parents still do – and his wide circle of relatives had made sure that he grew up soaked in his native culture.

But worse than racist jeers, worse even than discovering what dance talent really was and his apparent lack of it, was that wretched haircut, and it caused the young Irek the most heartache. 'It was common in the Soviet Union for children to have this style,' he says. 'It is supposed to make healthy hair. But only for a few years. My mother insisted, though, that I had it done just before I went to

Moscow. It was so embarrassing.' At least it was one drawback that nature easily rectified in a matter of weeks.

The move to Moscow added fresh dimensions to the fashioning of the ten-year-old Mukhamedov's personality. To the pressure of his parents' parochial and idealistic socialist philosophy was now added the intrusive judgement of more sophisticated values. His conscious recourse was to fall back on the naïve premise, proven, he thought, in Kazan, that working hard to please others brought a just reward. But it was Mukhamedov's natural aptitude to accept life as it presented itself that helped him survive – that and his indomitable will to succeed.

Life in Kazan has been a packed though pleasurable energetic flurry, and Mukhamedov found security in the discipline of the Moscow Ballet School's regime. 'We did not have a moment that was not organised,' he remembers. The children were woken at 7.30 a.m., and after a quick wash breakfasted in the canteen. All classes started at 9 a.m., whether dance or academic; in his first term Mukhamedov's first class of the day was ballet. At 10.35 the boys had fifteen minutes to return to their rooms one floor above the studios, change into school uniform and settle to their studies in the schoolrooms along the corridor from their dormitory on the third floor. As well as resuming the academic curriculum that had been interrupted by their move from their home towns, the first-year students began studying French, the universal language of ballet, and piano. Mukhamedov's formal musical education was not a success. While Terentiev, who had an infuriating aptitude for anything he tried, played brilliantly, Irek could not, he remembers, co-ordinate the different activities of his right and left hands. Perhaps the theory of musical notation is too closely related to mathematical principles for his impractical nature. Mukhamedov and arithmetic never went well together, and his true musicality was obvious, as it is today, when he moved; the weekly rhythm class, therefore, was no problem. The children were asked first to count out loud to a succession of melodies played on the piano, then clap and conduct to a variety of tempos and walk and run in time to the music, a bewilderingly simple exercise for Mukhamedov.

Terentiev also shone in the limbering sessions, held in the basement gymnasium, in which first-year students of both sexes usually concentrated on turning out their legs. Turning the legs through 45 degrees from the hips so that the knees and feet face outwards from the body, instead of forward as nature intended, is a fundamental, though highly artificial, requirement of the classical technique. It is, however, essential in order to develop the aesthetically clean and flowing lines that transform dancing into high art. There is a basic and extremely effective exercise for developing turn-out known to dancers the world over. Sitting on the floor, the soles of the feet are pressed together then pulled as far as far as possible towards the body. The knees are then pushed down sideways to the floor. That at least is the theory, but it normally takes many years of painful exertion to achieve, as indeed it did for Mukhamedov. Terentiev's were the only knees in the class to hit the floor right from the beginning. And, needless to say, he effortlessly slid into the splits and never found difficulty with his extension to the front or to the side. During the eight years of study at the Moscow Ballet School Mukhamedov's only satisfaction in his battle to equal Terentiev's effortless superiority was in the maths class. Terentiev was as much a dunderhead with figures as he was.

The first steps in partnering were taken once a week in the historical dance class. The boys were taught how to present their female partners and how to execute that curious toes-first balletic walk that, if not performed with a natural conviction, can look more artificial than tights and make-up. The boys and girls learned simple dances together, such as the waltz and minuet, bows and curtsys and basic *ports de bras*.

Ever since those early days Mukhamedov has not understood the Bolshoi tradition of the ballerina taking her curtain calls at the footlights, while her partner retires upstage out of the spotlight, regardless of the merits of their respective roles. Many British ballet lovers will remember their frustration when he first danced Spartacus in London in 1986. They were denied giving full vent to their enthusiastic appreciation of his performance by his always taking his bow three feet behind the ballerina dancing Phrygia.

The school day finished at five and after supper there was homework and preparation for the next day's lessons; lights went out at nine.

All meals were taken in the ground-floor canteen, which, apart from the theatre, is the biggest room in the building, capable if necessary of accommodating with ease the school's entire complement of staff and students. And it was here, away from the ballet studios where talent was the only yardstick, or so Mukhamedov thought, that the segregation between Moscow and Internat pupils was most obvious.

Although the lunch break was staggered across classes, there were always queues of children and staff. Everyone entered through the same door, but that was where equality ended. The Internat section was served on the left and the Moscow section on the right, the window side of the room. In theory anyone could sit where they wished, but the staff and the Muscovites tended to occupy the bright, naturally lit tables. The monthly fee of 65 roubles paid by the Internat boarders included their daily food, and they were issued every month with a card to present at the canteen cash desk, to be marked with each meal taken. The Moscow children, on the other hand, paid 1 rouble a day for food, which, as they lived at home, usually meant lunch.

Obviously the Internat food budget was considerably lower than its Moscow counterpart, as was clear from the fare on offer at the canteen's separate serving stations. There was rarely a choice for the non-Muscovite students; any variety of the menu must be bought from the Moscow side of the counter. Mukhamedov's sweet tooth particularly craved a Muscovite dish of grated carrot mixed with sugar and cream, but it was a luxury he could rarely afford as his parents, like most of the non-Muscovites, struggled to pay the basic fee, let alone provide pocket money.

Mukhamedov was always hungry, a complaint common to most growing boys. 'I feel absolutely certain that it was not enough food,' he insists, though after reading the menus of the time, that is a claim apparently hard to substantiate. For breakfast there was cottage cheese with bread and butter and tea, and sometimes porridge with slices of hard cheese or cold sausage. There was always soup for lunch, the main meal of the day, followed by a main course of meat or fish and fruit compote for pudding. Russian tea-time is very similar to the British institution, accompanied with bread and butter and cake. A light supper was usually made up of cold sliced meat or

fish, porridge, perhaps, or fruit and a peculiarly Russian drink called
kefir, which is considered essential for growing bones and is best
described as watered-down yoghurt. Even today, with the Russian
economy in ruins and the most basic of foods often difficult to find
outside the black market, the Moscow Ballet School and the
Vaganova Ballet Academy in St Petersburg somehow contrive an
adequate supply of food for their students. Sophia Golovkina and
Leonid Nadirov, the respective directors, have developed impressive
skills of coercion, blackmail and straightforward bullying to ensure
that their charges enjoy as rounded a diet as possible. An inconceivable state of affairs in the Brezhnev days of 1970; they were days of
plenty, despite Mukhamedov's hungry memories.

If any bond still unites the four young boys who shared an Internat
dormitory in Second Frunzenskaya Street, now grown and scattered
across two continents, it is the memory of Mukhamedov's Aunt
Galina and her carrier-bags stuffed with food. She knew about little
boys. And when she heard Irek complain about the canteen when he
stayed with her most Saturdays and Sundays, she sensibly reckoned
that any extra roubles she could find for her nephew would probably
end up in the Russian Cola machine. Hence her weekly food-laden
visits became an institution. They also became, for Mukhamedov
and his room-mates, a headache. Word soon spread among the
boarders that a group of new boys had a private and tasty food
supplement. It was an irresistible challenge to their older colleagues,
who exercised their *jus divinum* and frequently stole the lot. Any
resistance was met by the traditional cuff round the head, a crude but
effective means of communication with which Mukhamedov was
becoming all too familiar.

As in boarding schools the world over, bullying was part of the
learning process at the Moscow Ballet School. In the canteen the new
boys were expected to fetch and carry for their seniors, refusal or
reluctance earning a blow. There is a tradition in Russian ballet
schools that the pupils bow or curtsy to their elders, and many a
foreign visitor has been captivated by such a greeting, usually
performed without a break in the child's rhythm as they hurry
between classrooms. 'When you bow, you must look into the other
person's eyes,' remembers Mukhamedov. 'If you don't, you get a
slap and do it again.' Mukhamedov was fair game: not only was he a

Tartar, grounds enough for ridicule, but his tubby physique also singled him out. He was frequently cornered and prodded in the offending tummy and bottom, and cuffed until he cried.

In December 1970 Mukhamedov first set foot on the Bolshoi stage. The Moscow Ballet School puts its children on-stage as early as possible, a practice common to all the major ballet schools that feed their graduates into their own companies. Performances by students at the Royal Opera House, the Paris Opéra, the Maryinsky or the Bolshoi are as much a part of the school's routine activities as the morning class, French lessons or homework. There was no sense of destiny, then, no thrill of future greatness when the young Mukhamedov took his first step through the stage door that eventually led to international fame. He remembers chiefly the smell of the red powder dabbed on his cheeks, the difficulty of adjusting to the theatre's stage lighting and concentrating so hard on getting the steps right that he forgot on which side of the stage he was to exit after the curtain calls.

Following rehearsals in the school theatre the students were bussed to the Bolshoi, where they snaked up to their dressing-rooms. His appearances in the school performances were the only occasions on which Mukhamedov changed in the theatre's corps de ballet's quarters. When he returned to the Bolshoi Theatre as a 21-year-old professional, he was the company's principal dancer and had a room of his own.

One of the traditions of the Moscow Ballet School's youngest boys and girls is a défilé every year to the school performance, called 'Suvorovtsy', for which the boys are dressed as military cadets, the girls in party clothes. The children do a few steps, but mostly parade with that irresistible charm of children on-stage. 'Suvorovtsy', conveniently, requires a large number of boys and girls. Naturally, Terentiev and his partner led the crocodile of boys and girls on to the stage and Mukhamedov brought up the rear. Terentiev was the last to leave the stage at the end, after dancing a tiny solo that Mukhamedov was determined eventually to perform.

Yelagin was also fond of a work based on 'Snow White', a children's ballet created by Kasyan Goleizovsky (a popular choreographer of the time who had died earlier that year) with music by Alyat Rebikov, which Yelagin supplemented with music by George

Gershwin. His class occasionally performed this little piece for visitors to the school; Mukhamedov was always one of the dwarfs.

Shortly after the December performance at the Bolshoi the school broke up for the winter vacation and Mukhamedov went with his fellow students to Red Pakhra, the school's winter holiday camp. He remembers these ten annual days of freedom and good food as the happiest of his school years – outside the classroom that is. The children wore thick Russian winter boots, called *valenki*, that the Internat boarders were given free, and their cold-weather topcoats, which came from a pool of secondhand clothes in the camp wardrobe, also cost their parents nothing. There were sledges, skates and skis available, a cinema, no lessons and a large amount of free time.

Apart from two visits from his mother, Irek had little contact with his family that first year. He hated writing letters and left it to his aunt to keep Kazan informed of his health and progress. So he was naturally eager to see his family and friends after such a long absence when, accompanied by Galina, he returned home for the summer.

It had not been a comfortable twelve months. Thanks to the bullying from the older boys, he had cried a good deal and frequently nursed a sore head. But his gregarious nature had found compensation in the comradeship of Terentiev and his other room-mates. He had accepted the change of status from star attraction to almost bottom of the class, but doubts were in his mind about his answer to the challenge. He had worked harder than he had ever worked in his life. He had listened to Yelagin's corrections and achieved much, even moving nearer to Terentiev at the barre, and yet he knew it was not enough. At his first annual school assessment in June 1971 he gained three out of the five possible marks for ballet, the minimum required to avoid expulsion. Three marks out of five represented failure to him. His usual solution, work, had let him down and at the age of eleven this was a serious blow.

4

Growing Up

MUKHAMEDOV RETURNED HOME in Kazan with just one thing on his mind: food. After the turmoil of his arrival and the distribution of the scents and scarves and other knick-knacks that his aunt had bought with him in Moscow, he happily allowed Rasheda's cooking to obliterate all memories of the school canteen. 'There was nothing to do,' he remembers, 'but eat and explain my new life.' He amply succeeded in discharging the former obligation, but his unwitting failure to achieve the latter created a gap between him and his parents that has never been filled. But to all outside appearances Irek fitted smoothly back into the family routine. To Djavdat and Rasheda he was still the baby of the family, and Nail, also on holiday from school, made the circle complete.

Djavdat's conscientious service for the local gas company had earned him a small plot of land on the Kazanka riverbank, and the family, including Aunt Galina, went every day to the small summer-house he had built there. They settled down to a serious family recreation, talking, a process that in the past had served to cement them together, but this time triggered the shift of separation in Irek. All the usual parental concerns were examined. Did he get enough to eat? They already knew the answer to that one. Did he like his teachers? Was he happy with his room-mates? Had he been warm enough in the winter? As far as Irek was concerned, all was well. Except in ballet class. He told his family of Terentiev's gifts and detailed his own shortcomings, saying that no matter how hard he worked, he seemed unable to achieve the rapid results that had brought him such approval in Kazan. Only three marks for ballet after twelve months serious effort was a terrible set-back, and he could not disguise it.

Rasheda and Djavdat listened to their son and wondered if, after all, they had done the right thing in sending Irek to Moscow. They failed to grasp what an eleven-year-old could not be expected to articulate, that underlying his complaints was the first impact of real life on the beliefs on which he had been reared. It was the first skirmish in a twenty-year struggle to accept that life was not as simple as his parents' limited experience of it suggested, that rewards are not automatically reaped as a result of diligence and that in a more sophisticated society it is not generally accepted that hard labour has a virtue of its own. But, more significantly, it was impossible for the worried couple to have the slightest understanding of the complexities, or timing, of a ballet training. The infant Irek had danced a swath through two of Kazan's Pioneer clubs, whose purpose was basically to provide part-time recreation for their members, and had never encountered the competition of a natural talent equal to that of, say, Terentiev. That challenge remained an unknown quantity to his parents. They could never know how it feels to be faced with the physical embodiment of all you are working to achieve, and to know that your back will always be too short, your hips too broad and your ankles too tight to emulate your rival's perfection. At eleven that is a tough reality to cope with. Rasheda and Djavdat heard only their son's dismay and missed the resonance of resolve and commitment to this strange thing called ballet in his voice. They knew the course of training at the Moscow Ballet School was eight years long, but had no concept of the slow, careful construction of the regime, not realising that it took years, not weeks or even months, to train muscles and tendons to achieve turn-out, high extensions and elevation. Growing bodies must be strengthened with infinite patience as they approach adolescence, and the consequences of careless physical pressure can be crippling. The fact that time was on Irek's side was completely overlooked by his anxious parents.

It seemed to Rasheda and Djavdat, as they listened to their son blithely detailing the impossible odds against his achieving a successful career in ballet, that the philosophy on which they had built their own and their offspring's lives was simply not working for Irek in Moscow. Therefore Moscow must be wrong.

For now, however, more childish concerns were pressing. There was much swimming to catch up on and the two brothers devoted quite some time to the task. Irek's old school friend Vadim had a whole year's gossip on local matters to fill in and he was keen to hear of his friend's experiences in the capital. The pair of them went off to the country for a long weekend with Vadim's mother, to a Pioneer camp that she supervised.

Rasheda and Djavdat said nothing to Irek of their misgivings for his future as they prepared him and Aunt Galina for their return to Moscow. But Rasheda was determined to send him back to school with something to remember her by and, to Irek's mortification, his hair was cropped again. 'That was it,' he says. 'I was furious and I swore to myself it would never happen again.' And it never did.

Mukhamedov's second year at the Moscow Ballet School was one of consolidation. In his first ballet class Yelagin, his teacher, compensated for his previous year's poor marks by moving him to the centre barre, albeit at the very end. His new place, tight in the corner, was probably the most awkward in the room: even in an uncrowded class and even when you are only 1.37 metres tall, space is restricted and it is necessary to re-angle your body constantly to avoid painful collisions with neighbouring arms and legs. But he was in sight of Terentiev. And he had scored another bonus point: during the holidays he had grown an inch taller than his friend and rival.

No fresh demands were made of the second-year children; the school routine was much the same as the first year, and Mukhamedov was grateful for the sense of familiarity. Ballet class still came first in the morning, followed by school lessons, including piano, before and after lunch, then preparation for the next day, a couple of hours' freedom and lights-out. Few new steps were introduced in the ballet class, but a shift of emphasis required extra exertion. More effort in their jumps, simple though they were, was expected as the boys' physique strengthened, and simple enchainements in the centre brought a feeling of dance to the class work, an element that Mukhamedov keenly appreciated.

But while their son slotted back into his school routine, Rasheda and Djavdat decided in Kazan that it was not too late to start Irek on another path to the future that would be more congenial than that of the dispiriting world he had described during the holidays. Djavdat was dispatched to Moscow to bring him home.

Irek knew nothing of this until his father arrived unannounced in Second Frunzenskaya Street, told him of his and his mother's doubts and said they felt that Irek had better come home. A shocked Irek took his father to see Yelagin, and during a lengthy talk with his son's teacher Djavdat was easily persuaded of Irek's suitability for a career in ballet. 'He is a worker,' he was told, and nothing counts as much in the life of a dancer. Yelagin, who had nurtured the first steps of thousands of youngsters, knew better than most that natural talent often carried the seeds of its own destruction. 'Give him time,' he said. 'A technique built on years of thought and effort can prove more durable than a flashy facility. Irek is a good boy and I like him.'

Djavdat was convinced. A phone call to Kazan soothed Rasheda's fears and, after taking Irek out for tea, Djavdat returned home, leaving a relieved Irek to continue to grapple with his chosen life.

One of the four boys in the dormitory, Sasha Sahknovsky, having failed his first end of year assessment, had not returned to school; Andrei Sapaev now shared the room with Mukhamedov, Terentiev and Zaharchenko. None of Irek's three room-mates had relatives in Moscow, and they rarely spent their free time away from the Internat quarters. Gradually Mukhamedov spent more and more weekends with his friends in the school and fewer with Aunt Galina, visiting her no more than once a month. Nothing, though, could stop Galina's weekly visit to her hungry nephew with her eagerly anticipated food parcels. And nothing stopped the late-night raiding parties by the older boys.

Mukhamedov and his friends were no longer at the bottom of the pile. They were in their second year and began to flex their muscles, starting that subtle transition from persecuted to persecutor, but they had a long way to go. 'The seniors would now come to our room with brooms and tell us to clean their rooms,' Mukhamedov recalls. 'Now we were older, they expected more than trips for tea and *kefir* in the canteen.' Excuses sometimes worked, but more often than not brute force prevailed. Mukhamedov still provoked special attention, but he now accepted the sore heads as part of the pattern, and the routine was no longer strange and therefore frightening. He even ventured the odd 'no' to his persecutors, to test his own resolve. It sometimes worked, and it sometimes ended in tears. It did not occur to him to resent Terentiev's occasional exemption from the older boys' tyranny. Terentiev was, after all, the star of the Internat pupils; any special treatment he enjoyed was, it seemed to Mukhamedov, only part of the natural order of things. In his school studies, mathematics and piano remained the biggest problems, the romance of history and the imaginative leaps of literature the most enjoyable. The morning ballet class had already established an addictive grip on the young boy, and he was almost obsessively determined to prove to Yelagin that he warranted his place in the class. He did nothing but work, work, work, to prove his worth – evidence of a single-mindedness that might become a dangerous element in the emotional baggage a youth carries towards puberty.

The summer of 1972 was again spent in Kazan. Nail, who was preparing for his final school examinations, was immersed in a massive revision exercise and too busy for his young brother, so Irek and Vadim spent the days wandering the countryside, unaware that it would be the last of such childhood intimacy.

Rasheda and Djavdat were understandably proud of their sons. Nail was bright and was expected to do well in his final examinations and go on to university. Irek's teacher had praised his efforts and his character to Djavdat in Moscow. Although he had finished his second year with the minimum of three for all subjects, including ballet – marks that had caused such heartache last year – they were now sure that their upbringing would serve him as well as it apparently did Nail. The inscription in Djavdat's photographic record of his younger son's balletic progress for 1972 confidently reads: 'The school receives a medal, and the boys are growing up.'

There is always a bustle at the start of a new school year. In September 1972 the twelve-year-old Mukhamedov and his classmates were now in 3V, nearly halfway through the course of training at the Moscow Ballet School. They could not aspire to senior status in the school's pecking order, yet they no longer saw themselves as strictly juniors. Mukhamedov was only months away from becoming a teenager. A new element entered the business of claiming a dormitory as Terentiev and Zaharchenko now felt a compulsion to be based near the girls' quarters. While Mukhamedov remained gauche and awkward with girls, Terentiev led his contemporaries' pursuit of the opposite sex with as much precociousness as he did the ballet class. Then they had to find the right desks to occupy in the new classrooms, for the three friends had to stay in whispering range. And their new issue of school uniform was of a satisfyingly larger size.

The boys' expectations were high; the new term presented a fresh slate on which to register new achievements, both in and out of class, and, for Mukhamedov, better marks than last year. He was devastated, therefore, when Yelagin announced his choice of students for the annual class concert. Terentiev would star, as usual, and Zaharchenko would dance a few steps, but Mukhamedov's role was no more than a baton carrier in the finale. He and the other boys considered too unworthy to execute even a changement or two were to run on at the end to fill the stage for the final bow. It seemed a crushing confirmation of Yelagin's verdict at the end of the previous year of three marks for ballet.

For the first time in his short life Mukhamedov despaired. The extrovert boy, brought up on the Soviet work ethic, finally admitted defeat. His parents were right after all, he thought; after two years he had achieved nothing. He was too fat. He should give up and go home. 'I really, really nearly killed myself,' he says. For weeks he and the other boys who were not considered good enough to represent class 3V sat in disappointed silence to watch rehearsals.

But he complained to no one. He and his young colleagues already knew, after two years at an institution that operated in a strictly hierarchical structure, that there could be no questioning a decision and that resentment was futile. He was growing away from Aunt Galina, though he was grateful to know that she was there, and for her gifts of food. She had by now joined the others outside the school walls, including the rest of his family and friends, those who knew nothing of ballet. She could not understand. He felt worthless and very isolated. The last thing his teachers would do would be to express sympathy for his disappointment. None knew better than they that a great ballet company is built on discipline of an almost military nature, and, as they knew from their own experience, the sooner you learned to accept it, the better it would be for your future. Mukhamedov accepted it and did not search for the comfort of an explanation of his hurt from outside; he recognised that his old world could not comprehend the problem and his new would not admit there was one. So, trapped between an overwhelming sense of failure and an already deep commitment to a life in ballet, he worked out his own explanation.

He acknowledged that he was now part of the Moscow Ballet School and bound by its rules and its aspirations, which were foreign to an outsider; life within its walls was apparently harsh, certainly lonely and – even more baffling to the outsider – concerned with nothing but art. The Kazan credo, so confidently espoused by his parents and instilled into him since birth, whereby a dutiful action always brought a rewarding consequence, did not hold good in Second Frunzenskaya Street. His parents had been right last summer; those rules did not work in Moscow. He drew back from facing the truth, that Moscow was right and Kazan was wrong, and blamed himself for the verdict of failure that has been handed down to him from the school authorities. But, instinctively, he began to get an inkling of the real nature of work, to realise that the physical effort he expended each day in ballet class had a more far-reaching consequence than the instant gratification of the pat on the back he had so far come to expect. He became dimly aware that the future played a part in the scheme of things. Salutary and timely observations to ponder as you approach adolescence. Djavdat's comments in the photograph album about his sons growing up were only a little premature.

If any British mother or, particularly, father were asked to name a suitably healthy environment in which their adolescent son should spend his formative years, a boarding ballet school would probably not even be an option. Attitudes are rapidly changing in the West, but the vexed question of male dancers' virility in this country remains a music hall joke. Right from its beginning ballet was accepted in Russia as a serious art form on a par with opera, music, drama or painting and was therefore seen as a justifiable and natural pursuit for either sex. The historical and sociological reasons for the different attitudes towards dance in Russia and Britain are many and complex. Part of the answer may lie in the fact that powerful and dominant women, such as Ninette de Valois and Marie Rambert, founded and developed this country's ballet institutions in the 1930s when British dancers were seen as little more than chorus girls in vaudeville and seaside pier theatres. The aura of femininity still clings very powerfully to the word 'ballet'. But ballet masters, not mistresses, ran both schools and companies in Russia, starting a tradition of founding dynasties that continues to this day in such dancers as Lavrovsky, Messerer, Liepa and Fadeyechev, names that have been famous for generations.

Mukhamedov, then, grew up in a world in which the traditional masculine principles of discipline, work and competition were the norm, principles he had anyway absorbed from his parents since birth. But, although the basic precepts are important in the training of both sexes, the emphasis in the classroom in Russia encourages the essential difference between them. The pairing of the sexes in their free time at the school was a natural and eagerly pursued development; if not actively encouraged by the authorities, it was at least accepted as inevitable. Indeed, the marriage and divorce rate in the Bolshoi Ballet itself was, and still is, bewilderingly high, as Mukhamedov was later to discover. During the eight years he boarded at the Moscow Ballet School he was unaware of any homosexual activity among his fellow students. That, however, probably reveals more about Mukhamedov's blinkered dedication than the sexual mores at the Moscow Ballet School.

From his first day at the school Terentiev epitomised Mukhamedov's ideals as a dancer: 'he had everything from God'. But at twelve years old Irek was searching for a role model in life. Vladimir Karakulev was a Moscow boy, the son of a Red Army general and, as Mukhamedov recalls, completely without fear. 'I realised that if everyone else has two valves in their heart, Karakulev has four. If he was stabbed in the heart, his would go on beating.'

'At that age we all looked like little dancers, but Karakulev looked like a little man.' He was tremendously impressed by Karakulev's ability to stay under a cold shower for more than fifteen minutes. Mukhamedov could only manage three.

The winter of 1972–3 was severe in Moscow and the city lay under a carpet of snow. One evening after supper in early January 1973 Mukhamedov and Karakulev were fooling around in the school's central courtyard, a recreation area in which the children gathered together, gossiped and snatched fresh air between classes. Down the centre of the yard runs a small raised concrete platform supporting benches and triangular flower troughs, in all about a metre in height. A couple of older girls were strolling round the courtyard, deep in conversation, and were ignoring the young boys. Karakulev could not resist the challenge. With the usual boyish exhortation of 'Watch this, Mukhamedov' to make sure the girls did, he cleared the bench with a single leap. Unfortunately, his attention-seeking stunt was upstaged by Mukhamedov, who, unable to resist the temptation to prove himself as dashing as his friend, followed suit, slipped, fell and broke his left wrist. As he lay in the snow in agony, his pride suffered a further blow from the girls' cutting observations on the stupidity of little boys. A chagrined Karakulev helped him back into the building, where Mukhamedov found the nursing sister. She took him to the local hospital for an X-ray later that evening. It confirmed that the wrist was broken, and his arm was put into splints for a month.

It meant, of course, four weeks without ballet classes, sitting again at the side of the studio as he had for the class concert rehearsals, watching his colleagues working. As a small consolation, at the end of the worst six months of his life Yelagin marked him up in his half-yearly assessment, giving him a three plus. By the time his mother came to Moscow to help celebrate his landmark thirteenth birthday in March, Mukhamedov was no longer a child. His more serious approach to work when he was fit enough to get back into practice earned him a mark of four in his final assessment, and he returned to Kazan for the summer holiday chastened and relieved to put the past twelve months behind him.

His friends met a less angry, more articulate youth when he joined them in the apartment block's basement for their evening smoking sessions. Their teasing provoked no more than 'So what?' instead of childish fury, and in response to the taunts about his life at the Moscow Ballet School he asked if their future would be any brighter than their aimless present.

Mukhamedov found that he had less in common with his childhood friend Vadim and that he could better exercise a newly found resource, his brain, in the company of his brother, Nail. Nail was on his first vacation from university, and the brothers spent many hours on the Kazanka riverbank with some of Nail's fellow students. With them Mukhamedov felt less compelled to justify his desire to dance, and more able to communicate the experience. As he did, for the first time, with his father. His parents were still toying with the idea of sending him to military academy, even though thirteen was already a little too old for the top officer training schools. Mukhamedov again blamed himself for the past year's disasters, but instead of just emphasising his own shortcomings, he was able to express some of his commitment to a life in ballet; he said he could now envisage no other pursuit, certainly not the military. Next year, his fourth, he explained, he and his colleagues would move out of Yelagin's class and on to a more senior level with a new teacher, who would advance the training in class, teaching new steps and new ideas. He realised for the first time that his chosen life did not come free and became aware of the sacrifices that Djavdat made to pay half his monthly salary to the school. The discovery only hardened Mukhamedov's resolve.

As a cruel coda to the emotional battering he had received during the past twelve months, Terentiev was chosen as the youngest representative of the Moscow Ballet School when it accompanied the Bolshoi Ballet to America that summer.

5

Alexander Prokofiev

MUKHAMEDOV'S FOURTH YEAR started as inauspiciously as 1972. The Moscow Ballet School was celebrating the two hundredth anniversary of its founding in 1773 by Filippo Beccari and an elaborate event was planned for that December at the Bolshoi Theatre. The preparations would be long and painstaking, and the children found themselves plunged at once into extra rehearsals.

'The best students from every class were chosen to be in a special ballet,' Mukhamedov recalls. High government and party officials would attend the bicentenary gala and the most distinguished leaders of the Russian ballet world would be there. The director, Sophia Golovkina, was determined that the occasion would boost her already considerable standing among the capital's ruling élite.

Mukhamedov had learned to grit his teeth the year before at the decisions made by his masters, and the practice came in handy yet again when he discovered his biggest contribution to the prestigious performance would be confined to a bow as the children exited; since he was relegated to second cast, he might never even appear at all. Mukhamedov was consigned to the sidelines once more as the school's artistic director, Maxim Martirosyan, choreographed show-piece variations for, of course, Terentiev and other school luminaries, such as Alexei Fadeyechev, son of Nikolai, the famous Bolshoi Ballet *premier danseur* and partner of the legendary Ulanova.

Not for the first time, he found consolation in his work. Two months into the term Alexander Prokofiev, who was one of Moscow's best known teachers and had a formidable reputation for toughness, took over class 4V. To the adolescent boys Prokofiev, with his long hair, ever present cigarette and caustic wit, seemed like a real man and brought a worldly air of sophistication into the classroom. The boys immediately felt more grown-up and relished the physical challenges that he presented to them. But, most of all, they were grateful for his insisting that they now wear tights and a T-shirt for class instead of the singlet and trunks that for the last three years had marked them as juniors. Prokofiev had been a dancer in the Bolshoi, but had retired early after sustaining an injury to his leg. Mukhamedov believes it was Prokofiev's passionate love of dance, which underpinned all the harsh corrections, sarcasm and perfectionism in his teaching, that woke an echo of inspiration in his own nature.

Yelagin's three years with the boys had laid down a solid structure for a classical technique – straight backs and legs, turn-out from the hips not the knees and correct *ports de bras* – building carefully on their developing strength. Now it was time to move on. Prokofiev's classes were harder than anything the boys had previously experienced. The barre work was more sustained, so that they started to develop the stamina that would eventually carry them through the rigours of a three-act ballet. He taught the basics of true pirouettes, leaving behind the childish exercise of revolving on two feet to practise the whipping motion of the head that keeps the eyes facing front as long as possible. It was with Prokofiev that Mukhamedov discovered his natural turn was to the left. A common phenomenon in many dancers, it is accepted as such in Russia, though less so in the West, and was to prove a mild source of friction when Mukhamedov joined the Royal Ballet. In the class centre work, when the students leave the security of the barre, the major advance was in jumping. With Yelagin all jumps had been confined to taking off from and landing on both feet. Now the boys were taught gratifyingly grown-up steps from one foot to the other, such as jetés and sissonnes. They learned how to jump over an imaginary obstacle and through the air, and to lift themselves upward from the hips rather than push from the feet. And to land softly.

'Terentiev's demi-plié' – the secret of a quiet landing from a jump that absorbs the force of gravity like the hydraulic undercarriage of an aeroplane – 'was as deep as his full plié, so he could straightaway land very quietly,' Mukhamedov remembers. During these exercises in ballon Prokofiev would ask the class pianist to play as softly as possible and unseemly thumps from his coltish charges were treated to comments of an extremely uncomplimentary nature, gibes that spurred Mukhamedov on to greater efforts rather than causing offence. One physical advantage over Terentiev that Mukhamedov now discovered was a natural give in his muscles, a softness of tone that did nothing to detract from his strength, but allowed him to develop the powerful elasticity in his elevation for which he is now famous. However, Prokofiev's most significant gift to 4V, particularly to Mukhamedov, was dance.

Yelagin's strict schooling had taught the children how to achieve the basic positions of a classical technique, for instance, arabesque and attitude, and how to move between them with, say, glissades and pas de bourrées. Prokofiev now introduced a fresh element: feeling. Steps were no longer to be merely joined together, they must flow together, from the first plié to the final bow. The boys were encouraged to feel the music and to dance every moment. Even the monotonous strength-building exercises like the endless battements tendus and changements were danced, not just executed. Épaulement, the lyrical use of head and shoulders described by the great St Petersburg-based teacher Agrippina Vaganova as 'the first suggestion of future artistry of classical dancing', turned into an exciting means of expression. All this created new worlds for Mukhamedov. This, he instinctively felt, was what he had been waiting for; this was what ballet should be, starting from within. At last the juices began to flow.

As if to seal this surge of optimism, Prokofiev moved Mukhamedov as near to the middle of the centre barre as he would ever get. He was finally standing next to Terentiev, and they were to remain side by side until they both graduated. There was further good news in store for Mukhamedov. One day when he was straining every sinew to achieve a correction Prokofiev had given him, the teacher turned to the class and said, 'Look how hard Mukhamedov tries. That is how I wish you all would work', and a little later he pulled the boy out to demonstrate the correct execution of a step. Mukhamedov was stunned. This was not the gratuitous head-patting he had taken for granted in Kazan, this was real and meant a great deal more. After the battering his confidence had had the previous year, this boost to his morale was vital.

The bruising he had experienced in the ballet class since moving to Moscow had started to mature Mukhamedov's character. He was coming to terms with the gritty values of the classroom, turning on them all his considerable powers of concentration. But ballet and its demands were taking on a reality that life outside the studio was not. He was still the same stolid, solemn youth that he had been when he arrived as a child, opening out only to his room-mates and closest confidants, Terentiev and Zaharchenko. He was still the butt of Tartar jokes and ridiculed for his stocky shape. While his two friends were in frequent trouble with their dormitory warden (and at the same time earning the admiration of their colleagues) for their nocturnal wanderings in the direction of the girls' bedrooms, Mukhamedov was known to the school authorities as a polite, well-behaved student, a conscientious, if not too bright, scholar, an unimaginative and safe example to his fellows. As sure an obstacle to popularity among his compatriots in Moscow as it had been in Kazan, it made him an obvious candidate for day school class captain. He was perfect for the job.

In charge of the registers for both ballet and day school, he covered any absences. The twenty boys and girls in the class were, in theory, collectively responsible for cleaning the classrooms, but knew they could leave it to Mukhamedov. In fact, they left everything to Mukhamedov – organising weekend trips to the zoo or museums, reading aloud the political pamphlets at the weekly Pioneer meetings – safe in the knowledge that the class misdemeanour report book would remain empty. It was a satisfactory arrangement for all: his classmates let him present a dutiful façade to the teachers behind which they got on with the serious business of growing up, and Mukhamedov was content to live by the familiar values of service and duty on which he had been reared.

On 27 December 1973 the Moscow Ballet School Bicentenary Gala took place at the Bolshoi Theatre. As Djavdat's album records, Mukhamedov appeared after all, albeit briefly, replacing a classmate who was sick. He was also one of six non-dancing children who recited a prologue to the performance, a poetic paeon to Communism, in front of the assembled pupils and dignitaries. Something about the timbre of his voice appealed to one Moscow girl who was dressed in her Young Communist uniform and standing to attention in the stalls, arm bent over her head in the awkward Pioneer salute. Maria Kovbas peered under her arm a little more closely at the dark-eyed youth. And liked what she saw.

Even at the age of twelve Maria – Masha – Kovbas was strikingly beautiful, with short chestnut hair and large blue eyes. She was a popular girl at the school, particularly among the older boys; perhaps the fact that her mini-skirts, then the essential mode for girls of the Moscow Ballet School, were more minimal than most had something to do with it. A few days after the gala Masha and Mukhamedov came together by chance and began a relationship that, beset by adolescent angst and adult mistiming, took fifteen years to be consummated.

On 7 January 1974 the school began its winter holiday at the Red Pakhra camp. Mukhamedov went as usual with his Internat colleagues, and shared a dormitory in the boys' section, as was also customary, with Terentiev and Zaharchenko.

The list of boys' names outside the room next door included one M. Kovbas. Masha was delighted to discover on her arrival that she was booked into the room next to the good-looking Tartar boy, but when the teachers eventually worked out that she was Masha, not Misha, she was moved down the corridor to a girls' room. Masha and Mukhamedov paired up quite naturally. The three boys spent their time with Masha and her room-mate Galina Pshenichnaya, walking in the forest, bundled up against the snow, pulling the girls on their sledges, and everyone accepted that Mukhamedov and Masha were sweethearts. But it was a chaste romance. While Terentiev and Zaharchenko disappeared into the trees with their girlfriends, it took all Mukhamedov's nerve to hold Masha's hand, let alone indulge in the adolescent experiments he was sure his friends were conducting in the snowy forest. And later in their room, when the two juvenile Lotharios compared notes, Mukhamedov maintained a discreet, not to say embarrassed, silence. Nevertheless, his pulse-rate quickened satisfyingly whenever he laid eyes on Masha, and she, on her first visit to the winter camp, was extremely pleased with the outcome.

Back at school, their romance blossomed comfortably. They would meet between classes, on the stairs or in the corridor, shake hands and talk. They never kissed, just shook hands. When they met in the mornings, when he walked her home at night, they shook hands. And the clasped fingers lingered and lingered. Only at thirteen can a polite handshake express such a welter of unspoken, turbulent yearning. During the summer Masha burbled about her new sweetheart to her family, dismissing scathing remarks about the social inconvenience and doubtful intelligence of the Tartar nation, and boasting of his handsome looks, how polite and considerate he was and how happy he made her. In Kazan, Mukhamedov wrestled with his hormones and said nothing.

Masha's thirteenth birthday fell on 12 September 1974, a few days after the start of the new school year, and she eagerly anticipated Mukhamedov's appearance at her birthday party. But what a present was in store for her. On the day before her birthday Masha's class followed Mukhamedov's into a geography lesson. One of the boys sat at Mukhamedov's desk and found his forgotten exercise book. Naturally, he immediately opened it and found Masha's name endlessly, and lovingly, inscribed on page after page. He also discovered a torn-out leaf used for passing classroom messages, the last of which had gone between Mukhamedov and his attractive neighbour, Tatiana Lavrova. 'Why do you chase after that little monkey in a skirt, Masha Kovbas?' she asked. 'She is too young for you. Why do you love her?' Anxious to hedge his bets and keep in the running with a popular girl he had admired for some time, he wrote back: 'I do not love her. She is just a tart in a mini-skirt with her bum hanging out.' Hardly able to believe his good luck at being handed such a juicy morsel, the boy pushed the book into Masha's hands, conveniently opened at the offending page.

Masha was furious. After the lesson the humiliated girl marched up to the unsuspecting Mukhamedov, waiting as usual in the corridor with a welcoming smile and an open hand. 'I never want to speak to you or see you ever again,' she hissed, thrusting the exercise book at him. Mukhamedov was baffled as he watched her walk away. His message to Tatiana had been pure bravado; it had never crossed his mind that Masha would see it, let alone take it seriously. He telephoned her that night. 'Apologise,' she said, 'or I will never speak to you again.' Still Mukhamedov failed to grasp the consequences of his gauche scribbling and begged her to tell him what he had done wrong. There is a popular hero in Russian folklore called Ivan Tsarevich, who figures in the 'Firebird' legend, nicknamed 'Durachok'. It is a word that translates as 'simple' or 'innocent', and this neatly applied to the fourteen-year-old boy.

He was banned from the birthday celebrations. While Masha endured the family's telling her how right they had been about that Tartar boy, but hoped he would ring again, Mukhamedov wrote to her saying how much he loved and missed her. He delivered the letter by hand to her apartment block, but since he did not know the correct flat number, it went astray and Masha never received the apology she needed. The romance was over – or so they thought.

Mukhamedov's preliminary skirmish with the opposite sex confirmed his suspicion that he was not much good at it, and after Terentiev won Tatiana Lavrova's heart, the only female he tangled with for quite some time was Terpsichore.

Mukhamedov had turned fourteen in March earlier that year, the age for good Soviet citizens to commit themselves to the Communist Party apparatus, and he duly applied to the school party committee for membership of the Komsomol (Young Communist Party), in which, theoretically, he would remain until eligible for the adult section at eighteen. He was an ideal candidate. The party wanted children like Mukhamedov, hard-working, well behaved, not too precocious but willing, and happy to do their duty. He was, after all, class captain; it seemed only natural that he should take on additional political responsibility, however limited. You must join Komsomol, the party officials told him; you will be a good example to the others. Mukhamedov conscientiously learned the Komsomol rule book by heart, answered all the questions correctly at the examination at the headquarters of the Lenin Area, the part of the city in which the school lay, and paid his 2 copecks for his membership card.

His parents were delighted. As they well knew, the privileges that oiled the wheels of Soviet society were simply not available to non-party citizens and membership was essential to success.

By now, 1974–5, the pattern of Mukhamedov's life was established. With Prokofiev, he had found a new meaning in ballet; class was not just a physical struggle, but a means of personal expression. Thanks to the understanding between pupil and teacher, the forging of his remarkable technique was firmly under way, and so too was the unleashing of the power of his stage personality that was to make Mukhamedov the artist irresistible. It would be many years before Mukhamedov the man found similar freedom.

Folk and character dancing has developed a tradition of its own in Russia, and is an intrinsic part of many of the great classics. The fifth-year students began twice-weekly character-dance classes. As a signal that the boys were, in fact, growing up, a practice period was introduced one evening a week. During this hour they were free to work on whatever they wished, though under supervision, be it for the bi-annual examinations, the end of term show or just for the love of it.

Mukhamedov kept his four marks for ballet under Prokofiev, and his place at the barre next to Terentiev. His confidence with girls still failed to keep pace with the growing certainty of his dancing, even when the long-awaited moment arrived when he and his classmates officially put childhood behind them.

The Russian equivalent of secondary education finishes at fifteen, and in June 1975, the end of Mukhamedov's fifth year at the Moscow Ballet School, class 5V sat their final examinations. It was vital to pass in all subjects to continue the next phase of study in the Moscow Ballet School, no longer schoolboys but students in the Institute section of the school. Always nervous at examinations, Mukhamedov managed to gather his wits together sufficiently to pass with a four in Russian language and literature, history and geography, and to scrape through mathematics with the bare minimum of three. His ballet mark remained a steady four. To celebrate he holidayed with Terentiev at his home in Ashkhabad before returning to Kazan, where he remained for the rest of the summer. He had lost touch with Vadim, his childhood friend, and felt isolated from his contemporaries in his home town. Mukhamedov spent his time with his family, restless and faintly bored, thinking only of getting back to Moscow.

6

Adolescence and Graduation

THREE BOYS LEFT Moscow in June; three young men moved together into the sixth-year dormitory in September 1975. No more school uniform meant jeans and flared trousers. They were no longer boys on probation in school but were starting their serious training for a grown-up career. That meant swearing, smoking, long hair, the Beatles and roubles in their pockets.

The Soviet government encouraged its young citizens to continue in education after the age of fifteen by providing an allowance – but it demanded political correctness in return. The better you had behaved yourself in the preceding years, the more you received. While Terentiev's and Zaharchenko's allowances fluctuated with their reputations, and end of term report, Mukhamedov's spotless schoolboy record, class captaincy and his membership of Komsomol earned him a steady 30 roubles a month. Immediately all sorts of doors opened, particularly café doors. He could now occasionally spurn school lunches and indulge his taste for dumplings and ice-cream at nearby restaurants, or pay for the sweetened carrots he so coveted from the Moscow counter of the canteen.

Zaharchenko looked after their tailoring requirements, cutting into trouser seams and adding material to achieve the seventies bell-bottom look essential at the time, it seems, on both sides of the Iron Curtain. Terentiev had acquired an enviable collection of jeans on his trip to America, but Mukhamedov raided the Internat wardrobe for trousers and relied on Zaharchenko's flair with a needle and cotton for fashionable embellishments. Freedom from school uniform also increased their chances of working the age-old dodge at the local cinema. No longer obviously under age, they took their chance in the box office queue, and if turned out, tried to persuade friendly-looking strangers to buy tickets on their behalf.

Shaving suddenly became an important part of the daily routine. Regular applications of the razor, teenage youths are told, encourage a manly growth of facial hair, but it took Mukhamedov some time to develop a five o'clock shadow, let alone the embryo moustache he subsequently sported. He pioneered the smoking habit in his room, a necessary attribute to a professional dancer in Russia, as anyone in Britain who has fought through the backstage clouds of cigarette smoke of visiting Russian companies will know. Girls took them seriously too, not that Terentiev and Zaharchenko had ever had much trouble making their mark. But there is a world of difference between holding hands on school outings, satchels strapped to backs, and inviting a girl to admire your flares as you play a Beatles tape and jive the night away – or, at least, until a grown-up packs you off to your rooms for lights-out at nine.

Outfacing the local Moscow boys now provided an extra frisson. The uniformed ballet school boys were, and still are, an obvious target for pavement banditry by the surrounding 'civilian' youth. In mufti, cornered alone by the roaming gangs, and obviously a foreigner, there was nothing to fall back on, remembers Mukhamedov; it was up to you and your own bravado to convince your friends, and yourself, that you acted the hero. When Mukhamedov turned sixteen in March, he was issued with his domestic passport. He was now officially adult, he could vote, drive, marry with his parent's approval; it is the age in Russia of criminal responsibility, access to adult films and, most important of all, vodka. The friends began to carve out their own little autonomous empire in Second Frunzenskaya Street, tentatively to throw their weight about, answer the older boys back and bully the juniors – except in ballet class.

Prokofiev worked the boys harder than ever and their academic studies placed more and more emphasis on the nature and history of art in general. In addition, twice-weekly pas de deux classes were added to the character and acting lessons. Pas de deux is a dance form at which Mukhamedov obviously excels. He has always been strong, and a natural concern for his partner gives his work a rare synchronisation and fluidity. Igor Ukhsusnikov, an ex-Kirov dancer who taught the boys pas de deux, liked Mukhamedov for his manly bearing; he quickly moved him to the front of the class and used him

Kazan: first steps.

Top left and right: Matyanova's star pupil, and *that* haircut.
Bottom: First day at the Moscow Ballet School, September 1970.

Top: Final-year barre work at the Moscow Ballet School, 1978. *Left to right:*
Irek Mukhamedov, Alexei Fadeyechev, Igor Terentiev, Vladimir
Terokhin.

Bottom left to right: Igor Terentiev, Alexei Fadeyechev, Irek
Mukhamedov, Yevgeni Zaharchenko.

Top left: Graduation examination, 1978: Mukhamedov in a character dance with Yevgenia Farmanyants.

Top right: Class concert, 1977: performing the Prince's variation from *Swan Lake*.

Bottom: Graduation performance, 1978: with Erica Lonzina in *Coppélia*.

'The class of '78', June 1978. *Back row, left to right:* Alexei Varonin, Vladimir Terokhin, Andrei Sapayev, Yevgeni Zaharchenko, Mikhail Batukhtin (Hlustikov); *2nd back row:* Vitaly Maliakin, Alexei Fadeyechev, Renat Gizatulin, Igor Terentiev, Irek Mukhamedov, Irina Vedeneyeva, Yelena Boychuk; *next row:* Svetlana Ivanova, Tatiana Lavrova, Svetlana Glukova, Irina Shabalina, Natalia Maximova; *front row:* Inna Varonina (teacher historic dance), Alexander Prokofiev (teacher boys' classical ballet), Ljudmilla Chistova (teacher girls' classical ballet), Yevgenia Farmanyants (teacher boys' and girls' character dance).

Top: With Natalia Stavro in the 'Carnival in Venice' pas de deux from *Saturnilla*, Moscow Classical Ballet.

Bottom left: Second round of the Fourth Moscow International Competition, June 1981: in the 'Diana and Acteon' pas de deux.

Bottom right: First round: with Galina Krapivina in the *Le Corsaire* pas de deux.

Top: Third round: with Galina Krapivina in the *Don Quixote* pas de deux.

Bottom left: Mukhamedov receives his prize, and an invitation to the Bolshoi, from Yuri Nikolaievich Grigorovich.

Bottom right: Third round: in a variation from the *Don Quixote* pas de deux.

Mukhamedov in his début in *Spartacus* with the Bolshoi Ballet, December 1981.

and his partner for demonstrating. Mukhamedov learned a trick from Ukhsusnikov that caused adolescent squirms in 1976 but has stood him in good stead ever since. 'When you are supporting promenades with the girl on pointe in attitude,' he says, 'Ukhsusnikov told us boys to aim our hand straight between her tits. We were embarrassed, but it's true – she will never fall over.' In the end of year performance in June 1976 the boys of 6V provided the corps de ballet while the graduating students performed the solos in *Classical Symphony* to Sergei Prokofiev's music, a ballet choreographed by Leonid Lavrovsky for the school in the 1960s. For the first time Mukhamedov executed a *double tour en l'air*, one of the basic and potentially most spectacular jumps in the male repertoire of classical steps, on the Bolshoi Theatre stage.

He loved and thrived on the extra work, and the added responsibility student status carried, but a subtle shift began to take place between himself and Terentiev. The dangerous consequences of too much talent started to show in his friend's work. While Mukhamedov could not rest until he jumped higher, turned more, danced better, six years of being the best took the edge off Terentiev's attack. He appeared complacent as Mukhamedov improved. Classes were no longer designed solely around Terentiev's needs and attributes, and the centre work, particularly jumps, was concentrated more and more on Mukhamedov. Prokofiev rewarded his young Tartar's guts with the maximum five marks at the end of the year, a standard he maintained until he graduated.

Back home that summer, Mukhamedov smoked and drank as an equal with his father and brother and the other male relatives who came and went on family visits – and made it clear to his mother his hair would grow as long as he wished. But as he moved into manhood, he began to realise that it would take more than alcohol and nicotine to earn his parents' understanding of his chosen profession. Rasheda and Djavdat, and Nail, were always supportive and proud of his achievements, but they had no notion what ballet was about or what it meant to him, and nor, he was forced to accept, would they ever have. The separateness inherent in growing up was nearly complete.

Prokofiev's stable of talent, which included Mukhamedov, Terentiev and Zaharchenko, had by now gained such a reputation for excellence in the school that Alexei Fadeyechev, who was considered to be the best of the school's Moscow section and for whom a glittering career in the Bolshoi Ballet had already been predicted, was transferred by his father from Pyotr Pestov's class to Prokofiev's for the final two years of his training. Fadeyechev, Terentiev and Mukhamedov – that was the line-up at the centre barre in September 1976, their penultimate year of study at the Moscow Ballet School.

The school performances for that year were *Swan Lake* and *Classical Symphony*, in both of which Terentiev and Mukhamedov played supporting roles in the corps de ballet to Fadeyechev's solos. There was also the first performance of Sophia Golovkina's production of *Coppélia*, a ballet that, one year later, was to prove pivotal in establishing Mukhamedov's reputation.

Adolescent excess nearly jeopardised it, however. He, Terentiev and Zaharchenko, used by now to asserting themselves, decided to fill in a particularly blank Sunday evening with a private party in their room at the school. The smuggled bottles of beer and vodka were soon emptied and, in their inebriated state, disposing of the empties through the bedroom window into the street below suddenly seemed a hysterically amusing idea. The satisfying smash of breaking glass echoing through the deserted Moscow streets confirmed their decision. Golovkina thought otherwise. So did the three hung-over friends the next morning, lined up outside her office. Prokofiev's observation had been pithy and realistic: if you must drink, do it quietly. Golovkina threatened instant dismissal, an unrealistic prospect considering the quality of talent paraded before her, even in the dilapidated condition in which it presented itself that morning. Abject apologies followed the dire threats and then it was back to class, where Mukhamedov was feeling his superior strength. Thanks to his stocky physique, he was still classified as second fiddle to Terentiev and Fadeyechev, with their skinny classical looks, yet that very physique gave him the stamina and power to achieve a control and height, particularly in the air, that the others failed to match.

A month before the summer break Mukhamedov was jostling for lunch in the canteen queue when he noticed a tall, dark-haired girl who was eating with a group of friends. The face was familiar to him – it belonged to an Internat boarder one year below him – but something about the way Tatiana Nyemtseva moved her head caught his attention. Overcoming his morbid shyness, he went over and introduced himself. The attraction was mutual and in the remaining days of the term the couple spent much of their spare time getting to know each other. He ignored his room-mates, veterans as they were of the girls' corridors, and their ribald advice on the fundamentals of a relationship, but knew the time would soon be right to venture further than a handshake.

September 1977, and the dream was over. Mukhamedov was one of a very edgy batch of seventeen-year-olds suddenly facing their final year in the shelter of the Moscow Ballet School. Next May they would hope to graduate in class work, pas de deux, character dancing and repertoire; the academic examinations would follow a month later. A failure in just one subject in either group and the vital piece of paper – the all-hallowed diploma that granted professional status to the recipient – would be withheld. And in the document-ridden Soviet society that would mean the end of a dancing career before it had begun. The Internat boarders began casting around for prospective companies: Perm, Riga, Novosibirsk, Odessa. During the holidays Rasheda and Djavdat had urged Mukhamedov to apply for the Kazan company, but for a young man determined to make his own way in life, settling back in his home town was unthinkable. For the Internat students, the Bolshoi Ballet did not figure in their plans, though it might in their dreams, for they knew perfectly well that the few places that became available would, in time-honoured custom, be the exclusive reward of the Moscow graduates. The Moscow Classical Ballet Company was the only realistic alternative, but it was a small company with only fifty dancers, compared with the Bolshoi's two hundred. The odds against securing a place were enormous.

For the non-Muscovites there was also the problem of acquiring a permit to live in the capital if they were unsuccessful in their attempts at securing employment there. A traditional recourse for Internat boys at the school was to marry a Moscow girl, which automatically bestowed residence status. Options were weighed, stakes claimed and serious dating embarked upon that later resulted in at least three weddings of convenience, and three extra Muscovites, for the class of '78. Mukhamedov had made an almost conscious decision to fall in love with Tatiana Nyemtseva. It was an obligatory rite of passage for a youth of his age, as Terentiev never lost an opportunity to point out. Since her family lived outside Moscow, marriage to Tatiana could be only for love, not a passport. Meanwhile, there was work to do. Classes for the boys of 8V took on a new impetus and they paid the sort of urgent attention to Prokofiev's corrections that he wished he had seen during the past four years. The evening practice sessions were suddenly packed with guilt-ridden youngsters hoping to make up for lost time. Fadeyechev began rehearsals for the role of Franz in the school's second performance of *Coppélia* (Golovkina had turned down Prokofiev's suggestion of Mukhamedov for understudy, saying that a stand-by was unnecessary), Terentiev for a variation from *The Nutcracker*. Mukhamedov was given his first solo to learn, the first variation in the pas de trois from *Swan Lake*, Act I, which in the Soviet version is danced by the Prince.

Prokofiev was disappointed with Terentiev's efforts, since last-minute exertion could not compensate for past laziness. His elevation was poor and his whole performance lacklustre; a natural turn-out, he discovered, was not enough. Prokofiev withdrew Terentiev from the end of term performance. In the afternoon of 6 November 1977 Mukhamedov danced his first solo at the Bolshoi Theatre. There were no flashes of destiny in the young dancer's soul, no prescience of future glory. He cannot even remember which dressing-room he used, just the overwhelming sense of relief he felt as, exhausted by nerves, he completed the final pirouette and left the stage without falling over or banging into the scenery. That was only the start of the momentum that was rushing Mukhamedov to the end of his boyhood. Fadeyechev injured his knee during rehearsals for Franz, and a replacement was urgently required – *Coppélia* was in its final stages of rehearsal. Mukhamedov learned the role in three weeks and in January 1978 danced Franz, his first principal role, at the Kremlin's Palace of Congresses Theatre.

His ascendancy was complete. He could not compete with Fadeyechev's name, nor his Moscow status, but Mukhamedov was now top of the pile in the Internat section. He and Tatiana had become lovers earlier in the term and at last Mukhamedov joined in his room-mates' nocturnal wanderings. 'The school theatre was the best place to meet at night,' he recalls. 'There were many secret places to be alone.' And accommodating teachers looked the other way. Life was good for Mukhamedov. He now had principal status at the school, he had a lover and a growing confidence; what he did not have was a job. As the May graduation ceremony drew nearer and the prospect of a place in the Bolshoi was as remote as ever, he auditioned for a Moscow-based modern jazz group, Souvenirs, but heard nothing. In desperation he turned to the Red Army Folk Dance Ensemble; at least he would be stationed in Moscow. The Army was unimpressed. OK, come back tomorrow and enlist if you want to, he was told. He somehow resisted the offer.

Directors from all over the Soviet Union gather to attend the Moscow Ballet School graduation performances, held in the Bolshoi Theatre. In 1978 they took place from 15 to 17 May, watched by, among many others, the Bolshoi Ballet's Yuri Grigorovich, and Vladimir Vasilyov and Natalia Kasatkina from the Moscow Classical Ballet. Aunt Galina was there, but, though officially invited, Djavdat and Rasheda were unable to take time off work. Mukhamedov danced Franz in the third act of *Coppélia*. After the show the anxious graduates made their way to their classrooms to learn their fate. Each student had a form that listed the country's towns that supported their own ballet company and which of those companies wished to engage that boy or girl. Mukhamedov's list was headed by the Moscow Classical Ballet. 'I agree,' was his relieved response. Terentiev had, to no one's surprise, been offered a place at the Bolshoi, but discreetly turned it down. Tatiana Lavrova was to join the Moscow Classical Ballet and, deeply in love, he wished to dance and be with her.

Not until late June, when the results of the academic examinations were announced, did the graduates receive the diplomas that officially bestowed on them professional rank. Fadeyechev and other well-connected Moscow students won a prestigious red document for the family scrapbook, but Internat dancers had to be satisfied with a more mundane blue souvenir. Terentiev married his Tatiana, and while Mukhamedov's girlfriend went off on her family holiday, he and a group of friends accompanied the newly-weds on honeymoon. The wedding festivities, largely spent in an alcoholic haze, meant the two friends missed the last-night party at the Moscow Ballet School at which graduates say goodbye and thank you to their fellows and teachers. It was a slight to which Mukhamedov attributed an apparent coolness a few months later between himself and Alexander Prokofiev, who had been his friend and mentor for the last five years.

7

The Moscow Classical Ballet Company

RARELY DOES A dancer's first appearance as a professional make banner headlines. Nijinsky's humble début, for instance, was not even with a ballet company; he danced one of the four temple blackamoors in the opera *Aida*. Still, it was at least in an opera house – the Maryinsky in St Petersburg – and in Russia. Mukhamedov took this low-key approach yet further. His first professional steps were taken not in a theatre, let alone an opera house, but in a Roman amphitheatre thousands of miles from his homeland, in Busra Al-chem, on the western edge of the Syrian desert.

At the beginning of July Terentiev, his wife Tatiana Lavrova and Mukhamedov had arrived for their first day of rehearsals at the Moscow Classical Ballet Company headquarters, which occupied the third and fourth floors of the old Moscow Ballet School, across the street from the Bolshoi. They were shown to the office of the company directors, Vladimir Vasilyov and Natalia Kasatkina, who delivered the first-day exhortation familiar to young dancers the world over. You are all soloists, they were told, there are no corps de ballet dancers in this company. (The beginners were left to learn for themselves that some are more soloist than others.) Work hard and you will soon be principals. And don't waste time staring at that building across the road, the directors added, pointing through the window at the huge bronze statue of Apollo and his rearing horses clearly visible on the roof of the Bolshoi's portico. Don't even think of dancing in that theatre – you must be proud to be members of Moscow Classical Ballet. 'No, no, no. I will give my life to Moscow Classical Ballet,' was Mukhamedov's predictable reply. No sooner had the three friends finalised residency registration at the company hostel on the Riazansky Prospekt (though Mukhamedov opted to live for the time being with Aunt Galina) and gladly accepted the dizzyingly grand salary of 160 roubles a month than they were issued with passports, driven to the airport and flown out to Syria on the first of an almost endless series of foreign tours that was to be a feature of their lives for the next decade.

The first performances of the tour took place in Busra, 113 kilometres south of Damascus, when the Moscow Classical Ballet presented *The Creation of the World*. Choreographed by Vladimir Vasilyov and Natalia Kasatkina to music by Andrei Petrov, the ballet was a perfect vehicle for the initiation of newcomers. A minimum of rehearsals were required for them to walk on as part of the amorphous mass of humanity that brought the work to an end. Vasilyov and Kasatkina had originally created the work for the Kirov Ballet in St Petersburg in 1971, when a young man called Mikhail Baryshnikov made a striking impression as Adam. There were no ripples of future fame for Mukhamedov – that was to come later. His task now was to learn his trade.

The company of between fifty and sixty dancers, which is small by Russian standards, was originally named the Young Ballet. It was founded in 1967 by Igor Moiseyev and had a specific brief from the government to tour classical ballet to parts of the Soviet Union, and abroad, that larger companies could not visit. Ten years later Kasatkina and Vasilyov, reaching the end of their careers as leading dancers with the Bolshoi Ballet, took over the company. While they maintained the extensive touring obligations, they endeavoured to bring more gravitas to their little group by extending the repertoire to include their own modern works and by establishing a performance foothold in the capital. They offered themselves as an attraction at the cavernous Palace of Congresses Theatre inside the Kremlin walls. An unprepossessing hall, it has a vast platform stage and stark square lines. The eight-hundred-room palace was built at Khrushchev's bidding in 1961 to house the 22nd Congress of the Communist Party of the Soviet Union, as well as for state functions, galas and receptions. The glass and concrete pile became the focal point of government-subsidised coach trips from all over the Soviet Union. Posters in factories throughout the country tempted workers with the prospect: after a day's sightseeing in Moscow, enjoy an evening at the ballet – in the heart of the Kremlin! The crude but effective marketing ploy has kept the arena-sized auditorium full ever since.

It was in this comparatively rootless and contrived working environment that Mukhamedov cut his professional teeth. And it was at the Palace of Congresses Theatre that he made his Moscow début with the company on 23 August 1978, walking on, again unnoticed, in *The Creation of the World*. He made more of an impact three days later when he danced his first professional solo role, partnering the company's leading dancer, Natalia Stavro, in a virtuoso pas de deux, the 'Carnival in Venice' excerpt from *Saturnilla*, a little known, early work by Marius Petipa to music by Cesare Pugni. It was a crucial test for the eighteen-year-old. He had been given precedence in a solo role over Terentiev, so, he felt, the directors must have faith in him. His future depended on how he handled himself in this large part – he had to do well. 'Stavro was a bit big for me,' he remembers. 'But it was easy. I put her on my shoulder and ran. Everything worked.' He was unaware of effortlessly covering the huge stage; if the unfamiliar following spot was blinding, he did not notice. He turned with ease and jumped spectacularly. 'I was hypnotised,' he says. The surge of power he experienced that afternoon was to take over his whole life. He now knew beyond any doubt that the stage was his milieu and that ballet was all he needed.

Kasatkina and Vasilyov joined other company members congratulating the jubilant young man after the show, and Mukhamedov eagerly awaited Alexander Prokofiev's verdict, knowing his former ballet school teacher had made a special point of attending the performance. 'What was the matter with you?' Prokofiev asked. 'Your eyes were frightened. Why were you so scared?' Mukhamedov was stunned. Why was the man who had meant most to the growing schoolboy so grudging in his comments? Had he not done enough to earn at least faint praise for his first professional success? Was Prokofiev repaying Mukhamedov for his insulting absence from the school graduation party? After graduating from the Moscow Ballet School, which had been his home for so many important years, the dancer had been shocked to learn that he could not come and go in the building as he wished. When he visited Tatiana, he was forced to telephone her from the foyer or ask a student to take her a message. He had been deeply hurt when told that he no longer belonged there. Now, stung by Prokofiev's coldness, he resolved to have nothing more to do with the place, to put his schooldays behind him and to concentrate on his professional life. Which, perhaps, was precisely what Prokofiev intended.

It was about this time that Naum Azarin, a nephew of the great Bolshoi ballet master Asaf Messerer, joined the Moscow Classical Ballet from the city's Stanislavsky–Nemirovich-Danchenko Theatre. Azarin was a well-known and highly respected teacher of the day with a special gift for bringing out the potential in young professional dancers. Building on Mukhamedov's success in the 'Carnival in Venice' excerpt, he began coaching Mukhamedov in the *Don Quixote* pas de deux, one of the most famous bravura works in the classical repertoire. It was a collaboration that was to turn Mukhamedov from a talented young hopeful into a legend.

Having put childish ways behind him, or so he thought, it was time for Mukhamedov to learn about life in a small ballet company. Terentiev and his new wife were naturally busy with each other and their new home in the company hostel, while Mukhamedov lived at his aunt's flat. The bonds of friendship inevitably loosened. Terentiev's laziness, apparent in the later years at school, was growing, and caused a further awkwardness between the two friends. He found excuses not to dance full out at rehearsals, complained of minor ailments and, though still respected for his talent, gradually gave up his place as the favourite for success. Mukhamedov's affair with Tatiana Nyemtseva, in her last year at the Moscow Ballet School, had also cooled off. They still met and made love, but not often. She found occasional consolation with other boys at the school, and he became more and more involved with his life's true absorbing passion: ballet.

Mukhamedov was gradually drawn into a circle of older men within the company, some happily married, some on the brink of divorce, but most of them single, who enjoyed a masculine lifestyle that is peculiarly Russian. A great deal of spare time was spent in the steam baths, eating, smoking and drinking vodka – there was an odd piquancy, Mukhamedov found, in becoming increasingly inebriated and simultaneously cleaner – and talking about women. When they tired of theorising about the opposite sex, they invited a few of them round to one of the group's bachelor flats for yet more vodka, and research of a more practical nature. Mukhamedov happily paid his 10 roubles into the kitty for these stag sessions and learned a great deal about the traditions of the theatre, the ways of men and the facts of life, but retreated from exploring the earthier delights of the women only too anxious to give him a helping hand. Group sex frightened the life out of him and, using his love for Tatiana as an excuse, he would leave as the sessions became steamier. Anyway, he had to be in condition for the next day's class and rehearsals; his more worldly companions, who liked him no less for it, probably remembered how that felt.

Vasilyov and Kasatkina were pleased with their new recruit, and no wonder. Not only did he have talent and a boundless enthusiasm, but he was malleable too. Instead of demanding attention and praise for his early achievements, he was almost embarrassingly grateful and compliant – a director's dream. Later that year they rewarded him with the lead role of the Shepherd in their version of *The Rite of Spring* and were further impressed by Mukhamedov's refusal to count out Stravinsky's notoriously difficult music, whose fiendishly complex rhythms had defeated dancers for sixty years. They had created the work at the Bolshoi in 1965 for Yuri Vladimirov, one of the most forceful of the Soviet-style heroic dancers that the Bolshoi Ballet had then produced. The ease with which Mukhamedov coped with all the choreographic tricks that Vasilyov and Kasatkina had thrown at his formidable predecessor astonished them.

In January 1979 Moscow was waiting for Yuri Grigorovich's new production of *Romeo and Juliet* at the Bolshoi, but the Moscow Classical Ballet managed to upstage its seniors with Vasilyov and Kasatkina's version. Mukhamedov was Tybalt, a part that he felt comfortable in and relished for its dramatic possibilities. 'The character is bad, awful,' he says, 'and I like it' – a precursor of his hypnotic interpretation of one of the great monsters of all time, Ivan the Terrible. He had less affinity with his next leading role, in the same choreographers' *Gayaneh*. He was the romantic hero, Armen, but the small amount of dancing the part required frustrated him and the choreography seemed awkward; he found the long, slow central pas de deux difficult and trying to perform chaine turns backwards across the stage self-defeating. Besides, the villain, Kurd, had all the best steps to Khachaturian's rousing tunes. It was not a success.

In the summer of that year Tatiana Nyemtseva graduated from the Ballet School and, like all her colleagues in the Internat, was scrambling for a job and a means to stay in Moscow. Naturally she turned to Irek. He was already a prominent figure in the Moscow Classical Ballet Company; if not yet a star, he clearly had a bright future and was therefore not without influence with his masters. Surely, she felt, he would ask Kasatkina and Vasilyov to allow her to be at his side. The couple had discussed marriage in the early flush of their affair, but had grown less committed to their relationship since Mukhamedov's graduation. In March earlier that year, during a tour of Armenia, Mukhamedov had accepted a birthday present in the bed of a girl in the company after a particularly drunken party. Nevertheless, marriage to Tatiana was still an option. She did not need to spell out her expectations to her boyfriend when she auditioned for the company in May, but Tatiana had badly miscalculated. Mukhamedov knew that if he succeeded in per-suading the company directors to enlist her, it would lead inevitably to pressure to marry. At the age of nineteen he was already dancing principal roles in a well-known Moscow ballet company scarcely a year after his graduation, he was appreciated by his bosses and he had found a teacher in Naum Azarin with whom he felt a special affinity. He was profoundly grateful that all he had ever wanted in life seemed to be materialising. There was no choice. He had lost his virginity to Tatiana because he thought the time was right; he felt he loved her because he had been brought up to believe a man was honour bound to do so if he slept with a woman. There was nothing in his feelings for her to compare with the real driving force in his life, his will to succeed in his chosen profession. He said nothing on Tatiana's behalf to the company directors, leaving the decision to them, and waited for her audition with some trepidation.

Tatiana arrived at Pushetchnaya Street certain that Mukhamedov had spoken for her, and was devastated when she was informed after class that she would not be admitted to the company. By chance the couple came face to face on the stairs, she angry and uncomprehend-ing, he red-faced and uncomfortable. Mukhamedov mumbled an apology, wished her luck and fled. Tatiana eventually found work in her home town of Odessa. In spite of his betrayal, and in the best romantic fiction tradition, she never stopped loving him, as Mukhamedov was later to discover.

But there is little time, or energy, for self-doubt and castigation when you are a fit young dancer discovering every day that you can make your body respond to hitherto impossible technical demands, and, to Mukhamedov, self-absorption had always been anathema. Any guilt he felt about Tatiana was soon burned up in the impetus of his work. Under Azarin's guidance, he was learning that his natural co-ordination was an asset worth more than a naturally high extension. 'I felt my whole body worked together for the most complicated steps,' he remembers, when he rehearsed for the *Le Corsaire* pas de deux. Azarin was a great admirer of Rudolf Nureyev, having closely followed his short career at the Kirov and in the West after his defection, and would encourage his charge to experiment with some of Nureyev's more difficult combinations. To Mukhamedov's amazement and delight, they were successful more often than not. A high extension was also important, of course, and the lack of it created problems for his stocky, tightly knit frame. He diligently forced himself into splits every day to loosen his hips and improve his turn-out. He was extremely dissatisfied with his pirouettes, for they were never consistent enough. But this daily battle was now his life's blood. He added *Le Corsaire* to his repertoire during his second year in the company, as well as appearing as a soloist in a Goleizovsky work to music by Prokofiev entitled *Memolyotnosti*.

Mukhamedov fell into a routine on performance days. He would rise early, breakfast and go to class; there were usually no rehearsals in the afternoon of a performance, and he would sleep for a couple of hours, wake around five, drink some coffee and go to the theatre. It was a pattern he was to follow for the rest of his life.

It takes only a cursory glance at his roles so far with the Moscow Classical Ballet to show that Mukhamedov's categorisation as a demi-character dancer was already virtually complete. *Romeo and Juliet, Gayaneh, The Rite of Spring*, and the three virtuoso pas de deux, though admittedly from the classical repertoire, all emphasised his bravura technique, his powerful physique and overtly masculine attack. Caught up at the time in the thrill of his first appearances on-stage, he was grateful for the opportunities afforded him. Only later in life did he find the restrictions this type of role placed on him irksome.

In the late summer of 1979 the company repeated their tour of the Middle East, a part of the world that held no attraction for Mukhamedov. But that year it was to be the scene of a meeting of significant personal consequence for him: he became involved with his first wife, Ljudmilla Kudriavtseva. Ljuda had joined Moscow Classical Ballet from her home town of Perm, where she had been a star pupil of the famous ballet school there, shortly after Kasatkina and Vasilyov had taken the company over. She was (and is) a small, vivacious red-haired dancer, of the type described as 'useful', since they can be relied upon to serve a choreographer's needs, usually in the ensemble; Ljuda, however, was occasionally rewarded with a small solo. Mukhamedov, busy coping with the increasing demands of his budding career, had rarely come across this particular corps de ballet dancer, who was three years his senior, but of course knew her face. One night in September at the company hotel in Baghdad, during one of the regular post-performance parties at which he drank too much vodka, Mukhamedov enjoyed the attentions of the pretty red-head, as would any fit young man with normal appetites. And Tatiana was only a memory. They left the party early together and made love.

Mukhamedov's attitude to women was quite straightforward: they were there for sex, a mutually enjoyable pastime preferably conducted with the minimum of speech. He still found genuine companionship with his male friends in the company, whereas conversation with a woman seemed a contradiction in terms. The pragmatic Ljuda found this arrangement perfectly satisfactory, and their affair developed along contentedly lustful, if fairly non-communicative, lines. Eventually, however, Ljuda woke to the challenge that her young lover presented. 'She began to treat me as if I were nothing,' Mukhamedov remembers. 'So I felt I must make her feel I was important to her. I told her I loved her and paid her a lot of attention.' Soon they were seen everywhere together, and their friends accepted that Ljuda and Mukhamedov were seriously involved.

At this stage in his life any woman could have filled the gap that Ljuda occupied. Nearly out of his teens, he was almost a man, and was acquiring a certain standing in life through his gradual but steady success in the company. A man must have a woman, he thought, to complete the picture of social acceptability, and Ljuda was pretty, a good dancer and a willing lover. Thanks to his single-minded obsession with ballet, he felt he lacked most social graces; his shyness was compounded by his awkwardness with the opposite sex in general. Ljuda, naturally gregarious and never at a loss in company, was a strong-willed woman who appeared to know what she wanted. She provided, in fact, precisely the buffer he needed between himself and the emotional realities of life so that he could fully concentrate on his dancing. He convinced himself he loved her and was prepared to make himself responsible for her – by no means an ideal basis for a relationship, though worse have been known. Mukhamedov left Aunt Galina's flat and moved into Ljuda's room at the company's hostel. Galina was horrified. She was losing her surrogate son to another woman, and she intuitively knew that he was not ready for this type of commitment. He was naïve and impulsive and easily led, fair game for an older manipulative woman. Galina, intensely proud of her nephew's achievements in dance, feared for his future. She was correct, of course, in one sense, but she underrated his strength of purpose when it came to ballet.

This was Mukhamedov's first foray into a domestic life, Aunt Galina being the only other woman with whom he had shared a home since he had left his family in Kazan. Life with Ljuda quickly settled into its own routine. He recalls how literally Ljuda interpreted his stated desire to look after her; she rarely went to the shops, only occasionally cooked and never washed the dishes. For the first time in his life Mukhamedov not only bought the potatoes, but peeled and cooked them too; he continued to wash his own practice clothes and, weary after a day's rehearsal and performance, would try to keep the place clean. As always, he did his duty and at first it was fun. He could come and go as he pleased (depending, that is, on Ljuda's demands), he could smoke and drink as he wished and sex was no longer furtive. To Mukhamedov the whole adventure was like growing up – looking after his woman made him feel a real man. To begin with he even tolerated her gibes about his Tartar nationality and constant criticisms of his dancing. Being hen-pecked was all part of it, or so he thought.

He was dancing Tybalt and Armen, his biggest roles to date, during the initial phase of their affair, and expected Ljuda to share both the success and problems he encountered in what was an immensely stimulating stage of his young career. Gradually her negative responses grew more and more disheartening, and so he no longer discussed his work with her at all. It took a remarkably short time for him to shut her out of his professional life altogether. A bad mistake on Ljuda's part, as, to the most casual observer, it was quite clear where Mukhamedov's priorities lay – the way to his heart was through his dancing. And an early danger signal he himself was reluctant to recognise was his reaction to the inevitable dressing-room banter concerning their relationship. Mukhamedov would react angrily to his colleagues' coarse observations on the nature of his feelings, a sensitivity he had never shown when confident of his love for Tatiana.

Two months after Mukhamedov moved in with Ljuda a new girl, Svetlana Kubasova, joined the Moscow Classical Ballet from Saratov in southern Russia, and had to be provided with accommodation in the capital. There was a shortage of space in the hostel, and as the company officials were unaware of Mukhamedov's new abode, she was allocated the spare bed in Ljuda's room, a farcical situation that Mukhamedov found intolerable. He asked his aunt if they could move in with her. 'Of course *you* can,' she replied, 'but not with Ljuda.' The more he encountered opposition to his affair with Ljuda, the stronger became his loyalty to her, so he gritted his teeth and put up with the bizarre sleeping arrangements for the next twelve months. Ljuda's answer to the *ménage à trois* was marriage. As man and wife they would be entitled to a place of their own, like the Terentievs, and could at least apply for a flat, even if it would take some time to materialise. Marriage was now the spectre at the feast for Mukhamedov. He had narrowly escaped the issue with Tatiana, and with Ljuda he hoped to achieve the best of both worlds, enjoying the benefits, such as they were, of living with a woman while avoiding a basic commitment. But one truth he knew with absolute certainty was that ballet came first.

That year Rasheda and Djavdat travelled to Moscow together to see their son, and to deliver their annual thank-you gift, a Tartar sweetmeat, to Kasatkina and Vasilyov. They stayed as usual with

Galina and were visited by Mukhamedov, alone. He felt that introducing Ljuda to his parents might be misconstrued as an admission of an honourable intention he did not have.

Since joining the company, Naum Azarin had taken a particular interest in Mukhamedov, recognising the potential scope of the young man's talent, sensing that he was more than a jumping machine. Azarin made sure that he coached the dancer not only in the classical repertoire, but also in the newer works. He would take Mukhamedov to his flat to show him videos of Rudolf Nureyev's performances in the West, and urge him to watch how his fellow Tartar expressed character and mood through every step, no matter how athletic or simple. As they watched *Le Corsaire*, he said, 'See how he does the bow', that famous obeisance in three-quarter profile with fingertips to breast, and pointed out that every complicated aerial trick in Nureyev's *Don Quixote* rippled with Spanish arrogance. These sessions were conducted in secrecy, usually with the curtains drawn, as Nureyev was at that time officially reviled in the Soviet Union, condemned as a traitor to his homeland.

In 1980 Mukhamedov added Romeo to his growing repertoire. Azarin, having already realised that the young man benefited from being pushed, and hard, proposed that he enter for the bi-annual Soviet Union Ballet Competition, held exclusively for Russian dancers, later in the year. But Kasatkina and Vasilyov had other ideas. Stanislav Isayev, aged twenty-four, was the undisputed principal male dancer of the Moscow Classical Ballet; he still led the company in 1984 when they danced in Britain. He was also the director's favourite, possessing that fine classicism they felt Mukhamedov lacked, and they insisted that if anyone stood a chance of winning a gold medal and bringing prestige to the company, it was Isayev. In no position to argue, Azarin backed down and comforted Mukhamedov with the promise that he would compete in the following year's Moscow International Ballet Competition. 'Let Isayev have his chance,' said Azarin. 'If you compete against him, you will be certain to win the gold. It will be much better for you to appear in the International.' The argument might have been intended as a sop to Mukhamedov's pride, particularly as Isayev took the gold in the Soviet Union Competition, but it was a startlingly accurate prophesy.

Mukhamedov remembers that year of preparation as one of intense excitement. As the competition was in June 1981 and the first audition in late August, early September 1980, there was no time to lose. Azarin carefully chose a repertoire of works for his protégé. He would dance first *Le Corsaire*, then the 'Diana and Acteon' pas de deux from *Esmeralda*, a short extract from Kasatkina and Vasilyov's *Rite of Spring* and finally the *Don Quixote* pas de deux. Azarin asked Galina Krapivina, a former pupil of his from the Stanislavsky Ballet, to partner Mukhamedov. A tall, slender blond, she would perfectly complement his dark looks and, though she would not be a competitor, the exposure would be good for her.

As he had already danced the other pas de deux, Mukhamedov and his partner started rehearsals immediately on 'Diana and Acteon'. Mukhamedov's approach to his work took on a new and vital quality during the intense period of preparation that followed. There is a world of difference between working as one of a group as he had until then, however conscientious and caring the teachers, and being the focus of one man's attention, imagination and knowledge. Azarin's manner was both gentle and implacable; he would rarely raise his voice, but he would never give up. When Mukhamedov despaired of perfecting a step, or his legs gave out from exhaustion, he would quietly urge him to rest a moment, breathe quietly and try it again. Why not see if it would work from the other side of the stage? Or on the other leg? And somehow it happened. Never close the studio door on failure, he said; get something right before you leave. If you keep falling over on the pirouettes, get the feeling right, try to find something new in the music. Mikhail Lavrovsky had introduced a fiendishly difficult jump into the 'Diana and Acteon' pas de deux when he had danced it at the Bolshoi in the 1960s, a *double tour en l'air* with the right leg extended in front, the left tucked underneath and the arms reaching for the right foot. It required extreme strength and athletic daring. Lavrovsky had performed a series of the step diagonally across the stage, but Azarin told Mukhamedov that Lavrovsky's version was too easy. He wanted him to repeat it circling the stage – *en manège*. Mukhamedov was appalled at the suggestion, but tried.

Mukhamedov's confidence grew under this experienced tutelage and he successfully completed the first audition for non-Muscovites at the Tchaikovsky Concert Hall in September, dancing *Le Corsaire*, one of hundreds performing the same variation. The repetition of music and steps and the ensuing tedium for the judges was a danger against which Azarin had carefully calculated.

In January 1981, when Moscow Classical Ballet was on tour in Siberia, the directors reluctantly gave Mukhamedov permission to attend the competition's second and final audition at the Bolshoi. To make matters worse, his partner was also touring at the time and had no possible justification for leave of absence since she was not competing. So Mukhamedov was forced to perform the *Don Quixote* pas de deux alone. In a strange echo of his fateful audition nearly eleven years earlier at the Moscow Ballet School when he had been forced to improvise, he danced his variations, rested while the pianist played Krapivina's and completed the coda alone. He was relieved to learn that he had been as successful as in his previous attempt.

As he approached his twenty-first birthday, the pattern of Mukhamedov's life was established. At work he was absorbed; every day he met and coped with the challenges that Azarin presented both technically and artistically, instinctively drawing on reserves of strength, perseverance and creativity that were reflected in his dancing. A door closed tightly shut on that world when he went home to Ljuda. 'When I was dancing, I forgot Ljuda. When I was with her, I forgot ballet,' he recalls. The sense of freedom that had lightened the beginning of their life together had all but disappeared in a routine of mutual dependence. He remembers no loving affection between them, just her demands in return for her presence and his compliance as justification of his. They still shared their room with Svetlana Kubasova, but sex was never a problem for the couple. The trouble was, the only love was in his imagination. Her insistence that they marry continued, and Mukhamedov felt it was increasingly unreasonable to deny her, that by doing so he was not keeping his side of the bargain. In May 1981 they went together to the Soviet equivalent of the registry office and booked a wedding ceremony three months hence. They were issued with the special permits and coupons to buy goods at their local Magazin Dliya Novobrachnih (wedding shop) and Ljuda's ambitions were temporarily placated as she started to collect bed linen, crockery and all the other paraphernalia of the domesticity she craved. Mukhamedov's involvement in the Moscow Competition was barely discussed, partly from his choice, but mostly because Ljuda was simply not interested.

No special provisions were made by the company for Mukhamedov's rehearsals for the competition; after Isayev's success the previous summer, Kasatkina and Vasilyov felt the whole project was unnecessary and probably doomed to failure. Azarin would slip the combinations Mukhamedov was working on into other rehearsals, and if the directors found the three of them working together, they were firmly told to get back to the company rehearsals listed on the notice-board. Kasatkina also made it clear to Mukhamedov that immediately after the competition he was to re-join the company on its tour of Brazil to walk on in *The Creation of the World*. Moscow Classical Ballet departed for South America at the end of May, taking Ljuda (with her engagement document in her handbag) and leaving the company headquarters empty and free for a couple of weeks' uninterrupted work. Azarin was pleased with the couple's progress, and, as June drew nearer, exuded a cautious confidence, treading a delicate line between maintaining Mukhamedov's belief in himself and cushioning him against failure.

8

A Glittering Prize, the Bolshoi Ballet and *Spartacus*

ON 11 JUNE 1981 one hundred and twenty-six dancers gathered at the Bolshoi Theatre for the opening ceremony of the Fourth Moscow International Ballet Competition. They came from all over the world – Japan, America, France, Argentina and Austria. Thirty-four were there as soloists, forty-six as couples. One of Mukhamedov's colleagues at Moscow Classical Ballet, a young woman called Margarita Perkun, was competing as a soloist; and the other fourteen Soviet entrants included Nina Ananiashvili, Yuri Vasyuchenko and Andris Liepa from the Bolshoi Ballet and Konstantin Zaklinsky from the Kirov. Among the western contingent were Kim Glasgow and Kevin Pugh from Canada, Yannis Pikiris from Venezuela, Gigi Hyatt from Germany and Amanda McKerrow from America.

The competition is held every four years, and was founded by the Soviet government in 1969 (when Mikhail Baryshnikov was the first to win the gold medal) to rival the Varna Competition in Bulgaria, which had gained an unrivalled reputation for excellence since its establishment five years earlier. Both events have senior and junior categories with gold, silver and bronze medals; an overall supreme accolade, the Grand Prix, is awarded at the discretion of the judges for outstanding talent. Vladimir Vasiliev had won the Varna Grand Prix in 1964 and fellow Bolshoi dancer Nadezhda Pavlova had won the Grand Prix in the Second Moscow International Competition in 1973, but in its twelve-year history no man had so far succeeded in earning the Moscow Grand Prix.

The thirty-strong panel of international judges was heavily weighted by a formidable host of Soviet balletic power and dominance, including Galina Ulanova, Marina Semyonova, Oleg Vinogradov and Konstantin Sergeyev, and headed by the most powerful of them all, Yuri Nikolaievich Grigorovich, the man who had ruled the Bolshoi Ballet for nearly two decades and whose influence was reputed to reach far beyond merely the cultural life of the Soviet Union. There was also a distinguished collection of names from the rest of the world, among them Robert Joffrey, Yvette Chauviré, Hans Meissner, Alicia Alonso, Betty Oliphant and Elsa Marianne von Rosen. Altogether a nerve-racking array of famous and influential faces to confront the mostly inexperienced new dancers.

The competitors were split into two age groups, group A for those aged from twenty to twenty-eight and B for those from sixteen to nineteen. In the first round of the competition they were required to dance either a pas de deux or solo from the jury's published list; in the second they could choose any classical and any modern work; and in the final round they had to perform a pas de deux or two variations from the Russian classical repertoire. The first two rounds were to be accompanied on the piano and the grand finale was presented as an evening performance with the full Bolshoi orchestra.

Le Corsaire was a popular piece, and Azarin assumed that Mukhamedov would do enough to get through round one without much trouble; he relied on 'Diana and Actéon' to display the power of his spectacular jump; the short excerpt from *The Rite of Spring* was included merely to abide by the rules and give the dancers a breathing space; and *Don Quixote* was the *pièce de résistance* intended to show the judges an all-round classical dancer with a special gift for characterisation. But the first problem to overcome before the couple danced a step was how to make an impact on the jury. No matter how conscientious the judges, during a run of fifty or so *Corsaires* or *Don Quixotes* or *Swan Lakes*, eyes are apt to glaze over around number twenty-five, and performances blur into one after forty-nine of them. 'Pick a number after a hundred,' Azarin half jokingly urged Mukhamedov as he went forward to pull his place in the performance list out of the hat. To their amazement, the number he picked was one hundred and eight, almost the last to dance.

Mukhamedov realised the enormity of the judges' task and understood Azarin's fears when he learned that there would be five days of competition before he and Galina appeared before the jury. What chance had competitor number one to stay in the judges' memories? 'Go home and rest,' Azarin told him. 'Try to relax. I will watch the opposition.' They had a final fine-tuning rehearsal, and on

16 June performed *Le Corsaire*. It went well, but the following day they found they were placed only seventh. Mukhamedov despaired. He felt that he had done more than his best and if that had achieved such low marks, it was hopeless to continue. 'All right,' said Azarin, 'you're depressed, but you must either concentrate now on "Diana and Acteon" or retire.' Quitting was not an option for Mukhamedov, and they danced again two days later.

The Vaganova version of the 'Diana and Acteon' pas de deux is a standard and familiar work in Russia, but even so Mukhamedov and Galina made a striking impression as the Goddess of the Hunt and the ardent youth who pursues her. She was long-limbed and elegant in white, while he, wearing gold head-band and loin cloth, was dark and muscular. Everything worked: his partnering was impeccable, her pirouettes were sparkling and his jumps were moving aerial sculpture. The audience was by now expecting a thrilling variation from Mukhamedov, but was unprepared for the stunning perform-ance he gave. As he started the series of tours around the stage over which he had slaved for so many months, there were gasps of disbelief. When he finished, the theatre erupted. His legs were trembling so violently from exhaustion that when Galina entered for the final few bars of the coda, all he could manage was a shaky walk, instead of the athletic dash that was choreographed, and his final jeté into the wings was less than soaring. But the audience was ecstatic and gave them the biggest ovation of the competition so far. The judges placed Mukhamedov and Galina third. Mukhamedov was grateful for that; at least, he thought, he might get through the rest of the competition and finish with a diploma if nothing else.

As the final round was accompanied by an orchestra, a rehearsal with the musicians took place the next day, and Azarin cautioned Mukhamedov to do as little as possible so as not to give anything away. The conductor, Algis Zhuraitis, among the Bolshoi's most experienced musicians, has an amazing sensitivity for dance, and Azarin was confident that all would go smoothly without the young man dancing full out and thereby spoiling the impact of his performance.

The Bolshoi Theatre was packed on the night of 24 June. The last round of the Moscow International Competition is a highlight of Russia's cultural calendar, and all of Moscow tried to lay hands on a ticket. Mukhamedov arrived at the theatre at seven to prepare for the evening's performance; the film crews roaming backstage and through the dressing-rooms did nothing to soothe his jangling nerves. The crimson and gilt auditorium buzzed with opinion as one of the most knowledgeable ballet audiences in the world gathered to deliver its verdict on the young talent that had survived so far. Once the audience was seated, the judges made their own grand entrance; laden with flowers, they progressed down the centre aisle to their seats in the front row, acknowledging the applause as they went. Grigorovich came last, earning the loudest cheer, and once he was settled in his central position, the performance began. It seemed to Mukhamedov that he would dance the 208th *Don Quixote* pas de deux that night as the orchestra struck up the familiar opening melody again and again, and when he and Galina took the stage around eleven o'clock, he was sure the audience would be fast asleep. But Zhuraitis helped.

The opening *adage* started well, and when it came to the ballerina's unsupported grand pirouette, caught off balance at the last minute by her partner, the conductor created such a crash in the tympany as Mukhamedov's hands touched her waist, it frightened the pigeons roosting on the theatre roof. The pas de deux section finished with a roar of appreciation for the couple's style and brio, despite one clumsy finish to a fairly simple pirouette, and there was a deep hush as Mukhamedov walked on for his first variation.

The cheers started at his opening step, a *double saut de basque en dedans*, a difficult jump that was performed by Mukhamedov at a terrific height as he travelled through the air almost the width of the Bolshoi stage. But it was not merely his aerobatics, clean and clear as they were, that captivated both audience and judges. There was a passion and openness about the young man's attack that made his incredibly slow-motion jumps more than mere tricks. He broadened his chest and opened up his shoulders not simply with his arms, but with his spirit. It was an artistic nobility that over the next decade and a half thousands of the world's dance lovers were to find irresistible. He took three calls after his solo. An anxious Azarin was waiting in the wings, like a boxer's second, to encourage and calm him, and to remind him to breathe and not to forget his style as he entered and exited.

So captivated was the audience that it cheered Galina's next appearance, even though they knew she was not competing, and continued doing do throughout Mukhamedov's second variation, which included a *double tour en attitude* made famous by Vasiliev. Mukhamedov seemed to stand in mid-air for a moment, poised, perfectly placed and as Spanish as a Velázquez painting, before landing briefly and doing it all again, and again, and again. By now the applause had fallen into a rhythmic clapping in time to the music, and when Galina started her fouettées in the coda, Zhuraitis laid down his baton and ostentatiously crossed his arms, waiting for her, the music and the audience to finish. In the wings Azarin mopped Mukhamedov's face, patted his shoulder and quietly ushered him back on-stage for his final appearance. His *grande pirouette à la seconde* was brilliantly fast and his legs perfectly straight and placed – if he travelled slightly, nobody cared – bringing the performance to a spectacular and triumphant climax.

Anatoly Yelagin, Mukhamedov's first teacher at the Moscow Ballet School, was sitting in the circle and remembers the emotional occasion. 'I clapped so loudly,' he says. 'I was thinking, my God, it's my Irek, it's my wonderful Irek, such a wonderful dancer. It was a huge success.

'The auditorium roared like thunder. I thought the walls would collapse, that's how much the auditorium roared. It was unforgettable.'

Mukhamedov cannot recollect how many curtain calls they took, how many times they returned to face the wall of sound that filled the Bolshoi that night. He was exhausted and close to collapse through exertion and nerves, and as the music began for the competition's final entrants, Zaklinsky and Anna Kushnerova from Kiev, who were dancing the 'Black Swan' pas de deux, Azarin led him and Galina away to wind down, change and take refuge in his flat to wait for the results. Azarin's wife, Lilia, had prepared a light supper for them all and they settled down with a bottle of vodka to wait. The alcohol did little to calm their nerves as they lived through the night's experiences time and again. Azarin said he thought they would be in with a chance for a medal at least, and were they aware, he asked the exhausted couple, that they had received the biggest ovation of the whole two weeks that night? Mukhamedov hoped for bronze, he thanked Galina and they all blessed Zhuraitis for his help.

At four in the morning the telephone rang and they rushed into the hall. Azarin lifted the receiver. 'Yes, yes. Good, good,' he said, his face giving nothing away. 'I'm sorry, can you repeat that?' he asked the caller. 'Did you say Mukhamedov did not get the gold? Did you say Mukhamedov has won the Grand Prix?'

'It was incredible,' Mukhamedov remembers. 'I jumped, we screamed, I nearly fainted.' The fact that he was, and still is, the only man ever to win the Moscow International Competition Grand Prix barely penetrated the immense joy and relief of knowing that nearly a year's work had paid off so victoriously. The rest of that night is a blank. He knows only that he immediately telephoned his aunt, who in turn rang Kazan to learn that the early morning radio news had broadcast the results to the nation at the same hour as the call to the Azarin's apartment, and Kazan was already celebrating. The rest is lost in a cloud of vodka and euphoria.

Mukhamedov slept off the excess of alcohol and exhaustion the next day at his aunt's flat, where he had moved from the hostel when Ljuda left for Brazil, and woke to face another nerve-racking ordeal, the prize-giving ceremony and the prize-winners' gala.

The state television and radio companies, as well as the press, were still set up in the Bolshoi Theatre when Mukhamedov arrived that night. The stage was packed, this time with the jury and other officials on the right and the competitors to the left, looking painfully young and vulnerable as dancers do when neatly dressed in street clothes and stripped of the exotic allure of their profession. Yuri Grigorovich, the master of it all, sat alone centre stage. Margarita Perkun, Mukhamedov's colleague from the company who had won a gold medal, had a strange sense of destiny. She had to win a gold before it was too late, she had told friends before the competition; her mother had died young, and she was sure she would too. It was an unnerving premonition, even by the fatalistic standards of most Russians, and served to make her friends even more delighted at her victory.

After the interminable self-congratulatory speeches that are a feature of these events wherever in the world they take place, the master of ceremonies announced Irek Mukhamedov as the winner of the Moscow International Ballet Competition Grand Prix. He moved forward from his seat next to Margarita Perkun and accepted from Grigorovich a monumental Czechoslovakian green glass vase, a medal and an envelope containing 2,500 roubles in cash. The exchanges between the two obviously consisted of more than just a handshake and a few polite remarks. The next day cinema audiences and television viewers all over the Soviet Union watched Grigorovich engage Mukhamedov, nervously juggling vase, medal, roubles and flowers, in a fairly lengthy conversation when the ceremony was reported in the newscasts. When he finally sat down, the other dancers pestered him to know what had gone on between them. He could hardly believe it himself. Grigorovich, after congratulating him, had said that now that it was all over, he would like Mukhamedov to come to his office at the Bolshoi to have a chat. 'When?' asked the bemused dancer. 'Tomorrow morning, please,' was the polite reply that brooked no argument. Hardly had the conversation with Grigorovich sunk in than it was time for his speech of thanks. Dancers are notoriously bad with words, and Mukhamedov was no exception. As he reached for the microphone, he froze and forgot the two people most important to him, his partner Galina and Naum Azarin, but he thanked Grigorovich for the prize, thanked the jury for working so hard to choose a winner, thanked the orchestra, thanked the audience and stumbled, mortified, back to his seat. 'You forgot to thank the cat,' someone reminded him.

But the night had only just begun, and there was the winners' gala to get through. Mukhamedov was acutely conscious that *Don Quixote* must be better than it had been the previous evening if he was not to ruin his new-found reputation. The adrenalin rarely flows at the same sizzling rate at the second performance and half Moscow would be waiting for an excuse to scoff at the jury's decision to award him the Grand Prix. He called on every scrap of his considerable will-power to make sure that did not happen. At midnight Mukhamedov and Galina brought the celebration to a close with a performance of the pas de deux that easily bettered their prize-winning appearance.

The following morning Mukhamedov duly presented himself at Door 15 of the Bolshoi Theatre, the administration entrance, and was shown upstairs to Grigorovich's fourth-floor office. Azarin had

forewarned him that Grigorovich was almost certain to offer him a
place in the Bolshoi company – he could hardly do less to the winner
of the Grand Prix of the Soviet Union's première competition – so
Mukhamedov was in a state of high expectation, but ill prepared for
what ensued. Grigorovich did, indeed, offer him a place in the
Bolshoi Ballet. 'I would like to invite you to join my company,' he
said, 'as a principal dancer.' 'Thank you, Yuri Nikolaievich,'
muttered a breathless Mukhamedov, but there was more. 'I would
like you to dance Spartacus,' he went on, 'and Ivan the Terrible, and
join the rehearsals for Boris in *The Golden Age*.' Mukhamedov was
aghast. No one had ever danced Spartacus at such a young age. 'Do
not worry,' Grigorovich reassured him. 'I will help you.' *The Golden
Age* was Grigorovich's latest eagerly awaited work, and the Moscow
Ballet world knew that he was unhappy with Yuri Vasyuchenko, his
first choice for Boris. 'I want you as a partner for Natalia Igorevna
[Bessmertnova, the Bolshoi's leading ballerina and Grigorovich's
wife]. And if you agree,' went on the man whose word was the law in
Russian ballet, 'I want you to go with the Bolshoi immediately to
Turkey and dance "Diana and Acteon" with Nina Sorokina. You
will join the company proper on 10 September.

'The doors of the Bolshoi Theatre are open to you.'

To say that Mukhamedov's feet hardly touched the ground for the
next few days is a cliché, but true, though admittedly a certain
amount of time was spent with them propped up on a sofa
recovering from an endless stream of alcoholic celebrations. He did
manage to stagger to State Bank Number 7982 on Gorky Street and
deposit his winnings of 2,500 roubles, roughly equal to the same
amount in pounds, which remained almost untouched until he left
for Britain almost nine years later. The Moscow Competition
winners traditionally perform a celebratory gala at the Palace of
Congresses Theatre and in 1981 three performances were scheduled.
Mukhamedov was in such a state of exhausted intoxication, both
literally and metaphorically, that he only managed to dance the *Rite
of Spring* excerpt at the first, opting out of the other two altogether.
The sympathetic Azarin caused Mukhamedov the only twinge of
regret in an otherwise perfect world. Azarin had not needed to ask his
pupil to recommend him to Grigorovich, however obliquely, as he,
as much as anyone, was keen to work at the Bolshoi. Mukhamedov,

unwilling to hurt his friend, was reluctant to tell him that he had brought his name into the conversation that fateful morning, expressing his deep appreciation of his mentor's dedication. Grigorovich's only observation had been that he knew Azarin to be Asaf Messerer's relative. As everyone knew Grigorovich and Messerer were sworn enemies, there was nothing more to be said.

Margarita Perkun flew to Brazil to re-join Moscow Classical and Mukhamedov started rehearsing 'Diana and Acteon' with Nina Sorokina for his début with the Bolshoi Ballet. Sorokina was one of the Bolshoi's senior ballerinas and, at thirty-nine, her career was drawing to a close, but her partnership with Mukhamedov was in the Russian tradition of utilising experience to ease young dancers into top-level performances. She was the first to dance Phrygia to his Spartacus in the pas de deux from the ballet, though only during an open day for the KGB at the Bolshoi. Bolshoi répétiteur Vladimir Nikonov rehearsed the couple for a few days before the company journeyed to Turkey. To Mukhamedov's relief, working with Sorokina was a pleasure. 'I expected her to kick me and tell me how awful I was because she was a great ballerina,' he says. But, of course, she was gentle and helpful and the partnership was a success.

The Bolshoi Ballet was embroiled in controversy when he and Sorokina joined it in Istanbul. A corps de ballet dancer, Galina Chursina, had fallen in love and eloped with a Turk. As defections were still seen as treason in the 1980s, the company was confined to the hotel, under strict supervision by their accompanying KGB agents. There was class in the morning and the performance at night, and the rest of the day was spent sitting around the swimming pool, playing cards, chatting, waiting. Mukhamedov knew few of the other dancers, and the enforced idleness and isolation added to the sense of unreality he had felt since the upheaval of his brief but cataclysmic conversation with Grigorovich barely a week before.

After the ten-day stint in Istanbul the Bolshoi returned to Russia to start the two-month summer break on 1 July, and a few days later the Moscow Classical Ballet returned from Brazil. Naturally, Margarita Perkun had told the dancers of Mukhamedov's triumph in the competition, but neither she, nor even Ljuda, was aware of Grigorovich's invitation to join the Bolshoi. Mukhamedov and Ljuda were just a couple of weeks away from their wedding date, and he realised that he could no more marry Ljuda now, on the brink of an undreamed of future with the Bolshoi, than he could have married Tatiana during his early days with Moscow Classical. He had spent much time with Naum Azarin during the days between returning from Turkey and meeting Ljuda again, talking about the momentous opportunity he had been offered, how grateful he was to Grigorovich and how he would devote himself to both his new ballet master and the Bolshoi. Azarin agreed that there was a great deal to live up to, and urged him to put aside thoughts of marriage; he must dedicate every ounce of mental, emotional and physical energy to the colossal challenge facing him.

Mukhamedov was waiting at the hostel to greet the bus bringing his fiancée and erstwhile colleagues from the airport, and broke the news as they disembarked. After the back-slapping and general rejoicing from his friends, he followed a thoughtfully quiet Ljuda up to their room, as cold and shabby as when they had left it a month earlier. Although Svetlana Kubasova had discreetly left them to themselves, there was an uneasy tension between them. Ljuda had brought him a present of jeans and a T-shirt from Brazil; she silently noted the new green leather jacket Mukhamedov was wearing that he had bought himself in Turkey, and made no remark about his lack of a welcome-home present for her. She said little as he tried on his new clothes and told her of his conversation with Grigorovich. He was not just a dancer in the Bolshoi, he explained, not even just a soloist, but a principal, and was about to start rehearsals for Spartacus. 'This changes things for us, Ljuda,' he said. 'Do you not see that this is not the time for me to marry you?' he went on as he struggled back into his old clothes. 'I must concentrate on Spartacus.' This was what Ljuda had been waiting for, and she hit the roof. 'How can you treat me like this, after all I have done for you? All the help I gave you during the competition. I did nothing but worry about you in Brazil.' He tried to reason with her, but it was no good. 'Get out,' she shouted. 'I don't want you here if you do this to me.' She grabbed the nearest blunt instrument to hand, a small electric fire, and threw it at her lover. Luckily, it missed. As he was later to realise, a wiser man would have taken her advice and saved himself a great deal of heartache, but Mukhamedov was more loyal than worldly and offered to postpone the wedding. Could they not go back to the registry office and set another date, he asked. Ljuda finally calmed down and accepted his blandishments, asking at last if he would take her with him to the Bolshoi when they were married. 'Of course,' he replied, and retrieved his clothes from his aunt's flat.

The following day he visited the Moscow Classical offices to inform Kasatkina and Vasilyov of his move to the Bolshoi. He met with almost as tempestuous a reaction as he had had from Ljuda. They were shocked and furious. Not only had they been proved wrong in not backing him in the competition, but now their arch-rival Yuri Grigorovich had high-handedly poached the Grand Prix winner, thereby robbing their company of the kudos, without even informing them, let alone having the courtesy to ask. 'Your best place is here with us. If you work hard, you will soon be dancing more principal roles,' Kasatkina told him. 'What do you think you will dance at the Bolshoi – Spartacus? Ivan the Terrible?' 'Yes,' replied Mukhamedov. 'That is what Yuri Nikolaievich has promised. I start rehearsals for Spartacus in September.' They then made the young man even more uncomfortable by launching into a personal tirade against Grigorovich, accusing him of all manner of wickedness.

Grigorovich had set the date for Mukhamedov to join the company officially at 10 September, but now moved it forward a month. Mukhamedov was to start rehearsals for Spartacus as a principal dancer of the Bolshoi Ballet on 10 August 1981. But before he did so, there was a reception of a shamelessly triumphant nature waiting in Kazan for the winner of the Grand Prix.

Mukhamedov travelled with Aunt Galina to his home town and stepped off the train, only to disappear under a deluge of flowers. All Kazan, it seemed to the overwhelmed dancer, was there at the station to greet him and thank him for restoring civic and Tartar pride. Not for a long time had the town featured so lavishly in nationwide television and radio coverage. Their favourite son had even appeared on the cover of *Ogonyok*, the high point of a whole flood of magazine and newspaper articles. The Mukhamedov clan was there in force, and after a noisy tram-ride home to Gagarin Street, they crammed themselves into the crowded flat and settled down to some serious celebrating. The next day the chairman of the local Communist Party welcomed him officially, a particular pleasure for Djavdat and

Rasheda; in his office across Freedom Square from the town's rococo Opera House the chairman told Mukhamedov how proud Kazan was that he had added his name to its list of distinguished sons and daughters, and that he must be proud of his origins and uphold the honour of the Tartar nation. Mukhamedov left clutching a statuette of Musa Dzhalil, his boyhood hero, and headed for the Kazan Kremlin, where the Tatarstan Minister of Culture waited for him with similar sentiments and signed copies of Dzhalil's poems. These emblems of civic approval ended up on someone's mantelpiece; unfortunately, Mukhamedov cannot remember whose.

Mukhamedov and Djavdat spent a few lazy days together at the family dacha on the Volga, discussing the implications of his new job and the foolishness of marriage in his present circumstances. On returning to Moscow Mukhamedov had some disturbing news. Margarita Perkun's premonition of early death had been shockingly realised. She and her husband had holidayed in Yaroslavl and died in a car crash while driving back to Moscow to start rehearsals with Moscow Classical. She was twenty-three years old.

Mukhamedov walked through the Bolshoi Theatre stage door that August morning and felt completely at home. He had been hurt when Grigorovich had passed him over three years ago at his graduation; he had done enough, he thought, to earn a place in the Bolshoi Ballet. But now the decision had been reversed, and he cheerfully left the past behind to come to grips with the biggest challenge of his life, Spartacus. Just how demanding a challenge it was he discovered over the next four months of intense and solitary rehearsals. He had not needed Kasatkina to tell him of Grigorovich's reputation. The whole country, indeed the entire world, knew him as the Stalin of Russian ballet; stories of his cruel and profligate wastage of dancers were legion, and he was acutely aware that the Bolshoi was riddled with his enemies. None of it meant a jot to Mukhamedov. The great man had offered him a golden chance in life and the most important responsibility facing the young dancer was to justify Grigorovich's faith in him.

He felt a rightness about life as he walked up to his fourth-floor dressing-room, greeting the occasional familiar face. Although he was a newcomer, he knew enough about Bolshoi politics to realise that he would change beside the older, loyal dancers and would not be allowed to come too close and risk contamination with Grigorovich's known enemies, such as Vasiliev and Lavrovsky; he knew that Grigorovich would cocoon him in his own sphere of influence, but that was all right. He was in peak physical condition, and at only twenty-one was a principal dancer with the Bolshoi Ballet with everything to prove, and win. If Grigorovich was his Svengali, Mukhamedov was happy to put himself under his master's influence. He changed alongside Nikolai Simachov, one of the company's most experienced répétiteurs and a close aide to Grigorovich. Simachov was to teach him the choreography. After that morning's company class they entered one of the theatre's third-floor rehearsal rooms and an intense, isolated relationship that would write a fresh page of balletic history.

During the next four months Mukhamedov lived a hermit's life at the Bolshoi, a muscle-racking drudgery of class, rehearsal, midday break, rehearsal – day after day, week after week. He thought he was in heaven. To make your début with the Bolshoi Ballet as Spartacus (the first-century slave who led a doomed revolt against his Roman captors), which is acknowledged as the most testing male role in the current Soviet repertoire, was an unheard of gamble, particularly when barely out of your teens. Previous exponents of the role, such as Lavrovsky, Vasiliev, on whom it had been created, Vladimirov, Godunov and Gordeyev, had all been experienced artists in their late twenties and early thirties when they were given a chance in the part. But Mukhamedov felt no pressure, only pleasure; each day brought a new challenge, and fresh insight into the role and himself. His first task was to improve his splits. Audiences around the world were soon to gasp in disbelief as Mukhamedov hurled himself across the stage, legs cleaving the air in gravity-defying leaps. It all began with months of early morning, painful stretching exercises in a dusty Bolshoi rehearsal room. The step that worried Mukhamedov the most was a simple *double saut de basque en dedans*, the jump that had earned him such applause when he won the Grand Prix. Grigorovich's version was not so simple, and he had to land on the bent knee, not the straight supporting leg that nature intended to meet the ground first. 'I was afraid I would break everything,' he recalls, but he didn't.

Mukhamedov saw little of Grigorovich during this time. When the company reconvened in late August, he asked Mukhamedov why he was attending the classes of Asaf Messerer, whose popularity rivalled Grigorovich's own and therefore made him one of Grigorovich's least favourite men, knowing, of course, that it was a natural choice for Mukhamedov as Messerer was Naum Azarin's uncle. 'They are not suitable for you,' he told his new dancer. 'They have the atmosphere of a supermarket. He is not really serious about dance. I think Nikonov would be better.' Vladimir Nikonov's classes also proved unsuitable for Mukhamedov; although the barre work was thorough, there was hardly any emphasis on jumping. He finally settled down to work with Shamil Yagudin, a former company soloist and a fellow Tartar.

Grigorovich had promised to teach Mukhamedov the role of Spartacus personally when he recruited him, but his visits to the rehearsal studio were few and his criticisms limited to brief observations, such as 'Very good, Nikolai.' Simachov occasionally called on Mikhail Lavrovsky to fill in gaps in his memory, and Mukhamedov remembers with what awe he learned a few sequences from one of the original dancers of the role. The fleeting visits from Lavrovsky were the closest he came to contact with the senior company members, most of whom were at loggerheads with Grigorovich and treated the latest favourite with polite disdain. Vasiliev could scarcely bear to return his daily greeting, so Mukhamedov stopped trying.

When he needed company, and had the time, he would go downstairs and seek out his friends from the Moscow Ballet School. Alexei Fadeyechev, his superior in those student days but now a first soloist and also a Grigorovich man, was pleased to see his colleague, as were other such similarly placed new recruits as Nikolai Zagrebin, Andrei Sitnikov and Konstantin Uralski. More often than not Mukhamedov would venture no further from the theatre than to the TSUM department store next door for an ice-cream, sleep for half an hour in his dressing-room and dream of Spartacus. Then it was time for the next rehearsal.

He quickly grew into the charmed life he would lead for the next few years in the Bolshoi Ballet. He was treated with a cautious deference by a certain section of the company, not because he had yet earned it, but because he was Grigorovich's chosen. He accepted this as natural and devoted himself to his protector. But while his artistic development surged to an unforeseen level, his personal situation remained locked in a dismal domesticity. Today Mukhamedov might be accused of a selective memory of the most blatant kind, but he remembers no sharing with Ljuda of the momentous events that were shaping him then. He remembers only returning home shattered from rehearsing a part that was physically beyond most normal human beings, only to be sent out to queue for and then cook the evening meal. If he could, he would buy *pelmeni*, a Siberian-style half-cooked dumpling that he could boil for them both and eat quickly. Ljuda never seemed to have the time to clean their room, and Mukhamedov would do the housework before he left for class in the morning. Although he disliked the shabby little room in the hostel where everybody lived in each other's pockets, even after Svetlana Kubasova eventually left them to move in with her boyfriend, it was he who bought the necessary odds and ends to make it more comfortable. And it was in this period that Ljuda blithely agreed to care for the poodle belonging to the Moscow Classical Ballet's leading ballerina, Galina Shlapina. Conveniently for Ljuda, it was for the duration of a short Russian tour by the company, and, needless to say, it was Mukhamedov who cleaned up the daily mess of the shamelessly un-house-trained animal in their absence, and walked it night and morning. But the chores were easier to cope with than the emotional blackmail he now recalls. Tears were never absent for long as Ljuda reminded him of her hurt at his rejection. She required constant assurances from him that he loved her and that he would honour their next wedding date. 'When will you ask Grigorovich to take me into the Bolshoi?' was an almost weekly request. But the way of life had become a habit, and by now he believed the constant repetition of his avowals of love. There was no going back.

Simachov was pleased with Mukhamedov's progress in rehearsal. 'Just do the steps,' he said, 'and you will be Spartacus.' And it seemed to be working. Mukhamedov read the classic story of the slave uprising in the first century AD as recorded by Plutarch, watched videos of previous exponents in the ballet and enjoyed Kirk Douglas's lusty interpretation of the title role in the Hollywood film.

Mukhamedov had a taste of why Spartacus had such a reputation for being the ruination of the unready when Simachov decided it was time to run him through Act 1 on his own. The muscular exertion was intense, and the split jetés a particular strain on the stomach. When he finished, his trembling legs could scarcely carry him to the bathroom, where he was forced to remain for a while until his stomach cramps subsided. There was some time to go before he built up sufficient stamina. After two months' work, Natalia Bessmertnova joined Mukhamedov in rehearsal. She was the Bolshoi Ballet's prima ballerina and, though the part was created in 1968 on Vasiliev's wife, Ekaterina Maximova, Bessmertnova had made the role of Phrygia her own.

There was almost a twenty-year gap between them, of which Mukhamedov was acutely aware. Bessmertnova was a household name in the Soviet Union, as well as the wife of the artistic director. He felt like a child and was extremely nervous of even touching the legendary dancer. But as he had found with Sorokina, his fears were groundless. She wanted the partnership to work and passed on as much of her experience as she could. They discovered that they could work well together: she trusted his strength and instinctive chivalry, while he respected her knowledge and found her light to lift and co-operative. The couple also developed one of the secrets of a great partnership, the ability to hear the music as one.

Unlike in the West, in Russia a theatre's performance schedule is not planned months ahead. The number of ballets to be produced in a season is plotted, but the sequence and the casting is usually only fixed about a month in advance, an apparently random approach that has often had British managers of tours by visiting Russian companies tearing their hair out in lumps. After he had worked with Bessmertnova for four weeks, Grigorovich decided it was time for Mukhamedov's début, and his first performance of *Spartacus* was scheduled for 4 December at the Bolshoi Theatre.

Although his own rehearsals with Simachov had been long and immaculately detailed, he had the minimum of time with the company. As his performances drew close, only two or three rehearsals were called for him to slot into the ballet; he was given just one run-through on the practice stage at the top of the building and one dress rehearsal with the orchestra on the main stage. This was the first time that Mukhamedov came into close contact with his fellow dancers in the company, and he experienced some difficulty in coming to terms with the fact that he, at such an early age, was a principal dancer and most of his contemporaries were merely corps de ballet. He coped with the run-through, somehow managing to be in the right wing at the right time and missing none of his cues. Bessmertnova and Simachov lent what support they could and Grigorovich had no major criticisms. The dress rehearsal on 3 December was similarly uneventful, and suddenly it was the day of his début.

He had slept well on the night after his dress rehearsal, and with an almost fatalistic calm did class the next morning at the theatre, ate a snack in the third-floor buffet and went home to rest. The normally noisy hostel was quiet; as Ljuda was rehearsing with Moscow Classical, he had the room to himself and he again slept deeply that afternoon. It was a normal working night at the Bolshoi and no one took much notice of Mukhamedov as he entered the stage door, but there was nothing ordinary about the evening for him. To begin with, he did not climb up to the fourth floor to change but made straight for the principal male dressing-room just off the stage on prompt side, where his dresser and make-up artist were waiting for him. After the basic foundation and eye make-up had been applied – he had grown his own moustache and beard to outline the contour of his jaw – he went on-stage to warm up.

Gradually the other dancers came and went across the dark stage, already set up with the ballet's first scene, and one by one came across to wish him luck. As he loosened his muscles and tried out some of the ballet's steps, he was acutely aware of the enormous responsibility he faced. Two weeks earlier the last performance of *Spartacus* he had seen was Vasiliev's, but the man for whom the part had been created was now forty-one and Mukhamedov knew his new master expected him to take Vasiliev's place. He also knew it was impossible and unheard of to make a first appearance with the Bolshoi in the role, let alone at his tender age. Yet here he was only moments away from doing it. He must justify the faith and hard work everyone had invested in him: Simachov, Bessmertnova, the other dancers, not to mention Grigorovich. It was a Herculean task, and for now, he decided, he must just concentrate on the night's work. His own worth and reputation were not part of his reckoning, even then, on the verge of the biggest challenge of his life.

He returned to his room to dress and put on the body paint to tan his arms and shoulders. He received the good wishes of Simachov, almost as nervous as he was; Lavrovsky also dropped in, as did Grigorovich, who was gambling so much on him. Aunt Galina and his mother were in the audience and had already left presents of cakes and flowers on his dressing-table, including a sticky Tartar confection of honey-soaked pastry, a childhood favourite of his. As Khachaturian's overture came over the backstage loudspeakers, Mukhamedov left his room, walked the short distance to the wings, took his place in the line of slaves and waited for his first entrance.

'It was a rainbow dream' is Mukhamedov's memory of that night. He launched himself single-mindedly into the performance like a blinkered horse and thought only of the advice Simachov had hammered into his brain for the past four months: just do the steps and you will be Spartacus. His first 'soliloquy', tormented and chained, went well, and his arabesques were high and clear. The weeks of work loosening his hips paid off, and the character's hallmark jump, the famous split jetés repeated in a diagonal across the stage, soared free and vigorous. He spent the interval, his stomach again in knots, lying on the dressing-room floor with his legs above his head, stretched up the wall to reverse the flow of blood and calm his spinning brain. Before he had time to warm up for Act II, the orchestra was playing his music and he was back on-stage for the first big love duet with Bessmertnova and the lift that has appeared in Bolshoi souvenir brochures in virtually every country in the world. Carrying Phrygia upside down above his head by supporting her left hip in the palm of his right hand, Spartacus walks halfway round the stage, with their faces only inches apart and her pointed feet reaching for the sky.

Grigorovich hurried round in the second interval. 'Hold it, hold it as you are,' he urged, clearly pleased with the way the performance was going, 'and everything will be fine.'

Mukhamedov was by now so numb with exhaustion, emotionally and physically, he remembers little of the third act – only that there were no disasters, and that he had a great sense of accomplishment when he was held high above the stage in the final tableau, impaled on a mass of Roman spears. It was a success. As the curtain fell, Grigorovich embraced him and pinched his cheeks in a gesture of affection with which Mukhamedov was to become all too familiar. He had proved that night that he had the stamina and power to conquer the most physically demanding role ever created for a male dancer. It would not take him long to develop an interpretation that would rival Vasiliev's, widen the limits of the uniquely Russian balletic style that combines both heroic bravura and unquestioning faith in the future, and make his Spartacus an irresistible inspiration to theatre-goers across five continents.

Theatrical tradition in the West dictates that artists making first appearances are given good-luck gifts, flowers and parties by their fellows; in Russia it is the artists who invite their colleagues to celebrate their good fortune and give them a good time. Mukhamedov was no exception. He stocked up with vodka and champagne and threw a party in his dressing-room after the show. He had been unable truly to assess the audience's reaction to his performance at the curtain calls thanks to the Russian protocol whereby the male dancer remains upstage, allowing the ballerina to receive the applause, so the number and rank of his post-performance guests would be a guide to his personal rating. His family and contemporaries from school were there, of course. Bessmertnova appeared, albeit briefly, to congratulate him, knowing that she had found a new young partner to see her through the next decade. Among the other visitors were Mikhail Gabovich, his Crassus, Maria Bylova, who danced Aegina, and an extremely relieved Nikolai Simachov, grateful that his pupil had proved to Grigorovich that he, at least, had done his job well.

There was one of Mukhamedov's former comrades at the school who had danced in the corps de ballet in Act I and did not join the celebration. Indeed, she had done all she could during the past four months to convey how unimpressed she was by his leap to fame. Masha Kovbas had hurried straight home after her appearance, but never forgot how proud the company was of his performance that night.

9

Marriage

THE FIRST HURDLE was cleared. He had proved he could do the steps, and now he had to make Spartacus as much his own as had Vasiliev and Lavrovsky. Between his début in early December and the end of the season in June Mukhamedov danced five more performances of the ballet, fewer than one per month – a light workload dictated by the size of the Bolshoi company, which has stood at around two hundred dancers since the nineteenth century. *Spartacus*, then as now, was the ballet that everyone in the Soviet Union expected to see at the Bolshoi, and it was presented at least once a week; Mukhamedov alternated with Vasiliev, Vasyuchenko and Gordeyev. During that run, as Mukhamedov steadily grew into his new role, Maris Liepa danced his last performance of Crassus, the Roman general, the part he had created in 1968. His partnership with Vasiliev had never been bettered. He was a long-time critic of Grigorovich, even though his son, Andris, was a favoured member of the company. Nevertheless, he paid tribute to Mukhamedov in his farewell speech on 28 January 1982, saying that he was happy to pass the ballet on into the safe hands of a new Spartacus.

The Bolshoi was booked for a short tour of Austria and East and West Germany during May and June that year, and Grigorovich made a last-minute decision to try out his new star in his version of *Romeo and Juliet* while the company was abroad. Already deeply involved in rehearsals for *The Golden Age*, Mukhamedov was well served by his ability to learn quickly, at least by leisurely Russian standards, and he learned the ballet in three weeks; Bessmertnova was his Juliet. Mukhamedov danced one performance of *Spartacus* at the Vienna Opera House and it was only on later return visits that he discovered with what success. People who saw that performance would come to him and say how vividly they remembered the evening, evidence of the indelible impression he made in the role that has endured to this day. He had little time for sightseeing as he was once again closeted with Simachov, learning Romeo. His début in Vienna was marred by the public's disappointed reaction to Grigorovich's version of the ballet. It was considered inferior to Leonid Lavrovsky's production, which had first appeared in the West in the 1950s and had become synonymous with the Bolshoi Ballet. All the same, Mukhamedov won whole-hearted approval from his peers in the company, relieved no doubt that at last Grigorovich had chosen to promote a dancer worthy of his position.

His head spinning from the breakneck speed with which events were hurtling him along, Mukhamedov remembers little of his first visit to Germany, except the captivating glimpse of Hamburg's red-light district from the coach's windows and regret that, in spite of the fervent requests of most of the company's male dancers, there was no time in the schedule for a more leisurely inspection of the goods on offer. And he had *Don Quixote* to rehearse, *The Golden Age* to learn, and Ljuda was on his mind.

Just before his departure for Austria, he and Ljuda had returned yet again to the registry office. By now Mukhamedov felt he was running out of excuses to delay it any further. He had given Ljuda his word, a fact she never allowed him to forget, and the date was set for August, halfway through the summer break. Mukhamedov had gone to see Grigorovich, who he now felt was more of a father than Djavdat, to ask for his blessing. 'You are the second of my dancers to have asked me that question,' was Grigorovich's reply. 'And I will say to you what I said to Godunov, and you will pay no more heed than he did.

'It will be a mistake for you to marry now and, like him, you will certainly divorce. And before you ask, you have my permission to bring your wife to join you in the company.' In fact, Mukhamedov's future would mirror Alexander Godunov's more than Grigorovich could know. As well as marrying and divorcing the dancer Ljudmilla Vlasova, Godunov unexpectedly left the company, defecting in America in 1979.

Mukhamedov made his début as Basilio in *Don Quixote* on 20 June, towards the end of his first season, dancing with Nina Semizorova, who had recently joined the Bolshoi from Kiev, in a gala performance at the Palace of Congresses Theatre in the Kremlin. His first professional appearance in his homeland had taken place on the same stage almost exactly four years previously, walking on with Moscow Classical. It should have been a triumphant return for Mukhamedov, or at least an occasion for an understandable inner glow of achievement, but the performance was not a success. He found Semizorova's height awkward to work with, but a more serious hindrance was the indifference, if not animosity, of the audience – not the majority of the six thousand ticket holders, but the tiny yet significant few that formed the claques.

The Russian claque system is a curious phenomenon rooted in imperial favouritism: society's upwardly mobile sought advantage by cheering and, more importantly, being seen to cheer the artist most appreciated by the tsar or any other influential dignitary. This highly idiosyncratic method of judgement continued under Communism, when the theatres were used by the authorities as part of their propaganda machine. Tickets for performances at prestigious theatres such as the Bolshoi were usually peddled around the country by Intourist or other government agencies, leaving few seats available for genuine theatre lovers. But artists still needed applause and recognition, and when faced with an auditorium packed with worthy citizens usually bemused by their first theatrical experience, there was only one recourse for an ambitious dancer, singer or actor: make sure your friends get seats.

So grew the custom, still as strong as ever in Russia today, for an artist to woo a group of supporters with varying degrees of generosity, from the occasional gift of a ticket and perhaps some cash for flowers to treats at expensive restaurants, spending money and lavish parties. In return, the paid supporters are expected to supply bouquets commensurate with the artist's rank, real or imagined, and applause. The number of curtain calls a dancer records can be vital when promotion is discussed.

Alexander Prokofiev remembers how at school Mukhamedov was innocent and ignorant of *blat*, the influence or allegiances that further careers, a more serious version of our 'old school tie' network. 'No one helped him – no one,' he says. 'He got everything through his own efforts.' But now, out in the real world, it was dawning on Mukhamedov that compromises might have to be made. The consequence of his lack of co-operation with the organised applauders was made vividly clear during a concert performance some years later of the 'Kingdom of the Shades', Act II of Petipa's *La Bayadère*, with Nadezhda Pavlova. In the Bolshoi version the hero, Solor, exits before his variation and when Mukhamedov re-entered to start his solo on this particular night, a wag in the audience applauded as if he were finishing and taking his bow, a crude interruption found highly amusing by a certain section of the audience. This threw him slightly and the tight *manège* of *doubles assemblés en dedans* that climaxed his variation, always a tricky combination, were not as smooth as they might have been. A by now thoroughly flustered Mukhamedov exited stage left when his ballerina was waiting for him stage right. As the music for the well-known 'Scarf' pas de deux began, a mortified Mukhamedov was compelled to race across the stage to catch his end of the scarf in time, accompanied by sardonic applause from his detractors in the auditorium. He had already decided that something had to be done and was under the impression that Yuri Smirnov, a young man his own age who worked in the Bolshoi museum and was a leading claqueur, could provide a solution.

Smirnov, a stocky, fair-haired man, had a flair for organisation and a passion for ballet. He met the dancers of the Bolshoi through his friendship with Vladimir Golovkin, the son of Sophia Golovkina, and was introduced to Mukhamedov by Gedeminas Taranda shortly after the première of *The Golden Age*. He was a fanatical admirer of Grigorovich and Bessmertnova, whom he was already cultivating, and, according to Mukhamedov's recollections, was anxious to find any means to get closer to them. He offered friendship to Grigorovich's protégé, and soon educated him in the niceties of the claque system. It is completely foreign to Mukhamedov's nature to buy approval from any quarter, and the furthest he went to accommodate what he viewed as a necessary evil was to buy and distribute, through Smirnov, an occasional standing pass. 'I never provided cash for tickets or even flowers,' he says. 'Once they thought they could get cash out of you, they never stopped demanding it.' But he depended on Smirnov's superior standing in the claque hierarchy to muster support when needed for his performances.

To the inexperienced Mukhamedov, Smirnov appeared a worldly young man, and gradually he began to rely on his help and advice on how to conduct his affairs. Smirnov, perhaps realising that discreetly promoting his latest Spartacus would find favour with Grigorovich, started to take Mukhamedov to parties to meet celebrities and artists outside ballet and, indeed, outside the theatre. Smirnov ran errands for the company's stars, particularly Bessmertnova, and as Mukhamedov was the only one among them with a car, he went too. Mukhamedov had very effectively separated his dancing life from his off-stage life and now that Smirnov was on the scene, the compartmentalising went further. Ljuda had quickly rid them both of his established friendships and he knew she would not tolerate the time he spent with Smirnov, so he kept quiet about it.

When he got back to Moscow in June from Austria and Germany, Mukhamedov had telephoned Aunt Galina to give her the news of his wedding date, anticipating her reaction. And he had been right – she was appalled. She in turn immediately called Kazan and urged Djavdat somehow to talk some sense into his son. Djavdat travelled at once to Moscow and told Mukhamedov he wished to talk to them both, or at least to meet the girl who was to be his daughter-in-law. But by now the opposition to his plans had so entrenched Mukhamedov's loyalty to Ljuda that when Djavdat knocked on his door the day before the ceremony, he agreed with her not to allow his father into the room. Their acrimonious conversation took place on the street. The father was pleading with his son to think a little longer about the very serious step he was taking at such a vital time in his career, while the son was claiming his independence to do what he thought was right and resenting his father's interference. 'If you cannot give me your blessing, then I do not wish to see you at my wedding,' were Mukhamedov's irate last words, so a bitterly upset Djavdat returned to Kazan. Mukhamedov felt terrible. He was guilty about the shabby way he had treated his father, angry with Ljuda for forcing the confrontation and furious with himself for allowing it to happen. But he had given Ljuda his word; he was committed to a course of action he considered honourable and there was no turning back. Although he hated himself for it, he allowed himself to be carried along by events, finally relinquishing the responsibility for the relationship by firmly placing himself under

Ljuda's thumb. There was little conversation in their room that afternoon as they prepared the Russian equivalent of a wedding breakfast for the next day – good-quality caviare and smoked fish, fresh *blinis* and the ubiquitous vodka and Russian champagne – and it was a subdued bridal party that left the hostel the following morning.

After a year's delay, on 7 August 1982 Mukhamedov and Ljuda exchanged their vows and rings to become man and wife. Ljuda reluctantly agreed to the Terentievs' attending the ceremony, but neither family was there, and it was a dancers' party back at the hostel, which meant a great deal of smoking, drinking and eating, in that order. The food was good. The couple had taken their precious wedding coupons to the government subsidised Food Shop Number 40 for the special delicacies they offered their guests as they were normally difficult to buy in Moscow, except on the black market. A few days later the newly-weds left for a honeymoon at the Siberian resort of Lake Baikal, the largest, deepest and oldest pool of fresh water in the world. There, for a fortnight at least, they were happy together.

On the way back to Moscow they stopped off in Ljuda's home town of Perm, where she showed off her new husband to her mother and the rest of the family. The few days went well, and quickly, with Mukhamedov playing the part of a loving husband and proving popular with his wife's female relatives. But soon it was time to travel to Kazan, a journey that for different reasons neither partner relished.

Their apprehensions were justified. Rasheda and Djavdat did all they could to make their daughter-in-law welcome, concealing their bewilderment at her insulting behaviour in Moscow and organising a lavish celebration at their riverside cottage. They discreetly refrained from questioning, or condemning, their younger son and they were so proud of him anyway it was painful to watch. Nail was the only member of the family who broached the subject of his brother's cavalier treatment of their parents and was promptly told to mind his own business. Ljuda hated every minute. She was fully aware of the Mukhamedov family's feelings towards her, no matter how politely they tried to mask them, and she informed her new husband that she was returning to Moscow that afternoon with or without him. They caught the train back to the capital together.

The Bolshoi reassembled for the new season shortly after the couple arrived back in Moscow in the middle of September, and for Mukhamedov this meant intensive work on *The Golden Age* as the première was scheduled for 4 November. Almost immediately he was asked to substitute for Vyatcheslav Gordeyev in a performance of *Don Quixote* in the Kremlin Palace of Congresses Theatre in just over a week's time. He was obviously out of practice and threw himself back into class with a little too much vigour and not enough thought. He landed badly after a *double saut de basque*, a basic step for him, and broke a small bone on the outside of his left instep. Mukhamedov was in plaster for a month, which upset the Japanese promoters of a short tour by the Bolshoi; incessant and indignant demands for Mukhamedov's presence landed on the desk of the theatre's director. Finally, he was summoned to the director's office 'to discuss the matter of his dancing in Japan'. His entrance on crutches ended the discussion before it began.

By mid-October, when the company returned to Moscow from Japan, Mukhamedov was out of plaster and after another couple of weeks of convalescence he was able to continue rehearsals for *The Golden Age*. Grigorovich had worked on this ballet for the past two years, an inconceivably long preparation in the West, but a perfectly normal timetable in the Soviet Union. Many eminent Russian ballet and opera directors, such as Yuri Temikharnov, former director of the Kirov Opera House in St Petersburg, have refused offers of work in European and American theatres, horrified at the prospect of a rehearsal period measured in weeks rather than years.

The ballet is a simple tale of Communist ideals vanquishing bourgeois decadence, set to music by Shostakovich and with designs by Grigorovich's long-term collaborator, Simon Virsaladze. The hero, Boris (dressed in white), battles for the confused Rita (dressed in pink, then black, and back to pink again) with the villain Jashka (all in black). Boris, representing all that is good and noble about the Komsomol (Young Communists), naturally wins. The young Mukhamedov was born for the part of Boris, and replaced Yuri Vasyuchenko. Vasyuchenko had not had the success Grigorovich had hoped for since he recruited him in 1980 after he won the Soviet

Union Competition from which Mukhamedov had been persuaded to step aside in favour of Stanislav Isayev. His début that year as Albrecht in *Giselle* was reportedly a disappointment to Grigorovich, who had nevertheless proceeded to create on him the role of Boris. After his first performance of *Spartacus*, Mukhamedov took over. Having spent more than four months with the company, he was now in close contact with Grigorovich, and he vividly remembers the exhausting method of creation employed by the chief choreographer of the Bolshoi Ballet. 'Yuri Nikolaievich would say that he wanted a jump here, so I would do some. After some time, he would say which he wanted, then next day change his mind.' But work had never frightened Mukhamedov, and anyway he would have lain down and died if Grigorovich had asked him. His Rita was Bessmertnova and they built on their partnership in *Spartacus*, allowing Grigorovich unlimited scope in the pas de deux passages. Only one thoughtless incident marred their otherwise idyllic work.

Later in the season Mukhamedov and Vasyuchenko were interviewed on television about Grigorovich's highly successful new ballet. Mukhamedov, flattered by his first television interview, spoke of his approach to the work and his character, comparing the different qualities he and Vasyuchenko brought to the piece, and foolishly never once mentioned Grigorovich. When Yuri Smirnov called him that night, a delighted Mukhamedov asked if his friend had enjoyed the interview as much as he. 'You fool,' screamed Smirnov. 'Why didn't you thank Yuri Nikolaievich? Or at least say that it was his choreography? He will drop you from the ballet and Natasha will never dance with you again.' An abashed Mukhamedov begged his friend to make his apologies and appeared at rehearsal the next day red-faced and apprehensive. But, though the atmosphere was frosty for a few days, nothing was said and Mukhamedov was to remain unaware for some years of the political games that Smirnov played to please Grigorovich. Keeping him in an apologetic frame of mind towards his mentor was, Smirnov guessed, what Grigorovich wanted.

Mukhamedov's physical achievements in the new ballet were, if possible, more spectacular than those in *Spartacus*. Later Mukhamedov was to criticise the character for being too bland: 'I come on-stage the same, and I go off the same. Nothing happened to me.' That may be true, but the ballet showed the prodigious range of his technique and the hypnotic spell of his stage personality. After he left the Bolshoi Ballet eight years later, *The Golden Age* was never the same again. It was the only work created for Mukhamedov during his professional life in Russia and, at the date of this book going to press, Grigorovich's last.

The ballet's première at the Bolshoi in November 1982 was an enormous success. As the curtain fell on the closing tableau, with Mukhamedov and Bessmertnova, portraying triumphant Communist youth, the focal point of a stage filled with dancers and huge rippling scarlet banners, there was pandemonium. The claques had been superbly orchestrated and the stage gradually filled with flowers as the cast, and Grigorovich, took call after call. The rhythmic handclap and the calls of 'Bravo!' so characteristic of Russian theatres continued as the house lights went up and most of the audience started to leave. The sight of principal dancers making their deep and measured bows, first to the front, then to the left, the right and again to the centre, to the backs of a departing audience is strange to western eyes. But while those small knots of vociferous, paid supporters persevere, so will the dancers. Bessmertnova had already told Mukhamedov that he was invited to the first-night party at the Grigoroviches' flat, and after the performance he made his way to the address in the Svetenka district, one of the oldest and grandest areas of Moscow. It was his first visit, and a signal honour for a young newcomer to the company, however brilliant.

The five-roomed apartment is small by western standards, but of the highest quality; only top-ranking artists and high government and party officials have the *blat* to secure such accommodation. The building, a purpose-built nineteenth-century mansion block, is immaculately maintained and has smooth, efficient lifts, in itself a mark of its prestige. The Grigoroviches live on the fourth floor. The walls of the entrance hall are a tribute in posters, photographs and paintings to the couple's lengthy careers. In the drawing-room Grigorovich displays the bulk of his Tibetan treasures; ancient statues of Buddha and other deities line the ormolu-mounted upright piano and cram the walnut display cases. Faded but exquisite embroideries of eastern pantheons hang on the wall, while a single crystal chandelier is reflected in the walnut-framed mirror. Antique

Russian tapestries line the firescreen and mantelpiece and a wolf-skin is thrown over the back of Grigorovich's favourite armchair. The overstuffed, bourgeois-looking apartment exudes the permanence of years and the comfort of money.

When Mukhamedov arrived that night, the flat was also packed with people – not only a select number of dancers, but the élite of Moscow's artistic life. And it was Mukhamedov's night. Grigorovich pinched his cheeks with special vigour and told him how great a dancer he would be – in his ballets of course – and with a flourish introduced him to the company. It was an occasion to foster conceit in any young man in his position, and he left the party in the early hours flattered, certainly, by the attention he had received and more than ever convinced that Grigorovich was the centre of the universe around which he was grateful to orbit.

Before his marriage, Mukhamedov had never mentioned to Ljuda his conversation with Grigorovich and the permission he had received for his wife to leave Moscow Classical and join the Bolshoi, but now the time had come. Ljudmilla Kudriavtseva was engaged as a corps de ballet dancer and, with a startling lack of tact, greeted her new colleagues with the news that the Bolshoi now had a new ballerina, the wife of Irek Mukhamedov. Eager to justify her place at the side of her increasingly famous husband, she demanded that he put in motion her application for the 1983 Soviet Union Ballet Competition and make arrangements for her preparations, all of which was acceded to merely on the strength of her married name. She chose not to be known as Mukhamedova, however, convinced that Kudriavtseva would soon carry similar status.

His marriage had rekindled the natural domesticity in Mukhamedov, and his desire to start a family. He had been given a chance in his chosen profession beyond all his expectations. Just how extraordinary his life had become was brought home to him one day when, as he was dozing on the metro on his way to class, a stranger pushed a scrap of paper into his hand and hurried away. It was a hastily scribbled but elegant poetic tribute to the effect that, though Mukhamedov was travelling underground, his dancing made him one of the brightest stars in the heavens. Heady stuff indeed. But he needed children of his own to make him feel a real man, and with the woman he had married. Ljuda would have none of it. She had her career to think of, she told him, and anyway she was sure she could not stand the pain of childbirth. Children were out of the question. The danger of marrying with so fundamental an issue unresolved had occurred to neither of them. Again, either through over-confidence or lack of interest, Ljuda misread her new husband. The only factor that would guarantee Mukhamedov's lifelong loyalty to a woman would be her role as the mother of his children. Just a few years later he was to be grateful that Ljuda had frustrated his wishes on this particular issue.

Meanwhile, there was the problem of their living quarters to solve. As Ljuda correctly, and frequently, pointed out, it was totally unsuitable for the principal dancer of the Bolshoi Ballet to live in a communal hostel. And since the building belonged to the Moscow Classical Ballet, they no longer had any right to be there. Mukhamedov approached the Bolshoi branch of the Equity Committee, a nationwide, semi-official organisation and the epitome of the British quango. The Equity Committee is a prime example of how socialist theory and a desire intrinsic in the Russian character to please everyone all the time can go hideously wrong. It was set up to ensure a just and equitable distribution of the good things in life, such as cars, apartments, dachas and extra food supplies, to all areas of Soviet society. A fine, philanthropic notion that took no account of the infinite capacity of human nature to swindle. The system's inbuilt opportunities for bribery, personal gain, preferment and all manner of corruption were soon realised. Mukhamedov, though, was one of the privileged ones. By the time he applied for a flat of his own his name, and its association with Grigorovich, one of the most influential in Moscow, meant no ten-year queue for him. He and Ljuda almost immediately took possession of a flat recently vacated by a senior theatre official.

The apartment was one grade up from the communal home in which Aunt Galina lived, self-contained but small. An archway led off the sitting-room into the one bedroom; there was a small kitchen and an even smaller bathroom with toilet and sit-in bath. The location was hardly picturesque – the flat was in one of those ubiquitous Soviet concrete blocks built in the 1960s, sandwiched between the Park of Economic Achievements and the vast 3,500-bed Kosmos Hotel, north of Moscow's outer ring road and halfway up the Prospekt Mira – but they had their own front door and a modicum of privacy, which was a great deal more than millions of their fellow Soviet citizens enjoyed. Mukhamedov did a small amount of decorating, do-it-yourself not being one of his more notable talents, and stocked up with the basic items of furniture. It was not long before Ljuda was pestering him for bigger and better premises. But Mukhamedov was now fully preoccupied with ballet.

10

Artistic Growth and Domestic Stagnation

IREK MUKHAMEDOV WAS the principal male dancer of the Bolshoi Ballet for nine years, and in many people's opinion the last great artist at the end of a great company's golden years. He started off in 1981 as a young dancer of immense power with a versatile technique built on years of battling with physical shortcomings. He was endowed by nature with a strong elevation and muscular stamina, and many of his detractors thought that was all there was to him. But when Mukhamedov left the company and his homeland in 1990, he was recognised around the world, not only in Russia, as a dancer with a unique inspirational gift. Like all true artists, his performances transcend his particular discipline; his dramatic powers are acknowledged as being as considerable as, say, those of an Olivier or a Burton, and his musicality profound and revealing. Many great performers develop a stage magnetism, a 'look at me' persona, to rivet the attention, but not Mukhamedov. He uses the art of ballet and the medium of the theatre to fuse together in his person the separate elements of music, scenery and steps, thereby revealing a deep humanity that finds an echo in us all. There may be a quality about him that not many of us possess. Call it what you will – talent, genius or soul – there is no doubt that something out of the ordinary happens to him when he steps on to a stage. That ingredient is there thanks not only to some special divine dispensation, but also to years of gruelling hard work.

Mukhamedov built on the success of *Spartacus* with the essentially athletic role of Boris in *The Golden Age*, but it was the next Grigorovich ballet, *Ivan the Terrible*, in which he made his début on 25 February 1983, shortly before his twenty-third birthday, that he felt gave an impetus to his artistic, as opposed to his technical, development. The part of Ivan was full of melodrama, for the story is told through intense acting passages as well as spectacular staging.

Ivan the Terrible was premièred in February 1975 after an incredible four-year gestation period. Inspired by Eisenstein's film, it deals with the sixteenth-century reign of Tsar Ivan IV, known as the Dread, or Terrible. In the process of uniting a splintered nation Ivan sacked Kazan, defeated the Boyars and created a secret police force, providing a typically sweeping historical background against which Grigorovich could highlight Ivan's infatuation for his wife, Anastasia, and his despair at her death, as well as his personal battle for survival in a corrupt court and his inexorable descent into madness. After Djavdat saw the ballet, he expressed his concern that his son, born a Muslim and a true Tartar, was portraying the man who slaughtered a great majority of the Tartar nation when he razed Kazan in 1552 and, moreover, clung to the Christian cross. 'It's only acting, Father,' Mukhamedov replied. The overriding memory of most members of an audience who have enjoyed Mukhamedov's performance as Ivan are his eyes, glittering with madness and bloodlust, or glowing with adoration for Anastasia. 'I was mesmerised by your eyes,' a fellow dancer once said to him. 'They changed colour during the ballet.' Bessmertnova danced Anastasia and they both had a tremendous reception. Mukhamedov felt that the evening was his, however, and in his enthusiasm forgot the strict rules of etiquette governing Bolshoi curtain calls and stood downstage of Bessmertnova to receive his applause. Yuri Smirnov was furious, but no one else seemed to mind. His role in *Ivan* provided a link with his past after he joined the Royal Ballet. When Grigorovich asked him to re-create a jump he had devised for Yuri Vladimirov when he had created the role of Ivan for him in 1975, Mukhamedov declined and substituted one of his own that Naum Azarin had made for him. During rehearsals for *The Judas Tree* in 1992 he showed the jump to Kenneth MacMillan, who liked it so much he incorporated it into the ballet.

Reflecting on Mukhamedov's remarkable career in 1994, his former teacher Alexander Prokofiev was to describe Mukhamedov as carrying on the tradition of Vasiliev, Lavrovsky, Vladimirov and Maris Liepa. In eighteen months, and dancing just three roles, the 22-year-old dancer had already make his mark on the history of the Bolshoi Ballet.

Shortly after his début as Ivan, Mukhamedov was partnered by the Kirov-trained dancer Ljudmilla Semenyaka as Anastasia, his first encounter with the beautiful, brilliant and notoriously temperamental ballerina. She was light, experienced and extremely easy to work with and they looked well together, but he discovered that she has one drawback: she will, if the mood takes her, talk non-stop throughout a performance. From her first entrance as Anastasia into Ivan's court, entrancing the deranged Tsar in an unearthly golden glow, she provided a commentary on the progress of their partnership – 'I'm off balance. I'm too high. I'm too low. You're late. You're early' – until the exasperated Mukhamedov could stand it no longer. When she complained in the 'Vision' scene, 'Put me down, put me down. You're hurting my liver', he turned downstage, still carrying her aloft, and growled, 'One more word and I'll drop you in the orchestra pit.' They finished the ballet in silence. Since the defection of Alexander Godunov, Grigorovich had been trying to find another partner for Semenyaka. He hoped it might be Mukhamedov, and tried again, casting her as Juliet when Mukhamedov made his Moscow début as Romeo in April 1984. But the young man preferred Bessmertnova. She was more passionate than Semenyaka – and quieter.

In June 1984 Grigorovich staged his new production of *Raymonda*, one of the great full-length ballets of the Russian classical repertoire. It was virtually unknown in the West until an exiled Rudolf Nureyev, in his quest to re-create his balletic heritage, mounted the work for Sadler's Wells Ballet (now the Birmingham Royal Ballet) in 1964 and later in Australia, Switzerland and America. *Raymonda* was created in 1898 by Marius Petipa when he was eighty years old, and was his last three-act work for the Maryinsky company in St Petersburg. It is a sprawling epic with a typically flimsy plot concerning a beautiful Hungarian damsel, Raymonda, Abderakhman, a Saracen invader who covets her, and Jean de Brienne, a handsome crusader who saves her. Nothing memorable there, but what rescued the ballet from extinction was the fabulous score by Alexander Glazunov and some of Petipa's most inspired choreography. By now Mukhamedov was at the height of his powers, unable, it seemed, to put a foot wrong on-stage, and already being talked about at home and abroad and all, he felt, thanks to

Grigorovich. So when Grigorovich came to him and explained that he wished to give the opening night of *Raymonda* to Alexander Bogatyrov, Mukhamedov's senior by a decade, saying, 'I must give him a chance before it's too late', Mukhamedov was eager to acquiesce. Indeed, he was happy to do anything the director wanted. Semenyaka and Mukhamedov were scheduled to dance the second performance.

Mukhamedov never thought for a moment that Grigorovich could do any wrong, or that there might be another motive for casting him, the man who was now generally acknowledged as the Bolshoi's leading principal male dancer, in second place. But Grigorovich had chosen him for his heroic spirit, not his princely bearing, for his athletic prowess, not the precision of his fifth position. There were many men in the Bolshoi hierarchy of dancers eligible to dance the Siegfrieds, Albrechts and Basilios, but a true Spartacus was rare, and for Grigorovich Spartacus was all that mattered. Bogatyrov was a *premier danseur* in the classical tradition, well suited for Jean de Brienne in *Raymonda*; Mukhamedov was Spartacus and Grigorovich intended it to stay that way.

No matter what his feelings on the matter might be, Mukhamedov seemed destined to be labelled 'demi-character' or, as he prefers to define it, 'demi-classical'. From his earliest days at the Moscow Ballet School his build, temperament and attack apparently made it inevitable that he should not be given the classical roles. Anyone seeing him win the Grand Prix in 1981 dancing the *Don Quixote* pas de deux would have been struck only by the clarity and precision of his technique, but Grigorovich chose to focus on the power of his jump and the boldness of the man, and developed the grandeur of the artist, rather than his nobility. In spite of his winning performance in the pas de deux, Mukhamedov danced the full-length *Don Quixote* just three or four times during his career at the Bolshoi. Dancers need to dance the classical parts regularly, for if they do not, the muscles are accentuated in the wrong direction; they must be kept stretched and elongated and, above all, soft in tone. The arms and back forget the formal lines and shapes and, most difficult of all to recover, the feeling goes. Grigorovich's choreography for *Spartacus, The Golden Age* and *Ivan the Terrible* demanded and developed tremendous stamina and flexibility in Mukhamedov, and considerably enhanced the athletic brio of his technique. To redress the one-sided emphasis of Grigorovich's dramatic and free-flowing style, Mukhamedov needed a strong diet of *Swan Lake, Giselle, The Nutcracker*, but he did not get it.

Grigorovich would often say to Mukhamedov, 'You are the leading dancer of the Bolshoi. You can dance whatever you wish.' But by the age of twenty-four, when most young dancers are still experimenting and extending their range, the pattern was set for Mukhamedov, and when ballets such as *The Sleeping Beauty* were mentioned, the thought of standing on-stage doing nothing frightened him to death. Nureyev invited Mukhamedov to dance his version of *The Sleeping Beauty* in Paris in 1989 and he eventually danced in that production three times, but, he recalls, 'I thought it was too late by then.' He never danced *Swan Lake* in Russia, only abroad, and he remembers the hilarity among his fellow dancers when he first danced Act II of *Swan Lake* in Mexico City in 1984 with Semenyaka. The company gathered in the wings, shaking with laughter as their muscular hero played second fiddle to a fairy-tale swan and confined his macho vitality to a couple of jetés. 'You'll be lovely in Chopiniana [*Les Sylphides*],' they taunted. When he made his début in *Giselle* in 1986 with Nadezhda Pavlova, he was acutely uncomfortable, particularly in the first act, as he grew more and more nervous, wondering how to stand, what to do with his arms; he relaxed only in the last five minutes of the ballet in his solo and the dramatic extended coda that follows. He had not solved these problems when he made his first appearance in *The Nutcracker* with Pavlova a year later. It says much for Mukhamedov's versatility that both Rudolf Nureyev and Anthony Dowell saw him as a natural Prince with a range greater than his repertoire at the Bolshoi, a faith that his performances in London have more than justified.

By 1988 overt criticism of his leadership of the Bolshoi Ballet had led Grigorovich to make a nod in the direction of modernism and show an interest in the outside world by inviting Roland Petit, the director of the Ballet National de Marseille, to mount his 1959 ballet, *Cyrano de Bergerac*, never considered one of his most successful works. Petit agreed to go to Moscow on condition that he had Mukhamedov as his Cyrano, and thus started an intrigue that left the politically naïve dancer floundering. Mukhamedov, knowing the ballet's poor reputation, wanted nothing to do with it, especially as it was common knowledge that the whole project was taking place against Grigorovich's better judgement. But to make sure of Petit's arrival, Grigorovich had to assure him of his star dancer's involvement, while at the same time he was determined he would have nothing to do with it. Mukhamedov got hopelessly lost. He heard through Smirnov of Grigorovich's assurance and agreed to dance the opening night of *Cyrano*, completely missing the point of his director's double bluff. He hated the ballet, did not get on with Petit and annoyed Grigorovich by dancing in someone else's work. Grigorovich retreated to his dacha in despair.

Some good came out of the sorry affair for Mukhamedov, however, who at the time was a very heavy smoker. At the post-performance party he was suddenly attacked by violent cramp in his legs, and he shocked both himself and the other dancers by falling dramatically off his chair and writhing on the floor in agony. The spasms soon passed, of course, but he was left convinced that his lungs were not supplying enough oxygen to his blood and, rightly or wrongly, never smoked another cigarette.

However limited Mukhamedov considers his time with the Bolshoi to have been in retrospect, his artistic development was a remarkable process in itself, indeed almost random and accidental. Unlike his famous predecessors, Vasiliev, Lavrovsky and Godunov, Mukhamedov was under the protection of Grigorovich, not his guidance. Once Grigorovich had made the decision to give him the roles, in itself a staggering example of artistic prescience, Mukhamedov was on his own. Nikolai Simachov taught him the steps, strictly in his capacity as répétiteur, Mukhamedov remembers, not as coach or producer. Grigorovich rarely discussed the roles with him, even when creating Boris in *The Golden Age*. The steps tell the story, was his maxim – a sound enough doctrine, but Mukhamedov did so much more. Like Nureyev, he turned into a professional loner; there was no guiding figure in the background who developed his maturing mind and body. The nearest to an *éminence grise* Mukhamedov ever had was Naum Azarin, during his spell with the Moscow Classical Ballet, but after, under Azarin's tutelage, he had won the Grand Prix and joined the Bolshoi, they had drifted apart. He discussed his work with no one, certainly not his wife, and relied on his instincts during performances to create the character he was portraying. The stage was his world and, apart from an awkward *Giselle*, there was no self-doubt, no hesitation. He never agonised over whether or not to do this or that; if he felt it was right, he did it.

He had known how to work from his first plié in Kazan, and his meeting with Terentiev at the Moscow Ballet School taught him at an early age that he had a battle on his hands when it came to his technical development. He was determined to win it. There was no one company teacher on whom he relied; after his unsatisfactory time with Nikonov, he stuck with Shamil Yagudin and later transferred to Boris Akimov. But whichever class he attended, the fight was a private one.

Classes are a challenge in logistics for the Bolshoi Ballet administrators. Allowing for absences through illness, there may be anything up to two hundred dancers arriving at the theatre to do their morning class when the whole company is resident in Moscow. There are two large studios on the theatre's sixth floor, and two smaller ones on the auditorium's gallery level; the rehearsal stage is on the roof, under the huge dome that crowns the building. The company classes commence at 10 a.m., three for the men and one for the women. An hour later there are three more women's classes and one for the principal dancers of both sexes. Mukhamedov usually joined in the company class as the other principals, taught by Asaf Messerer, were largely known to be unsympathetic to Yuri Grigorovich and were therefore to be avoided by the director's protégé. Anyway, Mukhamedov agreed with Grigorovich about the levity in Messerer's class, which suited many of the dancers' temperaments, but was at odds with his own serious approach to work.

On a non-performance day, which for the company principals was more often than not, as they appeared on-stage about four times a month on average, life followed the military pattern of short bursts of intense activity separated by long stretches of boredom. Mukhamedov would rise at eight and drive to the theatre to start classes at ten. He would rehearse later with, say, Bessmertnova or Semenyaka, killing time until their class finished at midday by drinking coffee and chatting in the third-floor canteen. Or he might visit the buffet in the stalls that opened every day for the public, where there was often a better choice or food and drink. As the only schedules for the day's activities were posted outside the fourth-floor company offices, he frequently joined the milling crowd of dancers round the notice-board wondering where on earth he was supposed to go next, and ended the day in the company sauna and plunge pool under the Bolshoi stage.

In the Royal Ballet, which currently has a complement of eighty-four dancers, the company will appear throughout an evening's performance, be it a selection of one-act works or a full-length ballet. It is very different for a company such as the Bolshoi, which employs about two hundred artists. The Bolshoi corps de ballet often changes with each act, and even the soloists will perform just one item in a ballet such as *The Sleeping Beauty* or *The Nutcracker*; over one hundred dancers will appear during the course of an evening. And the Bolshoi never employs extras for walk-on parts. Every spear carrier and back-row lady-in-waiting is a fully-fledged member of the company.

Irek Mukhamedov is very rare in that he joined the Bolshoi at the rank of principal. It is a general rule that all new recruits enter the corps de ballet, from which it takes a superhuman effort to escape. Much depends on the reputation a young graduate brings from the Moscow Ballet School and, of course, where you were born and, most important of all, what *blat* you can exert. If a newcomer is lucky to have a senior teacher such as Marina Semyonova, Marina Kondratieva or Nikolai Simachov take an interest in them, it could lead to small solos. Promotion out of the corps depends largely on the amount of solos performed during the year. The annual rise in salary determines a dancer's status and if the directors feel that an individual's work that year does not merit an increase, his or her rank remains the same, and frequently does so until retirement, which for a corps de ballet dancer in Russia comes at thirty-eight. Salary and rank even determine where you stand on the Bolshoi stage. Corps de ballet dancers in the 1980s received between 120 and 180 roubles a month, coryphées 180 to 200 roubles, soloists 220 to 300 and principal dancers 350 to 550. The top figure is earned only by such stars as Vasiliev, Bessmertnova and Mukhamedov.

One of the fundamental differences in attitude between the Bolshoi and the Royal Ballet that Mukhamedov discovered when he came to Britain was the approach to class work. Classes in Russia are always used to improve technique, except in the case of leading dancers who have a performance the same evening. 'I was amazed,' says Mukhamedov, 'to hear the word "relax" used so often in class at the Royal Ballet. The morning after a strenuous day's rehearsal, teachers here will say, "Don't push too hard." In the Bolshoi they are *always* pushing for more from you. At the Bolshoi class is the basis of your work.'

During rehearsals at the Opera House Mukhamedov was also shocked by the extensive use of dance notation to teach the company's repertoire to the dancers, a system of recording choreography by writing the steps down in the form of a series of symbols. 'You do what is written.' he says, 'regardless of a dancer's individual gifts and physical requirements.' This rigid conformity, Mukhamedov feels, strikes at the heart of the growth and development of the art, and ignores what he sees as a vital ingredient of dance that is largely ignored in Britain: personality. Nor can he understand the British attitude to veteran dancers. At the Bolshoi no principal dancer is coached or privately rehearsed in a role or a ballet in which the teacher or répétiteur has not danced, a tradition that ensures a knowledgable handing down of the truth of a ballet. In Britain, he says, once leading dancers have finished their career, they are disposed of. Thus an irreplaceable fund of knowledge and experience is lost, instead of being absorbed back into the company. One component, however, that is common to ballet companies the world over is politics. However hard Mukhamedov tried to stand aside from the warring factions when he joined the Bolshoi Ballet, fate, and Yuri Grigorovich, decided otherwise.

When he joined the Bolshoi, Mukhamedov was fully aware of the rift that divided the company – indeed, there was no one in the international ballet world who was not. On the one hand Grigorovich was viewed as the greatest director in the company's history and its only hope for the future; on the other he was reactionary, unproductive and slowly strangling a great national institution. But Mukhamedov remained unconcerned with the rights and the wrongs of the situation; his only desire was to dance. Grigorovich had given him the chance and therefore he would be eternally grateful.

The most onerous burden any ballet director has to deal with is telling a dancer that his or her short working life is drawing to a close and that it is time to move aside for younger blood. Without exception, in interview after interview, directors raise this problem as insoluble and infinitely painful. For dancers, age is the enemy that wins the battle decades before the average human being succumbs. During his thirty-year rule of the Bolshoi Ballet Grigorovich has faced this issue more than most. And when the dancers concerned are Maya Plisetskaya, Valdimir Vasiliev, Ekaterina Maximova and Mikhail Lavrovsky, one can appreciate the enormity of the task. These are not just artists with powerful temperaments, they are intelligent, creative and independent people, high achievers who naturally demand their own place in the sun. A high octane recipe for disaster.

Grigorovich once said to me that all his favourite dancers are now his enemies and that it is in the nature of things for him to be betrayed. He had nurtured Vasiliev's and Lavrovsky's choreographic aspirations, and felt they had turned on him when they experienced some success. Vasiliev, for example, refused to give credit for his help with his first ballet, *Icare*, in 1971. After the première of Grigorovich's ballet *Angara* in 1976, created to celebrate the sixtieth anniversary of the Russian Revolution the following year, Vasiliev won an award for his performance. In a televised interview after the ceremony he lambasted the ballet and Grigorovich's choreography. Both incidents could be excused as the natural reaction of youth kicking at the restraints of a guiding hand, but the split never healed and loyalties in the company were polarised between the two, Grigorovich representing reactionary attitudes and Vasiliev the future.

Mukhamedov arrived at a time when this conflict was reaching a particularly bitter phase. Looking back, he thinks that Grigorovich was determined not to fall into the same trap with his latest protégé. 'I saw him as my father,' he says, 'but Yuri Nikolaievich treated me not as a son, but as a little boy.' Grigorovich saw him fulfilling a particular purpose in the Bolshoi, he feels, and kept him firmly in his place. He is the first to agree that it was demeaning for the company's principal dancer, and Bessmertnova's partner, to play delivery boy with her shopping two or three times a week, though he did it quite gladly at Smirnov's behest. She occasionally rewarded them with lunch or tea and when Grigorovich was at home, they would join him for a drink and a chat. But Mukhamedov remembers Grigorovich only going over personal reminiscences of the old days and telling stories of his personal triumphs, never expounding on ideas or beliefs that could, perhaps, have stimulated them both. There were no discussions of ballet or art in general that might have deepened Mukhamedov's understanding.

Invitations to birthday parties and other celebrations soon followed these impromptu meetings, and Mukhamedov mingled with some of the most famous names in Soviet cultural circles. As at most Russian parties, the evening would end with the company sitting round the supper table exchanging toasts, and as it came time to raise his glass to his young star, Grigorovich was often fulsome with his praise. 'When Leonard Bernstein saw *The Golden Age*,' he would tell his guests, 'he rushed backstage and said, "Where is that Mukhamedov? I must see that Mukhamedov – what power!"' Or he would lean forward and say, 'For me the best dancer in the world is Vakhtang Chabukiani, and your dancing reminds me of Chabukiani.' Grigorovich would affectionately pinch Mukhamedov's cheeks until they were red, and send him home grateful and flattered. 'I thought I was something special to Yuri Nikolaievich,' he says, 'both as a person and as a dancer.'

Work, then, was the cornerstone of Mukhamedov's life during his nine years with the Bolshoi – and the countless heroic performances. He vividly remembers how precisely he fitted into the Soviet philosophy of the day, believing in the importance of the individual's contribution to the common good. His mother and father were fiercely patriotic, and Mukhamedov, like many millions of his fellow citizens, was passionately proud of his country. Aunt Galina, a veteran of the Great Patriotic War, was more so than most and, although she refused to join the Communist Party, she urged her favourite nephew never to forget he was a Russian when in a foreign land, to keep a national flag in his suitcase and never to do anything to dishonour it. He took tapes of Russian music on tours abroad and grew nostalgic as he listened, longing to be home. 'I remembered the queues for bread and potatoes,' he says, 'and couldn't wait to get back to Moscow to join them.'

When friends discussed the fortunes made in the West by Baryshnikov, Makarova and Nureyev, he felt nothing but scorn for them. They might be millionaires, but he would rather have his self-respect, and Russia. Nor did he envy their fame. To the Communist rulers, individualism among ordinary folk represented a threat to the fabric of Soviet society, and a good Russian was brought up to believe that gratitude to a superior for preferment was the key to success, not pictures in a glossy magazine. The Mukhamedov of the 1980s counted on the fact that the harder he worked, the more glory would reflect on the Bolshoi Ballet, Grigorovich and Russia. It sounds a grimly altruistic approach to life by western standards, allowing little room for enjoyment, but it produced the artist we know today.

Something was developing in Mukhamedov every time he stepped on-stage, free of the clutter of self-promotion – strength of purpose, understanding, reliability. Most important of all, his emotions were engaged; he felt, he knew, he communicated. What a tragedy for him, then, that none of it was happening off-stage.

Mukhamedov's position in the company was in many ways a lonely one, partly because he operated behind the curtain of Grigorovich's protection, a privilege that led to a certain artificiality in day-to-day relations with the other dancers, and partly because of his rank. He rarely mixed with his contemporaries on a free and easy basis at work; only at parties could he relax with his old friends from the Moscow Ballet School. Next morning in class and rehearsal, however, he was the principal.

The hierarchy in most Russian companies is more obviously rigid than in British companies. The dancers are expected to know their place, and this fundamentally different emphasis caused a certain confusion for Mukhamedov when he left Russia. In addition, in a company that numbered up to two hundred dancers, fraternisation between the upper and lower strata was physically difficult to achieve and artistically impossible. Then there were the internecine factions, the everyday shifts of party loyalties – who was with Grigorovich or who backed Vasiliev – which were vitally important when it came to sharing a table in the canteen.

Mukhamedov gradually recognised that his marriage was lowering his personal standing among his peers. Ljuda, he recalls, was not popular among many members of the company. Of course, it would be highly unlikely for any one person to find favour with all the individuals in such a large group, but the general consensus was that she was pushy and loud, and not particularly intelligent. Mukhamedov found himself bracketed with his wife, and was known as *bulizhnik* (meaning 'stone' or, less politely, 'thick') among the claques, as Smirnov lost no opportunity to remind him. And the nickname stuck.

Ljuda, Mukhamedov says, led him by the nose. He remembers that life in their little flat in north Moscow was very similar to life in the hostel. Now that she was in the Bolshoi, she was even more exhausted at the end of the day, and Mukhamedov, in spite of Spartacus, Ivan or Boris, still went out for the milk and bread before breakfast, queued for food after work, swept the place clean and did the washing-up. Mukhamedov grew to look forward eagerly to his mother-in-law's annual visits from Perm; they represented, for two weeks of the year, domestic bliss. No more shopping, suds-filled sinks or dust-pans and brooms. He would come home from work and find his supper on the table, and if his slippers were not actually warming in the hearth, his home life came a little nearer to what he had dreamed of.

He was earning a top salary at the Bolshoi – 550 roubles a month (more than twice the national average) and $200–300 per performance abroad – but never saved a copeck. No sooner had he earned it than Ljuda spent it. On foreign tours his mission on shopping expeditions was to follow in her wake and pay the bills. As a corps de ballet dancer Ljuda received a very low per diem allowance abroad and it was his dollars that bought the fur coats. He recollects buying her four at least, as well as a wardrobe of dresses she rarely wore. He remembers nothing good or anything particularly bad about this period of domestic stagnation, just a mundane routine. He resisted her requests to ask Grigorovich for bigger and better parts for her to dance. No matter how befuddled his personal judgements, his professional instincts told him that Ljuda would remain in the corps de ballet, despite her claims to the best legs in the Bolshoi, and he could never convince her that she ate too much. Any more than she could convince him that she would never bear his children.

Main picture: With Natalia Bessmertnova in *Spartacus*.

Inset: In the first interval of *Spartacus* Mukhamedov receives words of encouragement from Yuri Grigorovich.

Top: Natalia Bessmertnova, Mukhamedov and Yuri Grigorovich rehearsing *The Golden Age*.

Bottom: First night of *The Golden Age. Left to right:* Gedeminas Taranda, Natalia Bessmertnova, Mukhamedov, Yuri Simonov, Yuri Grigorovich, Simon Virsaladze.

Top: Mukhamedov as Boris in *The Golden Age.*
Bottom: With Ljudmilla Semenyaka in *Ivan the Terrible.*

Above: Mukhamedov with Nadezhda Pavlova in his last performance of *Spartacus*, Bolshoi Ballet, April 1990.

Opposite: Kazan, 2 May 1990. Three days before their flight from the USSR Masha and Mukhamedov bid a silent farewell to his family. *Clockwise from foreground:* Rasheda (his mother), Galina (his aunt), Djavdat (his father), a guest, the Aga Urmanchi, the Aga Urmanchi's wife, Masha, Mukhamedov.

Top left: With Darcey Bussell in Kenneth MacMillan's 'Farewell' pas de deux from *Winter Dreams* at the London Palladium, July 1990.

Top right: Mukhamedov with Kenneth MacMillan after his début with the Royal Ballet in the 'Farewell' pas de deux at the Royal Opera House, Covent Garden, August 1990.

Bottom: Mukhamedov and friends after his début as Des Grieux in MacMillan's *Manon* at the Royal Opera House, January 1991. *Left to right:* Monica Mason, Masha, Mukhamedov, Kenneth MacMillan, Sasha Agadjanov, Deborah MacMillan, Anthony Russell-Roberts.

Mukhamedov as Des Grieux in *Manon*.

With Viviana Durant in *Manon*.

It was on the foreign tours that Mukhamedov became aware of his growing reputation. The Bolshoi Ballet came to Britain in 1986 for the first time in twelve years, to dance a three-week season at the Royal Opera House, Covent Garden. They took London by storm. The critics were unimpressed by the standard of the choreography on show, complaining that little progress had been made since the company's last visit in 1974, but the quality of the dancers astounded London almost as much as it had during the company's first visit in 1956: Bessmertnova, Semenyaka, Nina Ananiashvili, Semizorova, Andris Liepa, Alexei Fadeyechev and Irek Mukhamedov, who more than fulfilled the expectations of him created by the enthusiastic reports of admiring visitors to the Soviet Union. He was lionised for his performances in *Spartacus*, and was nominated for that year's Laurence Olivier Award for Ballet for his overpowering interpretation of Ivan the Terrible. He suddenly noticed that people stared at him in the streets, followed him when he went shopping and asked for his autograph. The following year in New York the same thing happened; when he arrived at the theatre to warm up a couple of hours before the performance, there were queues of people already around the box office holding placards offering to pay any price for tickets for Mukhamedov. The attention brought a thrill of pleasure, especially as it confirmed that he was not letting Grigorovich down. His triumph in Britain in 1986 turned sour, however, when the company went on to Paris, where the season was not a success. The Parisians hated everything, Mukhamedov recalls, and *The Golden Age* most of all. As the ballet's hero was created for him, he felt particularly driven to prove Paris wrong.

In the final performance of the work, straining every sinew and already tired from his exertions in London, he performed a forward hand flip in the first act with more enthusiasm than expertise. He landed badly on his bottom and felt something give. He continued the performance in considerable pain and finished the evening flat on his back, virtually unable to move. The company doctor decided to send him straight back to Moscow, where he would jump a famous surgeon's six-month waiting list for an urgent consultation. Ljuda refused to accompany her husband, saying that Mukhamedov had plenty of friends and relatives to care for him in Moscow, and that as she had never yet visited Holland, she intended to continue the tour. The decision did little to raise her standing in the company.

By the time the Bolshoi and Ljuda returned to Moscow Mukhamedov's back had made a full recovery. Following his and Ljuda's short separation he began to realise that sex had become a habit and then, even worse, a duty. Neither had the imagination, or indeed the will, to rekindle a fresh spark between them. Despite his own puritan moral code, Mukhamedov was as aware as anyone else that sex was the main recreation among his colleagues, especially on tour. Although he maintains he was completely unaware that he could have had a queue of women at his bedroom door, one admirer managed to undermine his defences during a tour of the States in 1987. Mukhamedov succumbed one night to a corps de ballet dancer, an indiscretion that was all the more unforgivable because she and her husband were reasonably friendly with him and his wife, and they frequently went out as a foursome.

Mukhamedov was racked with guilt, and vowed never to weaken again. A couple of months later, however, Ljudmilla Semenyaka was invited to appear at a gala at the Kennedy Center in Washington, DC, and she asked Mukhamedov to partner her in the *Le Corsaire* pas de deux. On that trip Mukhamedov met President and Mrs Reagan in Washington, dined with Rudolf Nureyev in his apartment in the Dakota Building in New York and found consolation in the arms of Semenyaka. These peccadilloes, tame by Bolshoi standards, were outrageously out of character for Mukhamedov, and caused him considerable anguish.

He was either unaware of or reluctant to admit it, but chinks were appearing in the emotional armour-plating behind which he had felt so safe for so long. Like it or not, he was no longer the talented boy that Grigorovich had recruited. He was a mature artist with a repertoire of roles developed through the depth and understanding of his personality, yet he clung to the remnants of his adolescence, living out unrealistic ideals of true love and fidelity. Something had to give.

11

Masha

MUKHAMEDOV'S TEENAGE SWEETHEART, Tatiana Nyemtseva, joined the Moscow Classical Ballet in March 1988. While he had made private vows when he finished his brief fling with Semenyaka that he would never again cheat on Ljuda, Mukhamedov's newly liberated libido decided otherwise. Their relationship resumed as if not a day had gone by. The words of his father – 'the Mukhamedovs never divorce' – still rang in his subconscious and he was consequently in a continuous state of guilt, but after twenty-eight years of dawdling his sex drive would not now be denied and demanded compensation for lost time. No sooner had he left Tania's bed than his eye was caught by another schoolboy crush of his, Masha.

Masha Kovbas, the little girl Mukhamedov had loved and lost at the Moscow Ballet School, was now Maria Zubkova, a rising soloist with the Bolshoi Ballet, married to Oleg Zubkov, an official in Gosconcert (the state agency that controlled all Soviet entertainment), and as larged-eyed and glamorous as the schoolgirl had promised. Her long legs and fiery performances since she had joined the company in 1980 made her even more popular with her male colleagues than she had been with the boys at school and she was universally known as 'Playboy' – as much a tribute to her jealous husband, who made her as unobtainable as any centrefold model, as to her body. Her talent too had fulfilled its early potential, and even though she had no more *blat* than Mukhamedov, her future with the Bolshoi was considered exceptionally bright.

No one in the company knew that her marriage had completely broken down and that she was desperate for affection, so her welcome response to the attentions Mukhamedov now turned on her with all the enthusiasm of a beginner came as some surprise to most of the dancers. As for Mukhamedov, he had by now become wholly accustomed to compartmentalising his emotions. He left his guilt at home with Ljuda, enjoyed his illicit thrills in Tania's bed and anticipated more with Masha, all the while relishing his mainstay role in life as Grigorovich's favourite and principal male dancer of the Bolshoi Ballet. For the first time in his life he was experiencing the doubtful delights of having his cake and eating it.

The Bolshoi summer tour that year took in Italy, Sicily and Crete, and the three weeks in some of Italy's most beautiful cities – Bologna, Venice and Florence – were spent innocently enough. It was the hot sun and sea air in Crete that brought him and Masha together.

The five days of their visit were spent in the idyllic surroundings of the beach outside Heraklion, lazing in the sun and waiting for the evening's class and performance. Mukhamedov was not the only man on the beach to covet Masha in her new gold swimming costume. His wife had formed a close friendship with Vladimir Karakulev, Mukhamedov's erstwhile schoolboy hero, a relationship that, when he thought about it at all, Mukhamedov assumed was as innocent as he wished his own liaisons were. The three of them made up a party on the morning of the last day, and when the two men, both strong swimmers, left Ljuda on the shore and struck out to sea, Masha and a girlfriend followed. They met in the surf; after a while Mukhamedov urged Masha to swim out a little further with him, and they left their colleagues to make their own way back.

What happened to Masha and Mukhamedov in the Sea of Crete is still discussed between them with a certain disbelief, but it is commonly called lust. He quite simply could not keep his hands off her. They waded ashore later in silence and, ironically, were snapped by Ljuda as they emerged from the shallows. The performance that night passed by as if it never happened. During the last-night party they slipped away to the hotel swimming pool, leaving Ljuda drinking with her cronies, and spent the night together in a darkened lounge.

The following morning Ljuda, who, Mukhamedov claims, had probably drunk herself to sleep the previous night as many of the dancers were wont to do on these occasions, apparently noticed nothing, and they went down to breakfast, sharing the lift with Masha on the way, before catching their flight to Moscow. None of their travelling companions gave the couple a thought as they settled down with their duty free drinks. After all, who would credit Mukhamedov, the solemn and stupid ballet machine, with the imagination to involve himself with the glamorous Masha? Only Igor Yurlov, a schoolfriend of them both, intercepted a glance between the unlikely lovers and guessed at the truth, but he held his tongue.

It was Yurlov who had first introduced Oleg Zubkov to Masha three days before her sixteenth birthday, when she was still a student at the Moscow Ballet School. Zubkov at the time was a well-known sportsman, a water-polo player studying economics at Moscow University and a well-dressed, educated young man with a good physique, a new car and an apparently plentiful supply of money – as well as an absorbing interest in young female ballet dancers. Even though she knew Zubkov was married and had a baby son, Masha fell deeply in love. Their relationship was never easy, according to Masha. He grew more and more possessive, trying to control her every move, how she dressed and made her face up, whom she met. So much influence did he exert over her that she became convinced he had the hypnotic effect on women allegedly possessed by Rasputin. The only time in her life that she could draw breath, it seemed, was when she was away on tour. No matter how hard she tried as their affair progressed, she could not get away. Eventually he left his wife, and in December 1984 they married. It soon became apparent that the only money that would buy them the good things in life was Masha's, earned on foreign tours. First there was the flat (6,000 roubles), then money he owed his first wife for his car (4,000 roubles), and so it went on. During the four years of their partnership Masha pleaded with him for a baby, but he constantly fobbed her off with excuses. Finally, early in 1988, Zubkov's behaviour had become so outrageous that she realised their life together was pointless, and that, whatever it might cost, she had to go.

At the end of 1987 her husband had accompanied a group of Soviet dancers on a tour of the United States, and started an affair with an attractive girl from the Stanislavsky–Nemirovich-Danchenko Company. 'He kept having headaches,' Masha says, 'and claiming depression to avoid having a normal life with me.' As if that were not enough, he started to compare Masha unfavourably with his new love, whom he called his 'Gioconda'. But there was more to come.

Maya Plisetskaya invited Masha to join her group of fifteen dancers for a short tour of America in April of 1988. Masha was delighted and accepted, but knew it would lead to all sorts of political complications with Grigorovich, Plisetskaya's enemy. When she asked Zubkov's advice, hoping he could find a compromise to enable her to stay in Moscow and perhaps do something about their marriage, she was horrified to be told to beg Grigorovich's forgiveness and never again to speak to Plisetskaya. Masha went to America determined to be free of Zubkov.

In those weeks in America she became a new woman; she was able to enjoy herself, relaxing at parties with her friends and dancing better than she had for a long time. A weight was lifted from her, and, although she anticipated trouble when she returned to Moscow, she had made the emotional break and knew it was just a matter of how and when. She had only a couple of weeks in Russia before the Bolshoi left for Italy, and Zubkov, sensing he might have gone too far, took her to his home in Sochi on the Black Sea coast for a short break, hoping that a spell on the Soviet equivalent of the Costa Brava would help restore good relations. It did not, but Masha wondered if one solution might be a baby for her, the 'Gioconda' for him and separate lives for them both, as she was sure that Zubkov would acquiesce to any demand to keep them even nominally together so he could hang on to the good life her dollar earnings brought them.

By the time the Bolshoi had reached Italy, then, Mukhamedov and Masha, if not prepared for a fundamental change in their lives, were both certainly poised to branch out. Masha, having long forgiven his schoolboy crassness, had always admired Mukhamedov, especially round the hotel swimming pools. Like the rest of the company, she was puzzled at his association with Ljuda, but by now accepted his remoteness as a fact of life. Mukhamedov was at last ready to take a gamble with a member of the company. Sleeping with Ljuda had become an increasingly unsatisfactory and infrequent business. Something to do with Karakulev, perhaps, or just the way of married life – he preferred not to think too closely about it. Tania was good for him and, content with the Moscow Classical Ballet, was less likely to see him as a sound career prospect in the way Ljuda had. That was a trap he was determined never to fall into again.

When the company returned from Greece, there were just three days in Moscow in which to turn themselves around for a month's trip to Japan. Masha's resolve to leave Zubkov had hardened. She had left all thoughts of a compromise with her husband and his 'Gioconda' in the blue waters of the Sea of Crete and as they bickered while she packed for the trip to Japan, she knew that she did not even care if he kept the home she had painstakingly put together over the years.

She and Ljuda would be travelling east together on a three-day sea voyage, along with the scenery, crew, orchestra and most of the other dancers, for only the company principals were flying to Japan. Mukhamedov could have asked for his wife to travel with him, but chose not to. Ljuda might have been looking forward to a refreshing deep-water cruise in the company of Karakulev. Mukhamedov brushed aside these troublesome considerations as he waved his wife, and his latest mistress, goodbye at the docks, made a hurried telephone call and went home to where Tania was already waiting.

Something strange happens when a ballet company goes on tour. An unreal sense of release from the day-to-day responsibilities of life often leads to all sorts of intrigues of sex and spite, an effect probably enhanced in a company leaving the grim confines and restrictions of the Soviet Union. The normally circumspect Mukhamedov found himself at the centre of a tangled mesh during the Bolshoi's month in Japan. And to complicate matters further, the whole company was housed under one roof; usually the principals stayed in a separate hotel, which provided a little breathing space at least.

On her birthday on 12 September, shortly after their arrival in Yokohama, Masha threw a party in her room, something normally forbidden by her husband. Mukhamedov, feeling bold, monopolised her all evening. When the management complained of the noise, Ljuda, also absorbed with her paramour, suggested they all adjourn to their apartment, where there was much more space. Very soon afterwards Masha and Mukhamedov slipped back to Masha's room. The first time Ljuda went in search of them, she found the door open and they all exchanged pleasantries; the second time the door was locked and they shouted their excuses; the third time she knocked there was silence.

Again, nothing was said between Mukhamedov and his wife the next morning, but his knowing full well that Ljuda had not drunk herself to sleep the previous evening made him feel acutely uncomfortable. The risk of a confrontation was too high. Where and with whom had she spent the night? He decided he would rather not know. That evening Masha and he went out for a walk, and she realised for the first time that her lover had no idea what he was doing. 'Don't take it all so seriously,' she suggested, alarmed at his black and white view of life that threatened to ruin everything, but he was not convinced and returned to his room without her. Whereas Mukhamedov had been trying to be discreet, Ljuda, who had lost track of Karakulev, made no effort in the hotel lobby to hide her annoyance at her friend's absence. By now, and however much Mukhamedov disliked it, tongues were freely wagging about his affair with Masha. It was time to cool off, he thought, and as was to happen regularly for some time to come, he stopped seeing Masha. But she saw how he looked at her in class, and she glimpsed him occasionally watching her in performance from the wings. She knew how to bide her time.

Sure enough, Mukhamedov asked to travel back to Moscow with the main company, instead of taking the direct flight with the principals, and on the first seaborne leg of the trip he and Masha spent all the time they wanted together, pleased with their choice of hiding place, a lifeboat, probably the most obvious venue on any ship. The night before the ship docked in the Siberian port of Nakhodka there was a disco on board and in the early hours, as the lovers made their way back to their respective cabins, Mukhamedov came across Ljuda clearly upset and repeatedly knocking on a door. According to Ljuda, admittedly, like everyone else, the worse for drink, Karakulev was inside with another girl. Her embarrassed husband managed to calm her and take her back to their cabin. But Ljuda's blood was up, and the next morning at breakfast she seized a knife when the suspect appeared and loudly threatened to kill her. She was restrained, and nobody took her very seriously anyway, but Ljuda was going to wreak her revenge, one way or another.

After breakfast the women went to pack while the men settled down to some serious drinking in the saloon, and Ljuda was told by an enthusiastic troublemaker that Masha was alone in her cabin.

Ljuda was bent on having it out with her rival and headed for Masha's cabin. Finding Masha was indeed alone, Ljuda grabbed her by the neck, Masha recalls, and threatened dire consequences if her husband was interfered with one more time. Luckily, Igor Yurlov had left the other men, including Mukhamedov, to their vodka and stumbled across the two women. He was about to escort Ljuda back to her own cabin when the ship's heavy rolling threw her back into Yurlov's arms. As she lost her balance and fell, Ljuda's heavily booted foot landed in Masha's groin.

A shocked Mukhamedov learned of the incident as they transferred to the train for the fifteen-hour journey to Khabarovsk, where they would catch a flight to Moscow, and stood outside Masha's compartment in case his wife planned another confrontation. Masha was off work for a month. The last thing Masha had expected was violence, however accidental, and the confrontation had left her shaken. She had discussed with Mukhamedov the tangled state of her relations with Zubkov and now felt more than ever the need for some time and space to clear her head. She thought it would do Mukhamedov some good too. He blamed himself for the whole affair, for behaving irresponsibly; he had gone too far, it was all getting out of hand and it was all his fault. They completed the last leg of their journey across the whole of the Soviet Union land mass from east to west, without further mishap. As the company arrived in Moscow, Ljuda, who was determined not to give her rival any respite, saw Zubkov waiting for Masha, and, much to Mukhamedov's embarrassment, rushed across the tarmac to him and demanded that he keep his wife away from her husband.

Mukhamedov and Masha had talked over the situation on the train and she had asked him not to contact her until she could see the future more clearly. With his feelings for her as ambivalent as ever, Mukhamedov agreed.

12

The Beethoven Auditorium

MUKHAMEDOV WAS GLAD to get back to Moscow. As any dancer returning home from a fling abroad would, he attempted to slot back into the conventions of city life. He did not attempt to see Masha, nor did he call Tania. For a few months he rested from the hurly-burly of dangerous liaisons and gratefully turned to a world of which he was master, the stage. As usual he was dancing his round of Spartacus, Ivan and Boris that season, a heavy schedule of heavy roles.

One day at the end of December 1988 he was resting at home after a performance of *Spartacus* and nursing a sore rib, one of the inevitable knocks and bruises a dancer takes on-stage, particularly in *Spartacus*, whose action often resembles some of the rougher contact sports. Shortly after breakfast the theatre rang. Yuri Vasyuchenko had suddenly been taken ill and Yuri Nikolaievich wanted to know if Mukhamedov would step in and dance Spartacus again the next night. Of course he would dance, if that was Yuri Nikolaievich's wish, but first he must have his sore rib attended to.

He drove to the Bolshoi to consult the theatre doctor and asked for an injection to block the pain until he could rest properly after his unscheduled appearance the following night. The doctor obliged and injected a painkilling drug into the left side of his ribcage. Mukhamedov ignored the coughing fit that immediately shook him and returned home to rest. He dozed in bed for most of the day, attributing his increasing breathlessness to a combination of his bruised rib and the painkiller. He slept badly that night and was appalled the following morning to find that he could hardly breathe. His breathing was alarmingly shallow and he told Ljuda that he felt as if he were dying. As she appeared unperturbed by his condition, he somehow drove himself to the local hospital, the Klifatsovsky Institute.

An X-ray revealed that his lungs were filling inexorably with water and showed a small, precise puncture in the wall of his left lung. The Bolshoi doctor had injected her painkiller not into his ribcage, but straight into his lung. Thanks to her carelessness and the length of time he had put off seeking help, Mukhamedov was drowning. So near death was he that the doctors at the institute did not bother with an anaesthetic and at once plunged a hypodermic needle into the cavity and drew off the considerable amount of accumulated fluid.

The institute informed the Bolshoi of Mukhamedov's condition. His only visitor was Yuri Smirnov, who told him that he had made arrangements for his friend to be transferred to a Group Four hospital, a Soviet synonym for privilege, where he would have the privacy of his own suite and twenty-four-hour medical supervision – luxuries enjoyed by high government and party officials as well as by Yuri Grigorovich himself and other star Bolshoi dancers. Mukhamedov was never able to cut through the Smirnov–Grigorovich political mesh to discover whether it had been his boss's instructions to give him the benefit of the Group Four treatment while Smirnov took the credit or whether it had been Smirnov's own idea. He spent a comfortable five days there, during which time his natural vigour quickly healed his wounds, and after another week resting at home he was able to return to class and his heavy performing schedule. Although everyone at the Bolshoi knew of the seriousness of his condition, Mukhamedov cannot remember receiving a letter or telephone call, let alone a visit, from his wife during his time in either institution.

In January 1989 lurid tales surrounded Mukhamedov's failure to appear at the Armenian Earthquake Disaster Fund-raising Gala at the Royal Opera House, Covent Garden. One of the evening's advertised highlights was Irek Mukhamedov dancing the *Don Quixote* pas de deux with fellow Bolshoi principal Nina Ananiashvili, but on the morning of the performance he did not turn up for rehearsals, and frantic phone calls from the Opera House established that he had not left Moscow. No explanations were offered by the Bolshoi authorities, so the Opera House was able only to insert a slip in the

programme regretting his absence. The Royal Ballet's Errol Pickford stood in for him at less than a day's notice, and scored a
notable personal triumph.

London buzzed with speculation. Injury was discounted, as were
religious prejudices – the Muslim Mukhamedov refusing to dance
for Armenian Christians – but Mukhamedov's popularity in the
West was not. Rumour about his possible defection was rife and the
story quickly spread that the Soviet government had lost its nerve at
the last minute and the KGB had hauled him off the London flight as
it waited on the runway. The truth was a little less bizarre.

On the night of 11 January 1989, when he should have been
receiving an ovation from a glittering West End society audience led
by Princess Diana, Mukhamedov was facing his own company and
delivering a stinging attack on Grigorovich's enemies that, he feels,
split and irrevocably damaged the Bolshoi Ballet for years to come.

In 1989 Mikhail Gorbachev's policy of glasnost had not yet
loosened Soviet society fully, but enough to allow limited debate on
hitherto forbidden topics. One of the most contentious in the Soviet
art world was Yuri Nikolaievich Grigorovich, artistic director and
chief choreographer of the Bolshoi Ballet. A tidal wave of public
criticism had gained momentum over the past twelve months or
more. Newspapers and magazines, including *Ogonyok* carried
articles condemning his iron grip on the company, which, it was
claimed, had stagnated for years under his rule.

Televised debates tore the Bolshoi's repertoire to shreds, accusing
Grigorovich of turning the company into a personal choreographic
showcase as well as ruining the classics with his clumsy adaptations.
By any artistic standards, his detractors demanded, Grigorovich
should go, or at least relinquish one of his positions to allow new
creative blood into the company. The committee of the Bolshoi
Ballet Collective, frustrated at the theatre authorities' continuing
delay in considering its views, had called a meeting to put their
demands for change to Vladimir Kokonin, general director of the
Bolshoi Theatre, and through him to the Soviet minister of culture.

A formidable array of 'old guard' dancers, including such legends
of recent ballet history as Vasiliev and Mikhail Lavrovsky, opposed
Grigorovich and backed the Collective's committee, and on 11

January they convened a meeting in the Beethoven Auditorium, a small concert hall cum lecture room in the Bolshoi Theatre complex.

The Grigorovich camp was running scared. How could they counter the combined opinion of such internationally acclaimed artistic heavyweights, honoured artists of the Soviet Union who were much loved by the public? Only one man could rival their accomplishments and equal their popularity, and would be prepared, into the bargain, to sell his soul to the devil for Grigorovich: Irek Mukhamedov. In addition, Mukhamedov was a member of the company's Komsomol committee, a duty he undertook as conscientiously at the Bolshoi as he had at the Moscow Ballet School and with the Moscow Classical Ballet. Titles mattered in the Soviet Union, and the official report would carry more weight with officialdom if Mukhamedov's name, rank in the company and party position appeared.

Smirnov was dispatched to urge Mukhamedov to speak. Grigorovich needs you, he was told; you must not let him down after all he has done for you. Think of all you owe him. Forget London – your duty is here in Moscow. Armed with a speech written by he knows not who and surrounded by a handful of supporters, among them Yuri Vetrov, Alla Mikhailchenko and Yuri Vasyuchenko, Mukhamedov was produced at the meeting like a rabbit out of a hat to slaughter the opposition.

Almost five years after the event he recounted the incident to me in his house in London; it was the first time he had spoken of it to a western journalist. The deep blush that suffused his face spoke as much of his guilt as his words did: 'I shall never forgive myself for what I said. There are no words to make up to those people for what I did that night.' Something of an overestimation, perhaps, of the damage the foolishness of one dancer can wreak on a great company, but I could appreciate his sentiments.

He had not read the speech through before delivering it, but the more he read, the more carried away he became with its message. You older dancers are what is wrong with the Bolshoi, was the gist of its argument. Your troublemaking will destroy us, and after Yuri Nikolaievich had given us everything. You are a bad example to us all. If you really want to help younger dancers like me, stand aside.

Leave the Bolshoi at once and leave the company to us and Yuri Nikolaievich.

He pointed at each of his illustrious predecessors in turn, saying 'It is you who have betrayed the Bolshoi by your actions today, not Yuri Nikolaievich, you who have betrayed your homeland that has given you everything.' You are yesterday's men and women, he concluded. Get out of our way.

The company listened to it all in a stunned silence. Disbelief slowly turned into scorn, then contempt and finally a weary resignation as they realised that Grigorovich had again outflanked them. The reformers knew that there were enough Grigorovich supporters present to lose them the vote, and, encouraged by the politically correct speech of the company's current star, any waverers would now firmly back Yuri Nikolaievich.

Kokonin, the general director, was delighted. See what the real star of the Bolshoi Ballet thinks of you and Yuri Nikolaievich, he told the meeting. Go away and behave yourselves. A saddened Lavrovsky briefly took the platform and warned Mukhamedov that it would not be too long before their places in the hall would be reversed, and it would be Mukhamedov listening to a new star telling him to move aside. Masha was at the meeting and was horrified at Mukhamedov's gaffe. How could this man, she thought to herself, with all his talent and determination, allow himself to be so shamelessly manipulated? She saw him outside the theatre the next day and asked him how he could do such a thing. Mukhamedov's reply, roughly translated, was 'Mind your own business.' He heard nothing from Grigorovich.

The establishment had won the skirmish, but the barrage of criticism continued. The Bolshoi Ballet Collective was part of a larger network of workers' representation and trade union organisations, led at the Bolshoi by the chairman of the theatre's Communist Party, Yuri Grigoriev, a singer in the Bolshoi Opera and a bitter opponent of Yuri Grigorovich. The dancers and Grigoriev took the battle to the next meeting of the Pan-Soviet Theatrical Union, at the Operetta Theatre, across the square from the Bolshoi. Feelings were running deeply against Grigorovich as the debate continued, and on the second day of the meeting, urged on by Smirnov and other senior dancers in the company, Mukhamedov once again spoke out in his master's support.

But the need for heavier guns to be brought up in Grigorovich's defence was now clear, and Smirnov recruited Mukhamedov to bring Mikhail Gorbachev into the fray. That his granddaughter, Oksana, had recently started studying at the Moscow Ballet School almost guaranteed his support. Together they telephoned leading figures in the country's theatrical and art establishment, asking them to back their efforts to maintain the status quo at the Bolshoi, and succeeded in persuading such luminaries as the well-known actor Innokenti Smoktunovsky and Askold Makarov, a former principal dancer with the Kirov Ballet and then director of the St Petersburg Miniatures Ballet Company, as well as other artists, painters and writers. In his crusading zeal Mukhamedov conveniently ignored the fact that many of the signatories to his petition, to the government, for example, Gorbachev and Grigorovich's staunchest supporter, Nikolai Gubenko, the Soviet minister of culture, had sons, daughters or other close relatives either at the Moscow Ballet School or in the company. His efforts paid off, however, and when Gorbachev summoned Grigorovich to the Communist Party Head-quarters one snowy March morning to reassure him of his support, Mukhamedov and Smirnov followed behind in his car. They waited outside to hear the result of the meeting, but at its conclusion Grigorovich left, Mukhamedov remembers, with scarcely a glance in his direction. He felt chastened, like a little boy who ventured too far into grown-ups' territory; but then, that was nothing new in his dealings with Grigorovich.

Meanwhile, as Mukhamedov continued to run around Moscow in pursuit of Grigorovich's salvation to the considerable amusement of his many enemies and to the despair of his few friends, Masha came to the end of her tether with her increasingly violent husband. Smashed crockery and tearful tantrums were one thing, but when Zubkov's rage left finger-marks on her throat, she reckoned that her physical survival meant more to her than the furniture and decided to go. It was a difficult decision and she could think of nowhere she would be safe from her husband. But she badly needed a modicum of comfort from someone.

Her feelings for Mukhamedov were confused at this point. Part of her felt he was fair game as the world in which they lived almost universally accepted that he and his wife were ill matched, and his recent sexual escapades seemed to indicate his dissatisfaction. On the other hand, it was clear from the path he was treading in the current political furore that Mukhamedov was determined to stick to the rules. Masha was aware that meant steadfast loyalty to Ljuda as well as to Grigorovich. But for how much longer?

On Sunday, 5 March, three days before Mukhamedov's twenty-ninth birthday, the company danced *Giselle*. Masha appeared only in Act I, Mukhamedov was in the theatre rehearsing and Ljuda was dancing in both acts of the ballet. Masha rang Mukhamedov's dressing-room in the interval and invited him to go for a drive. Masha realised that telling Mukhamedov of her intention to leave her husband would panic him, but she ventured the question, 'Why are you afraid of me?' She knew the answer perfectly well, that he was afraid of his own feelings, not her, and he confirmed it with a vehement denial and a blustering assertion that his life was wonderful and that he had all he could possibly want. 'OK,' she said, and turned the car back to the theatre.

Monday dawned bright and sunny, and Masha felt strong and confident as she drove home after morning class and rehearsal. The rest of the day was free, and she sat alone in her flat for a while before picking up the telephone and calling her Aunt Lala, Larissa Petrovna. 'Meet me in the street in half an hour,' she said. 'I'm leaving him.' She left most of her luggage with her aunt and went on to stay with a new girlfriend whose address Zubkov did not know, certain that her aunt's flat was the first place her husband would look for her. Sure enough, later that day he knocked on her aunt's front door and demanded to see his wife, but as Larissa Petrovna is 'built like a wardrobe', according to Masha, he went away without argument. Two days later, Mukhamedov's birthday, was International Women's Day and provided Zubkov with an opportunity to remind Masha that she still had a husband. He filled her car, parked as usual outside the theatre, with dozens of red roses. She stopped at her aunt's flat on the way to her temporary hiding place with her girlfriend and gave the flowers to Larissa Petrovna. As she drove away from the roses, she left Zubkov behind her for ever.

The events of March 1989 could justifiably be christened 'Mukhamedov's Follies'. There were no limits to the number or size of
hoops, it seems, through which he would jump to safeguard
Grigorovich's reputation and ruin his own. There was one lucid
interval, however. On 14 March he made his début in *Legend of Love*,
a work Grigorovich had originally created for the Kirov Ballet in St
Petersburg in 1961. Mukhamedov danced the hero Ferkhad to Alla
Mikhailchenko's Princess Shyrin in a ballet that has never been seen
in Britain in its entirety. Western critics have perhaps judged it
unfairly on the strength of the short extracts that the Bolshoi has
occasionally danced on tour, condemning it as choreographically
contrived and awkward as only Russian 'modern' can be. But it was
an innovative work in the 1960s, the second in a long collaboration
between Grigorovich and designer Simon Virsaladze, and one of the
first major ballets to break away from the Soviet diktat demanding
social realism in art, based as it is on a Turkish legend dramatised by
Nazim Hikmet. *Legend of Love* had been in the Bolshoi repertoire
when Mukhamedov joined the company in 1981; he had immediately wanted to dance the role of Ferkhad, but had had a long wait for
the ballet's revival.

Two weeks later, on 26 March, Maris Liepa, the father of Andris
and one of the greatest lyrical male dancers Russia or anywhere else
has seen, died at the age of fifty-two. His death certificate cited the
cause of death as a heart attack, but anyone who knew him was aware
of the deep melancholia he had suffered following the cessation of his
dancing career and the serious dependence on alcohol that had
marred his later years. In many ways it was inevitable, if unjustified,
that the director of the ballet company to which he was dedicated
should be seen as the cause of Liepa's unhappiness, regardless of the
fact that all dancers must cope with the same problem as best they
can. On the day following the announcement of Liepa's death the
Bolshoi Ballet marked Yuri Grigorovich's twenty-fifth anniversary
as head of the company with a gala performance. As Grigorovich
walked on-stage to accept the audience's applause and congratula-
tions, a woman demonstrator ran down the centre aisle of the theatre
waving a placard accusing him of murdering Liepa and shouting out
her anger. An embarrassed Grigorovich turned upstage, appealing
for someone to do something. Mukhamedov, only too eager to

oblige, jumped on to the rail of the stage box and over the orchestra pit; as she ran towards the exit, he chased after her. Mukhamedov, according to eyewitnesses, was embroiled in the ensuing fisticuffs, but he has always strenuously denied it. Theatre officials broke up the mêlée.

The woman was taken away by the police and Mukhamedov returned to the celebrations to have his cheeks pinched in thanks by Grigorovich. Pleased with the outcome of the evening, Mukhamedov was shocked a few days later to receive a summons from the authorities to answer charges laid by the Bolshoi Communist Party leader, Yuri Grigoriev, that he was responsible for the extensive bruising the woman had received during the incident. The charges were eventually dropped, at whose insistence it is almost impossible to establish.

It had been over three weeks since the two of them had had any contact when Masha gave Mukhamedov her aunt's flat telephone number where she had decided to take refuge from her husband. Political manoeuvring had recently proved more titillating than matters of the heart, but by now Mukhamedov was thoroughly charged up, sexually and professionally, the focus of attention on-stage and off. He had lost touch with Tania as he strove to re-establish his tarnished image as a model Soviet citizen, and felt rash and foolish at allowing himself to become embroiled in an affair with Masha. But he had acquired a taste for the female attentions he missed at home and no matter how much he thought he should, he could not resist Masha's invitation.

He asked himself round for breakfast – but Aunt Lala was there too. She suggested he take Masha out to dine at a restaurant *à deux*, but he found an excuse to stay at home tête-à-tête – and Aunt Lala was there too. Desperate to be alone with him one way or another, Masha proposed driving out to the Lenin Hills, a beauty spot a few miles south-east of the city popular with Muscovites for its spectacular views. Mukhamedov insisted on their being discreet and each using their own cars, and they set off in convoy for the park surrounding Lomonosov University, Moscow's oldest and largest, from which both Mikhail and Raisa Gorbachev graduated. They ventured no further than the car park and Masha carefully avoided ringing any of Mukhamedov's alarm bells as they chatted, until the we should marry each other,' she quipped, only half jokingly. That was the end of their day out in the park.

Car parks apparently satisfied Mukhamedov's need for anonymity and the next day they met in the Bolshoi compound. He had heard of the death of Naum Azarin, the man who had coached him for the Moscow International Competition and whose knowledge and grooming had launched him on his undreamed of career at the Bolshoi. Thoughts of death and immortality filled Mukhamedov's head that day and he spoke of his desire to father children. Unable to help herself, Masha did it again. No sooner were the words 'I would like to have your baby' out of her mouth than Mukhamedov was out of the car and heading for home.

While Mukhamedov dithered over his relationship with Masha, another opportunity arose for him to rush with no prevarication whatsoever to Grigorovich's rescue. The campaign to rid themselves of Grigorovich was rumbling on among certain factions within the Bolshoi Ballet, and they forced a confrontation on the opening night of a revival of Grigorovich's *Stone Flower* on 31 March. Mikhail Gorbachev led an official party to the occasion and the pro-Grigorovich group, not satisfied that he had done enough in support of their director following their letter to him, decided to call their opponents' bluff and demand on the spot action from the general secretary.

A year earlier the Bolshoi Collective had delayed the start of a performance of *Romeo and Juliet* to register its dislike of Grigorovich. Now his supporters tried the same tactic: the curtain would not rise on *The Stone Flower* until the general secretary unambiguously and publicly backed Grigorovich. There was turmoil backstage. Officials pleaded with the dancers, made panic-stricken telephone calls and generally ran round in circles as most officials do in such circumstances; the dancers, made up and dressed, either sulked in their dressing-rooms or gathered on-stage to provide mutual moral support; Grigorovich locked himself away in his office; Gorbachev waited in his box. Mukhamedov, who was not dancing that night, answered the summons for help from Smirnov and arrived at the theatre with his nerve-ends jangling with crusading fervour. He went to the director's office and was connected to the telephone in Gorbachev's box, the same box over which he had vaulted only a few days before to end the demonstration at Grigorovich's gala. 'We cannot start the performance, General Secretary,' he said, 'until you can assure us that Yuri Nikolaievich will not be replaced.'

Gorbachev replied that the minister of culture understood the dancers' feelings and was on his way to the theatre as they spoke to reassure them. Mukhamedov ignored all pleas from the Bolshoi officials to start the performance, and it was only after the minister, Gubenko, had addressed the company on the stage and given his unequivocal promise concerning Grigorovich's future that the evening's entertainment got under way. Mukhamedov felt pleased with his performance; he had done his duty by the man to whom he owed so much. But he had forgotten to telephone Masha, who had waited for his call for hours. When he eventually rang, she found his self-congratulatory burblings about Gorbachev and Grigorovich profoundly depressing. Would anything ever dent his devotion to his idol, the system and his own misguided perception of his part in it?

Once more she wondered at the dichotomy in his nature. In spite of being an artist with remarkable insight into human nature and the gift to reveal the truth to others, he apparently had no sense of perspective when it came to himself. She was weary of men and their games and felt it was time, yet again, to disentangle herself.

13

Trouble Abroad and a Dreadful Thirst

YURI SMIRNOV HAD long been urging Mukhamedov to take advantage of the country's loosening political restrictions and his own position at the Bolshoi, and offer himself abroad as a guest artist. Such independent action did not appeal to Mukhamedov, however. He was and is by nature and upbringing a company man, and by the age of twenty-nine felt, if not set in his ways, then established in both repertoire and reputation. But Smirnov was persuasive and found an alternative to Gosconcert called the Theatre Agency, which, though government controlled, specialised in individual artists rather than companies and offered to make all the visa and travel arrangements for 25 per cent of Mukhamedov's fees rather than Gosconcert's 50 per cent. When he agreed at least to test the reaction abroad, Smirnov was delighted and convinced Mukhamedov that he could not travel alone. Thanks to the dancer's sponsorship, Smirnov thus received his first passport enabling him to travel outside the Soviet Union.

Towards the end of March, at his friend's insistence and with very mixed feelings, Mukhamedov rang the Palais Garnier in Paris and asked to speak to Rudolf Nureyev, then director of the Paris Opéra Ballet. 'Would you like me to dance for you?' he asked the man whom he had been brought up to despise and who had not officially existed in the Soviet Union since his defection to the West. 'Of course,' replied Nureyev. 'Come at once and dance my *Sleeping Beauty*.' Grigorovich was told and his permission granted. Accompanied by Smirnov, Mukhamedov travelled to Paris in April with an image of Nureyev the traitor in his mind that immediately vanished when he met the man. 'I understood completely when I met him,' he remembers. Nureyev called him Mukhmudka, an affectionate diminutive of his name, but made it clear at once that he had no intention of laying a finger on him, except in a professional capacity, and told him how happy he was that Mukhamedov would be the first Russian, apart from himself, to dance his version of *The Sleeping Beauty*.

They were both perfectionists and found that they worked with the same almost obsessional approach. For the two weeks of his stay in Paris Nureyev and Mukhamedov spent every day in the studio, and Mukhamedov developed a profound respect for the dancer who was so vilified at home. Ironically, Nureyev was able to devote so much of his time to his fellow countryman because of a strike at the Paris Opéra that resulted in the cancellation of *The Sleeping Beauty* just before the first performance. Mukhamedov was deeply disappointed not to dance a step in public in Paris on that occasion, but found working with Nureyev sufficient reward. During his stay, Nureyev received a call from Robert Denvers, artistic director of the Royal Ballet of Flanders, who was desperately in need of a guest artist to replace his principal dancer, Pablo Savoye, as he had broken his foot during rehearsals. The comparatively young company, founded in 1969, was shortly to embark on a brief European tour, on which it was to make its first visit to Britain, dancing Nureyev's versions of both *The Sleeping Beauty* and *Don Quixote*. 'Would you like Irek Mukhamedov?' asked Nureyev. Mukhamedov returned briefly to Moscow with Smirnov to renew their visas and clear his rearranged absence from the Bolshoi with the theatre authorities – only to fly into further domestic turbulence.

Ljuda had been furious that Mukhamedov had chosen Smirnov and not her to accompany him when he visited Nureyev, and in her fit of pique she had raced round Moscow accusing her husband of at last revealing his true sexual proclivities. She claimed she had known all along that he was homosexual. That the accusation was met with great hilarity by those who knew Mukhamedov made no difference at all to Ljuda, and her accusations grew so scandalous that Grigorovich felt compelled to intervene. Bessmertnova summoned the hysterical woman to her dressing-room and made it clear that her behaviour would not be tolerated and she must control herself. When he got back to Moscow from Paris and learned of his wife's foolishness, Mukhamedov joined in his colleagues' amusement, but the incident deepened the gloom that he now felt surrounded his marriage, and his wife.

Masha had been true to her word since the *Stone Flower* débâcle; she had only seen Mukhamedov at rehearsal and had hardly spoken to him. Nevertheless, he managed, once again, to blunder through her sensibilities during that brief stop in Moscow. She made her début in the lead of *Love for Love*, a ballet choreographed by the French-born Vera Boccadoro for the Bolshoi in 1976, and a particularly splendid bouquet was prominent among the flowers sent to her dressing-room. A friend who was helping to arrange them all threw away the cards and there was therefore no way to identify them, but Masha felt in her heart that they were from Mukhamedov; she also assumed he had been present in the wings during the performance because of her. The following day, seeing him in the street, she thanked him for the beautiful flowers. 'What flowers?' was his crass response. *Plus ça change . . .* , thought Masha.

Mukhamedov, with Smirnov once again in tow, set off for Antwerp, where the Royal Ballet of Flanders was based, to rehearse with them Nureyev's *Don Quixote* before the European tour, whose first port of call was Northampton. Due to his last-minute involvement there was no national press or television advertising of Mukhamedov's appearance at the Derngate Theatre, so hardly anyone knew he was there.

As part of my duties as ballet critic of the *Mail on Sunday*, I travelled to Northampton to see the Flanders company, purely because I had never even heard of them. On entering the foyer I was staggered to see a handwritten notice on what appeared to be a leaf torn from a notebook, pinned to a pillar between posters for *The Grotbag Show* and a Mike Reid tour, announcing that Irek Mukhamedov would dance Basilio at that evening's performance of *Don Quixote*. I immediately rushed to the nearest telephone and called my editor in London to tell him that I had stumbled across the balletic equivalent of Pele turning up unannounced to play for Accrington Stanley. Ignoring his inevitable response – 'Will it hold till Sunday?' – I then put in an urgent request for an interview with Mukhamedov.

A clearly unhappy man appeared shortly afterwards to talk to me. As we settled down in the foyer coffee-bar, Mukhamedov was on edge and, even though he had not performed for a number of weeks (thanks to the Paris Opéra strike), he looked exhausted; his performance that night proved he was out of condition. Yuri Smirnov sat next to him as we talked and took his duties as Mukhamedov's minder very seriously indeed, intercepting my questions and, more infuriatingly, his answers. 'Mr Mukhamedov cannot reply to that,' was his stock response. But the most telling feature of our conversation that day, which was only to strike me some years later when I grew to know the dancer and his sense of humour better, was that hardly once did a smile break through the tense frown on his face. Few suspected it at the time – certainly no one in Britain – but Mukhamedov was beginning to unravel, a process that gained impetus during his visit to Northampton.

The opening night of *Don Quixote* went well despite Mukhamedov's being out of performance practice. (It was eerie to see empty rows of seats in Northampton's small civic theatre when three years earlier the man had crammed the Royal Opera House in London.) After a suitably convivial first-night party Mukhamedov and Smirnov left for their hotel, where they shared a room. Mukhamedov was on the verge of a deep sleep when, to his horror, Smirnov, a man in whom he had complete trust, tried to climb into his bed. He instinctively lashed out with his fist, only to be subjected to a barrage of blows from someone he had grown to accept as one of his true friends. Smirnov was furious at being rejected and beat Mukhamedov repeatedly about the face until, as the consequences of his actions dawned on him, he calmed down and began a fruitless attempt to apologise.

The following morning Mukhamedov woke with his face red and painful from the beating, and sporting a very obvious black eye. He was reeling from shock, not so much at the discovery that his friend was homosexual (though there was a risk it would give credence to Ljuda's scandalmongering) as at his betrayal. He told Smirnov that he never wanted to see him again and asked him to catch the first plane back to Moscow. Smirnov begged his forgiveness; he blamed his behaviour on the generous quantity of spirits he had drunk at the party and vowed never to touch him again. Smirnov reckoned that he was by now too useful to Mukhamedov, who would probably be unable to cope with the business of contracts, travel and currency as well as dance every night at the Derngate, and he was right. But Mukhamedov insisted that he take a room of his own and stay out of his way until he had completed his commitments with the company in Austria; after they got back to Russia he was never to contact him again.

Mukhamedov joined the other dancers for class and rehearsal later in the morning. He explained away his bruises as the result of a squabble with Smirnov over a snooker table, which provoked mutters about 'crazy Russians' from the Derngate backstage staff (who had suspected the worst from Smirnov, as I later learned), and prepared himself for the evening's performance. But it was not to be. A bomb scare forced the evacuation of the theatre, and the dancers, fully dressed and made up, spent the evening at the Mailcoach pub next door. The rest of the week in Northampton was uneventful, to everyone's relief, if punctuated by increasingly acrimonious bickering between Smirnov and Mukhamedov, who made no attempt to hide his growing dislike of his companion. And my story did hold until Sunday, though it took me a few more years to unearth the real drama being played out that week in Northampton.

The company travelled next to Vienna, where Mukhamedov for the first time in his life, at twenty-nine, danced *The Sleeping Beauty* in Nureyev's staging. Once he had arranged for the week's stay in the Austrian capital and had his tickets home in his pocket, he asked Smirnov to leave. He had already accepted that their friendship was over. 'He wanted to be my wife,' he says. As Smirnov was leaving for the airport, Mukhamedov gave him $1,500 to take secretly to Moscow, money that he had saved from his guest appearances and wished to keep from the clutches of the government. Mukhamedov had opened a bank account in Paris in which he had deposited his fee for his engagement with Nureyev and could have left the extra money there. Dollars were one sure way to keep marital peace, however, and he needed them in Moscow. He never saw the money again.

By now Masha, who had seen other men since the company's return from Japan the previous year, knew that Mukhamedov was the only man she wanted. She felt she understood why he was so publicly loyal to Ljuda and respected him for it, but the contrast between his blinkered behaviour with his wife and his personality on-stage gave her a glimpse of something more – after all, you do not earn standing ovations all over the world and have audiences rushing the stage to throw flowers at your feet by being 'thick'. Mukhamedov's relationship with Grigorovich gave her more disquiet. While Mukhamedov remained temperamentally innocent of factional intrigues, Masha, always a political animal, was acutely aware of Grigorovich's consummate skill at handling people, an ability developed over years as the head of a great national institution that embraced much more than just a ballet company. All her friends advised her against getting too involved with Mukhamedov, for she had only just broken free of Zubkov. 'Give yourself a chance,' they said. 'Don't make more trouble for yourself.' But she saw his eyes when he looked at her in rehearsal and how his face lit up when they met in the corridor and exchanged polite greetings. She could not ignore his body language when they sat together in a car – no matter how often he fled from her when she tried to get close. In spite of the apparently insuperable difficulties, she trusted her instincts, and was prepared to wait.

Shortly after Mukhamedov came back from Vienna, the Bolshoi flew to Switzerland to dance for three days in Zurich before beginning a two-month tour of England and Ireland. When he checked the details of the tour schedule on the Bolshoi Theatre's notice-board, Mukhamedov could not know that he was embarking on a twelve-month journey that would turn him inside out personally and change his professional life for ever.

Masha had some friends in the company who cared for her happiness, and during the party the night before the company left Zurich they orchestrated a treat for her. Mukhamedov and Ljuda were invited to join a group of Masha's friends, unusual in itself since as a couple they were not considered party material. On this occasion they were made particularly welcome and immediately plied with vodka. Ljuda reacted angrily when she saw Masha across the room. 'What is that woman doing here?' she demanded of Mukhamedov. 'What's going on?' But his assurances that everything was finished between them calmed her down, and the other guests, conspirators in the scheme, urged on her glassful after glassful in quick succession until, in barely half an hour, she was beyond caring how, where or with whom her husband was misbehaving. But, to be absolutely certain, Mukhamedov took Ljuda back to their room, and, after putting her to bed, locked the door and pocketed the key.

He called Masha from the hotel lobby and in the early hours of the morning they set out walking in the forested hills that surrounded the hotel.

'I was thirsty for Masha,' he recalls, and feeling guilty at last about his treatment of her. He apologised first for his thoughtlessness over the forgotten telephone call after the strike, then for his tactless if truthful response when she thanked him for the flowers. They remembered the beach outside Heraklion and the blue Sea of Crete, and made love under the trees. As they walked and talked that night, Mukhamedov gradually came to the uncomfortable realisation that his guilt, which at that topsy-turvy time in his life represented emotional commitment, was beginning to centre not on Ljuda, his wife, which is where it should have been, but on Masha, his mistress. And it frightened him to death. What could he hang on to if he betrayed such a fundamental principle of his life? As they approached the hotel in the dawn hours, he panicked. 'Forget it,' he said. 'I shouldn't have said those things. Don't speak to me or try to contact me again.' He rushed to his room, leaving Masha once again speechless with frustration.

The next morning the company was enormously entertained, particularly the group who had engineered the lovers' nocturnal tryst, by the solicitous show that Mukhamedov put on for his wife as they began their journey to Heathrow. Not only did he carry all her bags, which was customary for him anyway, but he sat her on his knee on the coach to the airport and kept telling her more loudly than was absolutely necessary how much he loved her, quite clearly making more effort to convince himself than Ljuda. 'Look at them,' said her friends to Masha. 'They are as stupid as each other. It is pointless – have nothing to do with him.' But Masha was convinced she knew better, and carried on waiting.

The Bolshoi Ballet's 1989 summer season at the London Coliseum was dominated by one man. Nicholas Dromgoole, dance critic of the *Sunday Telegraph*, said in August, halfway through the visit, 'Irek Mukhamedov and his breathtaking performances, especially in *Spartacus*, have amazed us all. He has left us in no doubt as to his status in the world's ranking of male dancers, he reigns supreme.' *Spartacus, The Golden Age, Romeo and Juliet*, even the *Paquita Grand Pas*, which he had added to his repertoire in December the previous year – all contributed to the almost pop-star-like adulation that greeted his performances.

But if Mukhamedov was the young lion in the public's eye, his colleagues saw him as less than heroic backstage. To their constant amusement, Ljuda still led him around like a lamb, spending his money like water – he mentions a designer-label dress he bought for her for £300 in the West End that he cannot recall her ever wearing, as well as a £4,000 kitchen complete with all equipment for the new flat they had applied for in Moscow – and complaining of everything from the inadequacy of the hotel bedrooms to the cost of taxis. She added another ludicrous twist to the comedy by copying her rival's haircut. Masha had had her hair restyled in Moscow, adopting a chic, shorter look that she still prefers today and that the Bolshoi men particularly appreciated. Ljuda just had to have the same.

Masha saw little of Mukhamedov during their first two weeks in London, but she remembers feeling his eyes following her whenever they were in a room together; he would always catch her eye in the mirror in class, but they never spoke. Early one morning, however, the phone woke her in her room at the Charing Cross Hotel where the corps de ballet dancers were staying. It was Mukhamedov, thirsty again. He had the evening off, he said; could they meet? He knew, of course, that Masha would dance only in the first act of that evening's performance of *Spartacus*, her room-mate, Marina Zyatik-ova – and Ljuda – in all three.

He arrived nervous and empty-handed and walked round the room, pretending to admire the furniture, the bathroom, the pictures – until even he felt ridiculous. He told Masha that, although he had promised her, his wife and himself that he would never see her again, he could not keep away. Their evening together kept to their established schedule, sex, talk, more sex, more talk, but as curtain down at the Coliseum grew nearer and Mukhamedov realised his time was up, he grew increasingly edgy. Masha was horrified and could scarcely believe her ears as he launched into the familiar rebuttal as he prepared to leave. 'Goodbye. Sorry – forget it. It's all over. It's all wrong,' he said as he headed for the door. The exasperated woman could find no more fitting farewell than the empty beer can she had in her hand and hurled it with all her strength at his retreating back. Mukhamedov ignored the thump on the door behind him, and hurried back to his hotel in High Holborn.

Mukhamedov was pushing Masha as hard as he dared. How many more times must he play cat and mouse with her before she told him she was finished? These were not conscious thoughts, nor even half-defined feelings, but the instincts of a man desperately ignoring the events overtaking him. At first his affair with Masha had been no more than a masculine fancy, proof of a late-flowering satisfaction in his drawing power with the opposite sex, but now he admitted he could not keep away from her. He was inexorably drawn to something other than ballet; a new element was entering his life.

He could talk to Masha, and more importantly, she would listen; for the first time in his adult life he felt more like a man and less like an 'it' when in a woman's company. A voice that he was as yet unwilling to hear was telling him that any woman would no longer do, it had to be Masha. He could neither accept what was happening to him nor renounce it, so he attempted to force Masha to end it. A naïve ploy, as he eventually discovered.

Two days later he again had the night free when the company danced another *Spartacus* and he returned to the Charing Cross Hotel and called Masha from the reception desk, but there was no reply. He hung around the hotel lobby, walked along the Strand, dawdled on the Embankment and when after two hours she had still not returned, he gave up and went home. The next morning Masha received an irate telephone call. 'Where were you last night? I waited for you for hours!' She made a few soothing noises and put down the receiver.

They met and made love in this stop-go fashion as the Bolshoi danced in London and Birmingham, Mukhamedov giving way more and more to his ungovernable need for Masha. Then they reached Dublin. Since he and his wife had moved into their little flat in the northern suburbs of Moscow, Mukhamedov had applied almost on a monthly basis for bigger and better accommodation more in keeping with his status, until Ljuda had approached Bessmertnova to intervene on their behalf. Why Grigorovich kept aloof from this request mystified them both, as a single letter to his friend the minister of culture would have produced suitable premises almost overnight. When he and Ljuda telephoned Moscow from

Dublin, they learned from her mother that the seven-year campaign had finally paid dividends and they were the new owners of a large, two-room, self-contained flat in Third Tverskaya-Yamskaya Street, in the heart of Moscow's Belgravia. Perhaps this was what he and Ljuda needed, he thought, a new beginning, and he spent his time in Dublin making plans with Ljuda to augment the kitchen he had purchased in London.

The company stopped for just a few days in Moscow before moving on to China. The new flat proved to be all that they could have wished for and they were delighted with it. It had high ceilings and large elegant windows, and the rooms were spacious; Mukhamedov was thrilled when he found that, with a little careful manoeuvring, he could stand and get a sense of space through the flat, into which their old place would easily have fitted twice. Ljuda's mother had already overseen the transfer of what little furniture they possessed and Mukhamedov put out feelers for more among his friends on the black market. Meanwhile, there was some celebrating to do. They bought generous amounts of champagne and vodka and invited a few friends round on their first night to christen the new home. The actor Nikolai Karachentov and his wife, Ljuda Porgina, were there, Nikolai arriving after his performance at the Lenininskiy Komsomol Theatre. Soon the conversation turned to the future: now that the Mukhamedovs had a lovely new home, wasn't it time to start a family, wondered the Karachentovs. Ljuda, as always, hastily demurred, citing her well-used excuses of her age, the pain, her career. Nothing, it suddenly seemed to Mukhamedov, would change. A new beginning with Ljuda was a fantasy, the flat would never be a home, at least not his idea of a hub of family life, and he began to feel that he would never live in this beautiful apartment that had taken so many years to obtain.

He visited Masha at Aunt Lala's flat, spent time with her alone in the morning, drove her out to the Lenin Hills, comforted her when she spectacularly crashed her new car and pretended that all was well with him and his new home. But the premonition about his future in it grew.

The seating arrangements on the flight to China were confused: Ljuda was not given a first-class ticket, so Mukhamedov opted to sit with her in economy class, and Masha found herself in first. As usual, the dancers enthusiastically consumed large quantities of duty free liquor to while away the flight and in no time at all the aeroplane was reeking of cigarette smoke and geniality.

Mukhamedov, wreathed in vodka fumes and in a playful mood, made his way up to the first-class saloon where Masha was sitting. 'Do you know I've fallen in love,' he said to her, far too loudly. 'Can you guess who it is? It's you.' The chattering dancers in the forward cabin suddenly fell quiet and watched in amazement Mukhamedov's clumsy attempts to kiss the by now thoroughly embarrassed Masha. She tried to quieten him, feeling the row brewing in the air around them, and was quite glad to see the back of him as he went to the forward toilet. No sooner had he disappeared than, as if on cue, Ljuda marched up the aisle searching for her errant husband. Masha breathed a silent prayer of thanks that she had not arrived a moment earlier and when Mukhamedov reappeared, watched her lover being ushered back to his seat through the ranks of smirking dancers. So, she thought, it was done – a public declaration, though not as romantic and certainly not as sensitive as she might have wished. Next time, she vowed, he will be sober.

A chance call of nature may have rescued Mukhamedov from one predicament on that flight to the Orient, but there was more trouble ahead that he could not escape. When Ljuda eventually settled him in his seat, he fell into a deep sleep; he was beyond bothering to adjust the rather uncomfortable cushions on which he was sitting, and nor did he care about the erratic air-conditioning blasting jets of cold draughts on to him. As the plane began its descent into Peking airport, Mukhamedov woke and, to his horror, could not move. The awkward position in which he had been lying had combined with the capricious air-conditioning to inflame the sciatic nerve in his right leg. It was with extreme difficulty that he finally struggled to his feet and prepared to leave the aircraft. Ljuda, realising that he had so far got away with his diversion into the first-class saloon, started to give him the tongue-lashing she thought he deserved. A combination of hangover, outraged dignity and excruciating pain soon brewed a high-decibel row that flourished as the couple crossed the tarmac. Even by Bolshoi standards it was too much, and Yuri Vasyuchenko tried to play peacemaker between the unhappy pair, without success.

In acute mental and physical discomfort, Mukhamedov travelled with the company to Hangchow, where he managed to cope with the *Nutcracker* pas de deux. The company's then deputy director, Viktor Tikhonov, helped to arrange for acupuncture to ease the pain, but it had a limited effect, and Mukhamedov found difficulty in raising his leg to the front and *à la seconde*.

It was Masha's first trip to China and she found little about the country attractive: the hotels they were booked into were fairly basic, the food was disgusting, the humidity enervating and the smell in the streets obnoxious. Worst of all, only the principal dancers received their per diem payment. Nobody in authority could give a reasonable explanation and the situation only fuelled the simmering bad feeling between the dancers and the directors. Ljuda, however, continued to spend Mukhamedov's money, stocking up with china and bolts of silk with which to decorate their new flat.

If the country depressed her, Masha found consolation with her lover, and for the first time in their relationship Mukhamedov made love to her without immediately regretting it. One day in Shanghai the dancers were treated to a sightseeing excursion; Mukhamedov was staying behind for a session of acupuncture, and he asked Masha to find her own excuse not to go. She borrowed Igor Yurlov's key, leaving a note of explanation for her friend in reception, and she remembers the time they spent together as the most relaxed they had so far enjoyed. Mukhamedov could not yet repeat his airborne declaration of love without a strengthening shot of vodka, but when Yurlov returned early and knocked on his bedroom door, startling its clandestine occupants, he no longer felt the need to escape. They met every day, sometimes alone, often just for a walk. Mukhamedov admitted he cared less and less for Ljuda, but he could not face the consequences of leaving her even though he now found the stimulation of Masha's mind as seductive as her body.

Mukhamedov was to dance Spartacus in Peking, the last stop on their ten-day tour of China, but his leg was no better, the acupuncture had proved ineffective and he was worried about those endless split jetés. He shared his concern with Masha – a remarkable departure for him, as he had long ago abandoned discussing professional problems with anyone, let alone with the women in his life – and she urged him to go to Grigorovich and ask him to recast the performances. When they arrived in Peking, he went straight to Grigorovich and said, 'Yuri Nikolaievich, my leg is still very painful. Could Vasyuchenko, maybe, do my performances so that I can rest and get better for Brazil?' No, he was told, there were to be no cast changes in the repertoire, and that was that. Mukhamedov was taken aback at this curt refusal of what he felt was a perfectly reasonable request. He was, after all, constantly being assured by Grigorovich that he could do anything he wanted in the Bolshoi since he was the company's most valuable asset. What, he wondered, had prompted this apparently thoughtless decision? The unanswered question stuck uneasily at the back of his mind, but, as usual, Mukhamedov made excuses for his master and danced Spartacus as scheduled, changing many of the jumps to his right leg and recklessly ignoring the danger of permanent injury, as, it seemed, did Grigorovich.

Mukhamedov and Masha spent their last night in China locked in Masha's bathroom (to the considerable inconvenience of the other revellers at the inevitable farewell party), safe in an unreal dream world, where talk of the future, babies and love posed no threat to existing loyalties – and provoked no guilt.

14

Brazil

THE COMPANY CAME back to Moscow exhausted by its visit to China. The heat and constant travelling had drained everyone's energy, and the dancers' few days at home were spent gearing themselves for what promised to be an equally gruelling five-city tour of Brazil. Ljuda busied herself with the purchases for their flat that she – or rather Mukhamedov – had managed to carry in their hand luggage while he tried to rest his leg and ignore the growing sense of foreboding about his new home. He saw little of Masha until the morning of their journey to Brazil, when he managed to make excuses to his wife and drive round to visit Masha at her aunt's flat shortly after breakfast when Lala had left for work. It was not a particularly dignified visit. On her way to the bus-stop Lala had come across a street vendor selling apples and, like all good Russians who buy up whatever is on offer, promptly bought 2 kilos and returned home with them. She pretended not to notice the scuffling behind the door following the sound of her key turning the lock, ignored the extra coffee-cup on the breakfast table and a flustered Masha, dumped the apples in the kitchen and left as quickly as she could. A sheepish Mukhamedov emerged from his refuge in the bathroom, finished dressing and returned home to collect his wife and his luggage.

The twenty-hour flight to São Paulo at the beginning of October 1989 was comparatively subdued by normal standards, most of the dancers being too tired to create much mayhem, though Mukhamedov caused a certain amount of gossip by openly stopping at Masha's seat to check that she was well. The company had two days' rest when they arrived in Brazil, and there was just class and a few rehcarsals before the season opened with a performance of *The Stone Flower* on 6 October. But it was a far from peaceful interim.

The members of the company were shocked when they arrived at their hotels (separate accommodation having been arranged for the principal dancers) to be told that only the principals would be paid their salaries in dollars; the soloists and corps de ballet dancers would receive their per diem allowance in cruzeiros, the local currency, and at less than their normal rate. Cruzeiros were not traded on the international market, so could not be taken out of the country. Coming as it did on top of the absence of any allowance at all in China, this made the dancers furious. Dollar earnings were their main source of income, and they appealed to Grigorovich to intervene with the Brazilian impresario, Tamara Teisling, to rectify the situation. Grigorovich promised he would stand by the company, Mukhamedov remembers, but as the discontent within the company grew, Grigorovich was nowhere to be seen. Mukhamedov would be paid $1,000 a performance, more than even Vasiliev had ever earned with the Bolshoi, but what use were cruzeiros to the rank and file dancers? Masha and he discussed what could be done and, without thinking, he took it upon himself to speak to Tikhonov, the deputy director, on the dancers' behalf, confident that he was once again acting in Grigorovich's best interests.

The coaches to transport the dancers to the theatre for the opening performance of *The Stone Flower* were booked for six o'clock, and the curtain was due to rise at eight. During the afternoon word went round the company to stay in their rooms when the buses arrived. At the appointed time a single coach left for the theatre, carrying only the principals – except one. Mukhamedov, who was not dancing that night and was in on the conspiracy, stayed behind to play his part in the ensuing drama. At six the remaining eighty or so dancers, instead of climbing aboard their transport, trooped up to Tikhonov's suite and demanded to see Teisling. Masha remembers Mukhamedov giving one of his more inspiring performances as he harangued the unfortunate impresario when she finally arrived forty minutes later. 'How dare you treat the Bolshoi Ballet in this way!' he demanded. 'This is not one of the run of the mill companies that you normally handle, this is the Bolshoi Ballet, and we will not be treated like this.

'My colleagues were promised dollars and have received nothing from you,' he continued, really getting in the swing, 'and they have eaten next to nothing for three days. We will not dance until you keep your word. If you betray the Bolshoi Ballet, we will betray you.'

Acutely conscious that the audience was, at that very moment, filing into its seats full of expectations for its night out with the Bolshoi, Teisling had little option but to take out her cheque book and write a personal cheque to Mukhamedov for $250,000 as her guarantee for the dollar payments. Teisling was furious, the dancers were delighted and Mukhamedov was full of himself again. Everyone, including a deeply relieved Tikhonov, left for the theatre, where Mukhamedov expected to report to Grigorovich that he had handled the situation satisfactorily and that he need no longer worry about this particular problem. But Grigorovich was still nowhere to be seen. He had returned to his hotel, Mukhamedov was told, when it became apparent that the company intended to delay the performance. He went at once to the company office and picked up the telephone. 'Yuri Nikolaievich,' he said when he heard Grigorovich answer, 'it's Irek.' 'I don't wish to speak to anyone,' said Grigorovich, and slammed down the telephone.

Mukhamedov stood for a moment unable to believe what had happened. He stared in stunned silence at the receiver, then slowly put it back on its cradle. He could not move. Had Yuri Nikolaievich not heard who was calling? Perhaps he had failed to recognise Mukhamedov's voice. Did he think it was Vasyuchenko, or Tikhonov? But he knew Yuri Nikolaievich had made no mistake about the identity of his caller. For the first time in eight years he had treated Irek Djavdatovich, his special star and champion, his son, with the contempt he reserved for the rest of the world.

Mukhamedov walked round the town the next day with Masha, deeply depressed and with only one topic on his mind. Why had Yuri Nikolaievich put down the phone? After all, Mukhamedov reckoned, he had been a good boy and had tried to make everybody happy by resolving the crisis with Teisling – why was Yuri Grigorovich not happy with him too? For three days Masha listened to him wrestling with what was the most shocking crisis Mukhamedov had had to deal with so far in his life. His expectations with Ljuda had never been very high, but ballet was his whole world and, until now, Grigorovich had been its axis. He remembered Grigorovich's refusal to alter the casting of *Spartacus* in Peking to accommodate his sciatica. Was that the action of a loving father to a devoted son? A bad-tempered telephone call was a triviality in itself, but it triggered a train of thought that forced Mukhamedov to face an unpalatable truth. Masha, fearful of pushing him too far, merely waited for her lover to find his own answers.

Could it be possible, he asked Masha, that he had outlived his usefulness to his master, the man he revered as the genius of ballet? Had he after all, nearing thirty, served Grigorovich's purpose as Vasiliev and Lavrovsky had in their turn? Slowly the awful implications of his speech to the company denouncing the Bolshoi veteran dancers dawned on him and he blushed with shame at what those great dancers must have thought of him and the irreparable damage that his foolishness might have wrought in the company. And he remembered Lavrovsky's prophecy that inevitably he too would find himself discarded. Perhaps, he said to Masha, Grigorovich did not love him as a human being, perhaps he only thought of his ballets and not his dancers, as his detractors had maintained all along. Masha heard the pain in his voice and understood how deeply he was hurt, but she knew that Grigorovich had misjudged Mukhamedov as much as Ljuda had. They had both assumed that his lack of maturity was irreversible, and that the strength of his character, so graphically expressed on the stage, could somehow be permanently emasculated. She hated seeing him so desperately unhappy, but realised that without a blow such as this to his simplistic view of life, he had no hope.

Mukhamedov at this time made no effort to hide his feelings for Masha. He bought her flowers and carried them back to her room, and gave her gifts of fruit; when she was involved in a small accident during a performance of *The Stone Flower*, he rushed to her side and visited her every day as she convalesced. His relationship with his wife was at its lowest ebb. They rarely slept together and when they spoke, they rowed. He did not tell Ljuda of his upset with Grigorovich, knowing her response would be to advise him to forget his silly feelings and remember where his – and her – future lay, with Grigorovich and nobody else. But while he clung to Masha as an emotional anchor, he was still unable to countenance a final break with his wife. It was all happening too fast. Betrayed and betrayer, he was out of his depth. It was no coincidence that in São Paulo he bought Ljuda the most expensive present he had ever given her: a pair of earstuds with a matching ring set with emeralds and diamonds, costing $4,000.

One Saturday night after the performance, towards the end of the season in São Paulo, there was a company party. It might have been somebody's birthday, but nobody in the Bolshoi Ballet bothered much about what was being celebrated – a party was a party. As it was taking place in Masha's hotel, Mukhamedov naturally intended to go. For reasons of her own, Ljuda declined to accompany him, and he and Masha were alone in her room until the early hours of the morning. Eventually, afraid of another pointless slanging match with Ljuda, Mukhamedov walked the few hundred yards back to his hotel around 2 a.m. in the morning. His bedroom door was locked and, although he knocked as loudly as he dared at that hour, there was no reaction from Ljuda. He called Masha from the lobby and asked if he could spend the rest of the night with her. She gladly agreed, and by the time Mukhamedov retraced his steps to his own hotel early on Sunday morning he was exhausted.

Mukhamedov, the star attraction that night at a gala performance, was due to dance the *Nutcracker* pas de deux and the second act of *Giselle* – by no means a strenuous night's work for him, but nevertheless he desperately needed some rest. The day was already scorching hot and he was glad of the hotel's air-conditioning as he walked through the lobby and up to his room, the door of which was now unlocked. He undressed, mumbling to Ljuda that he must get some sleep, pulled the duvet over his head and tried to forget about them all.

Ljuda was strangely silent as her husband climbed into bed; her bizarre behaviour over the next few minutes suggests that she was, quite simply, speechless with rage. When Mukhamedov was on the point of slipping into his desired oblivion, Ljuda at last gave voice to her fury. She ripped the bedclothes off him, snatched up his bunch of keys from the bedside table and attacked him with it while demanding an explanation for his absence the previous night. 'I was completely shocked,' he remembers. 'I had cuts all over my body, my head, everywhere. She was hitting me with metal – it was very painful.'

Painful and shocking the blows might have been, but they sparked the reaction in Mukhamedov that he had so fearfully avoided for so long. He grabbed her arm, took the keys and, almost without thinking, told his wife, 'I have had enough of this, Ljuda. It's over. I love Masha and intend to marry her. I want a divorce.' At last the words were out and could not be withdrawn. 'I do not love you any more,' he went on. 'Everything is over between us.' Ljuda's reply was to hurl the bedside lamp at him. 'How can you say you don't love me when you give me presents like that!' she raged, picking up the emerald and diamond jewellery. 'Here, take them back,' she added, throwing them at Mukhamedov. In hindsight, Mukhamedov regrets not immediately flushing them down the lavatory to bring his hysterical wife to her senses. By now half the occupants of their hotel corridor could hear the histrionics issuing from the Mukhamedovs' room. Everyone naturally held their breaths, eagerly anticipating what would come next.

'I will deal with Masha,' growled Ljuda. She threw on a dress and slammed from the room. 'She was out of control,' says Mukhamedov. 'I had to warn Masha.' He picked up the telephone and called Masha, told her briefly what had happened and that Ljuda was on her way to her hotel, beside herself with fury. He pulled on a pair of jeans and a T-shirt, and followed his wife to Masha's hotel.

This was the point of no return for Mukhamedov. He had almost resolved the unreal relationship with his wife, but, coming so closely on the heels of his doubts about Grigorovich, it left him reeling. In a matter of moments he had rejected nearly thirty years of unquestioning loyalty to the ethics of his upbringing. He could handle only so much. He knew that if he went into the room where the confrontation was about to take place between his wife and his mistress, irrevocable decisions would have to be taken, and publicly. He might even be expected to take control. He could not trust himself to cope; it was all too much. He concealed himself behind a wall and allowed events to overtake him.

Masha prepared herself for Ljuda's arrival quite calmly. Life with Zubkov had inured her to melodramatic showdowns, and she sat quietly in bed, waiting, trying to reassure her nervous room-mate. A couple of her friends in the hotel had also telephoned to warn her that Ljuda was on the way, as the distressed woman was making no effort to disguise her fury. When the knock finally came on the door, Masha told her girlfriend to answer it, and in Ljuda rushed like a whirlwind. 'She straightaway grabbed me by the throat and called me by some terrible names,' she says, 'but my arms are longer than hers and I pushed her into a corner and pinned her down.' Masha broke three fingernails as she tried to control her assailant. Her friend pushed between them and told Ljuda to pull herself together or she would have both of them to wrestle with. Masha wisely refrained from exchanging insults with her lover's wife and just listened as Ljuda threatened her with the dire consequences of her behaviour when her friends in the administration heard of what had been going on. 'How could you seduce my husband? He is so young and innocent, he has never been unfaithful before,' Masha remembers hearing her say. Then, threatening dreadful retribution, Ljuda left Masha's room and the hotel.

Mukhamedov was still in hiding, keeping watch on the building's entrance, and when Ljuda reappeared, her face streaked with tears, he kept silent as she unknowingly walked past him. He knew Masha too must be desperately upset and in need of his support.

He turned and walked away from them both.

Mukhamedov maintains that the next two hours or so in São Paulo are a blank. Even five years later he has no recollection of what he did, where he went, what he thought, and in a sense it is easy to see why. On one hand, by saying he would leave his wife for Masha he had made a bid for personal satisfaction; on the other, by so doing he had committed an act of betrayal so fundamental to his personal code of honour (however naïve that may seem to others) that it simultaneously seemed like a fatal blow of self-destruction. To put it another way, he had dug himself into a hole and could see no way of climbing out.

But two other human beings were involved in Mukhamedov's crisis, and no matter how confused, or craven, he felt that hot afternoon in Brazil, one of them at least was intent on breaking the deadlock. When Masha arrived at the theatre that night, she was warned that Ljuda had already arrived and was waiting for her in her dressing-room. Accompanied by a small group of fascinated dancers agog to savour such a promising scandal, Masha confronted her lover's wife. Ljuda looked terrible, she remembers; her hair was

dishevelled and her eyes were red from crying. She was also wielding
a very large and lethal-looking pair of scissors. 'Her eyes said, come
to me I want to kill you,' says Masha, but she stayed in the door-
way, surrounded by her enthralled colleagues, breathless to know
what Ljuda would do. Suddenly Masha's girlfriend, having previously seen Ljuda in action, lost her nerve and broke the spell by
calling for help and bundling Masha outside. Just in time to meet
Mukhamedov stepping out of his bus and into more trouble. Masha
told him what had happened, and he went through the stage door to
look for his wife, who, by all accounts, was still running up and
down the corridors waving her scissors and vowing vengeance on
Masha.

When he found her, Ljuda was at her wits' end, sobbing
uncontrollably, begging Mukhamedov not to leave her and asking
the age-old and unanswerable question: how can you do this to me?
The company's assistant directors, Viktor Tikhonov and Marina
Kondratieva, joined them and tried to quieten her. The company
masseuse took the scissors from Ljuda's hand and led Masha past the
little group to the first-aid room, where she would dress and make up
for the evening's performance. 'Ljuda,' said Mukhamedov, 'it is over
between us. I have carried you long enough; you must now stand on
your own feet. I love Masha and I intend to marry her. You and I
must divorce.' And, ignoring the crescendo of screams of rage from
his wife, he turned to Tikhonov and Kondratieva and declared, 'If it
is better for the company, I will go straight back to Moscow to avoid
any more scandal.' His mind was made up, he went on, and there was
nothing more to be said.

It was done. In front of his wife, the Bolshoi authorities and the
scattering of fellow dancers unable to tear themselves away from
such entertainment, he had made a public commitment to Masha.
The pretence was over and, for the time being, so was the indecision.
There was no question, of course, that the Bolshoi could continue its
tour without its star dancer, and Tikhonov and Kondratieva made it
clear to Ljuda that she was the one who would be on the next plane to
Russia if she didn't pull herself together and stop behaving so wildly.
Anyway, there was a performance to get through.

To be safe, Masha was escorted to and from the stage by a small
phalanx of male dancers that night and a company official gave up his

room for the couple. After dining on sausages and cold schnapps, they spent the night together openly and with the company's full knowledge for the first time, exhausted but content. They woke the next morning at the start of what they consider today to have been their honeymoon, but there was still a long way to go.

Mukhamedov's first task was to retrieve his few belongings from the room that he had shared with Ljuda. He was thankful for once that he had so few possessions – shaving gear and some clothes, which he threw into his small suitcase. Predictably, it was an unpleasant meeting, and difficult for both of them. He remembers her parting words as he left were to the effect that, although he might think he was leaving her, he need not assume he was no longer responsible for supporting her financially. He hurried back to Masha. They had planned to breakfast quietly in their room on their first morning together, but Mukhamedov opened the door to discover a celebration going on and the room full of women. Masha's girlfriends, who had followed the previous night's back-stage drama with great glee, had been fascinated to hear first hand the background to the story – and how the affair was progressing. When Mukhamedov joined the party, the girls made him feel like a conquering hero returning to a particularly man-starved harem.

The Bolshoi Ballet flew on that day to Curitiba, the next stop on its tour, and the lovers boarded the airport bus surrounded by back-slapping dancers and the inevitable ribald comments. Masha settled into her seat with her new man by her side feeling that life had not seemed so promising for a long time. At that precise moment the bus carrying the corps de ballet dancers passed by them in the hotel drive, and for a second she was face to face with Ljuda. Their eyes met, and Masha instantly knew that Ljuda intended to exact a heavy retribution. She said nothing to Mukhamedov, and they enjoyed the trip and each other's company, and toasted themselves copiously on the flight to Curitiba, ignoring Ljuda in the seat behind them as she tried to make sure that her husband never forgot she was still there. 'I was completely happy,' he says. 'Not since I won the Grand Prix had I felt so good.'

When they arrived at their hotel, however, Ljuda gave them a taste of what they could expect from her. Naturally, she had no intention of giving up without a fight, and a fierce one at that; as Mukhamedov knew only too well, his wife was a born fighter. She was sitting in the lobby waiting for them, Mukhamedov's key in her hand. 'Shall we go on up now?' he remembers her asking, rising to meet him as if nothing had happened. 'Ljuda, it's finished,' he said again. 'Face reality for a change. We are through,' and he arranged another room for himself. They were soon to learn that Ljuda had no intention of leaving them in peace. Quite the opposite.

A few days later they were together in the hotel bar when Ljuda approached them. Masha was worried that she intended to have another shouting match, but Ljuda sat down quietly and, talking to Mukhamedov as if Masha did not exist, discussed the new flat in Moscow. They needed a new sofa bed for visitors, and what about the wallpaper they had planned to buy? Mukhamedov was now sure that he would never live in that flat; anxious for the moment just to keep Ljuda quiet, however, he agreed to buy what she wanted. The next day he paid $2,000 for a sofa bed to be shipped back to Russia.

A touring ballet company, even one the size of the Bolshoi, is like a giant goldfish bowl. There is absolutely no hope of privacy, and every liaison, old or new, is scrutinised avidly. Mukhamedov's triangular adventures had all the ingredients guaranteed to provide endless delicious speculation with which to while away those boring hours of travelling or just hanging about in strange towns. The casting was perfect: Mukhamedov the star, Masha the glamorous seducer and Ljuda the poor wife, trying to hang on to her man. No wonder the company filled the canteen at mealtimes, eager at the prospect of more public twists to the plot.

The truth was, of course, that Mukhamedov and Masha were clinging to a slender thread of hope in their lives, and the combined burden of Ljuda's fight for survival, however natural, and the attention from their fellow dancers was one they could well have done without. One day they decided to avoid the scrutiny in the subsidised canteen and paid for their lunch at a nearby restaurant. It was no good. The next day the company, and Ljuda, joined them.

But the company's curiosity was not all prurient. The society in which the dancers lived was restrictive. None knew better than Mukhamedov that conformity was essential, that often only examples from above offered acceptable alternatives, and he found that he had unwittingly earned a certain kudos among the male fraternity by breaking free of his moribund marital bonds. He likes to boast that the divorce rate in the Bolshoi somewhat increased following his own break from an obviously unhappy marriage and that he gave heart to many a man previously too timid to follow his instincts when it came to an unwanted wife. And his fellows could not help but grudgingly admire the panache with which Mukhamedov, the stolid ballet machine, suddenly appeared in their midst with 'Playboy' on his arm, the girl whom many of them had spent years lusting after. Interestingly, he remembers only one girl in the company, outside Masha's small circle of intimates, who expressed approval of his action.

He also gradually became aware of other changes in attitude towards him. After his embarrassing confrontation with Ljuda when she had got hold of his room key, the Bolshoi administrators tried to make sure that he was given a room well away from her and usually one of a quality superior to those he had had before. Now that he was Masha's partner he realised how many party invitations he had previously missed out on, and company colleagues with whom he rarely mixed seemed genuinely glad to see him. On one free day most of the dancers repaired to the nearest beach, and a particularly lively group, about to embark on a trip in a sailing-boat, insisted he and Masha join them. He was surprised at the goodwill, not to mention copious amounts of wine, that surrounded them both until nightfall. Ljuda's good friend Vladimir Karakulev was also on board, but that only seemed to add spice to the fun.

Masha too was happier than she had been for many years and shared Mukhamedov's sense of freedom in their relationship, while she tried to ignore the niggling doubts at the back of her mind. She had learned at considerable cost how deep-rooted his fear of the unconventional was; she knew Ljuda would persevere, and where did Grigorovich figure in the future? She feared that it was all happening too quickly for her lover. She was happy if he was, but she was nervous.

One day Masha came home from a shopping expedition and presented Mukhamedov with a gift-wrapped parcel containing an expensive shirt and sweater. He was amazed and mystified when he discovered it all fitted. How had she known his size? It was the first time since his childhood that anyone had bought him such personal items of clothing. The next day they went out together and found him a pair of extravagantly costly shoes, then a coat, and Masha, with great pleasure, dumped the more disreputable of his clothes in the rubbish bin. He had worn most of them 'for a hundred years', he remembers. She persuaded him to go to the town's best hairdresser to have his hair cut properly, rather than butchered by backstage enthusiasts or airport barbers as it normally was, and started a habit that has become almost a passion. (In London his visits to a smart Knightsbridge salon are a source of endless satisfaction to him.) The cynics in the company shook their heads at what they saw as this hasty making over of the Bolshoi's ballet machine, and muttered grim premonitions of imminent disaster. But Mukhamedov had discovered the thrill of having a woman care for him as much as he cared for her, and it was an intoxicating experience.

15

Copacabana Beach and Disaster

MUKHAMEDOV REMEMBERS THOSE early days with Masha in Brazil as an idyll, a honeymoon. Indeed, not only did his romance with Masha blossom, but he himself began the slow process of growing out of, and away from, the ties that bound him to his homeland – and Grigorovich. Yet he was still naïve enough not to realise that his actions, however private he thought them, had already caused ripples of consternation among certain sections of the company.

One day he and Masha, on leaving their hotel for the theatre, came face to face with Grigorovich as he got out of his car. Mukhamedov, with Masha on his arm, eager to show her off and share his pleasure with the man he still saw as his father, called out, 'Good evening, Yuri Nikolaievich. How are you?' He remembers how awkward he felt when Grigorovich turned away without catching his eye and, muttering only a perfunctory greeting before hurrying inside, quite ignored Masha. But it needed no public demonstration of disapproval to prompt large factions of the Bolshoi Ballet to start hedging their bets once the novelty of Mukhamedov's conduct had worn off. It was all happening again, they reckoned. Grigorovich's young favourite was growing up and showing sparks of independence, just as Vasiliev, Lavrovsky and Godunov had done. It would be best not to be too closely allied to Mukhamedov if and when the bust-up came. Unpleasant talk – who did this Tartar think he was anyway, walking off with a good Russian soloist – also began to circulate. Such racist intolerance had been subdued as long as Mukhamedov was seen as totally subservient to Grigorovich.

And there was now considerable jealousy of Masha among the women, particularly in the upper ranks of dancers. Ljuda's balletic abilities had represented no threat even though she was Mukhamedov's wife, as evidenced by her lack of promotion, but Masha was quite a different proposition. With no political clout at all, she was already a senior soloist in the company. How much higher could she climb with Mukhamedov's and, assuming he could still count on it, Grigorovich's backing?

Ljuda's behaviour in Rio upset Mukhamedov and Masha, as it was meant to, but even among Russians there are few codes of conduct in love and war. On the first morning they discovered her sitting on the corridor floor outside their room, and at eight o'clock she knocked on the door and called out to Mukhamedov that she was ready to go down for breakfast with him. The couple discussed the situation and decided, unwisely as they were later to discover, that it would cause less trouble if he were to go with her while Masha breakfasted in the room. If Masha went, they reasoned, Ljuda would merely raise a scene, and Ljuda was probably counting on Mukhamedov's horror of the public row that would surely follow if he refused. Whatever his ex-wife's tactics, imagined by them or otherwise, it worked. Husband and wife duly appeared together in the mornings, Ljuda quietly and solicitously choosing the food from the buffet for Mukhamedov, who tried to pretend she was not there. Ljuda also began to telephone his room late at night, and when Masha answered, she would tell her it was time for Mukhamedov to go to bed. 'He needs his rest, Masha. You don't know him like I do.'

Soon rumours trickled back to Masha via various 'concerned' individuals that the Bolshoi authorities were worried that Mukhamedov was establishing a *ménage à trois*, and making no effort to conceal it. If the rumours leaked out, they told her, it would do irreparable harm not only to him, but to Grigorovich and the company as a whole. Was Masha sure she was doing the right thing? This bizarre arrangement continued for some days. Meanwhile, Ljuda came to Masha in her theatre dressing-room and asked her to join her for a cigarette and a sisterly chat. 'Masha, I understand how you feel,' she said. 'You want to be a ballerina of the Bolshoi and you want plenty of money.' Ignoring Masha's vehement denials, she continued, 'You and Irek were childhood sweethearts, I know, but we must work out a compromise.

'Irek is tired and a little bit crazy right now, but you know he still loves me and I love him. He just needs a rest and he will come to his senses.' Masha replied that she too loved Irek and she fervently hoped he would never come to his senses. 'I have an idea,' Ljuda went on.

'Irek will not listen to me, so you must tell him that he must come back and live with me. You must stay out of the way, Masha, and tell him to live again with me.' Hardly able to believe her ears, and baffled as to where the compromise lay, Masha told Ljuda that if she wanted to say anything at all to Irek, she must say it herself. Only he could choose what he wanted to do. But she found Ljuda's new apparent reasonableness chilling.

The next night the Bolshoi was invited to a grand party thrown for them by Tamara Teisling, the impresario. Ljuda insisted that she would go with the couple, but neither Mukhamedov nor Masha was willing to provide any further fuel for the gossip-mongers, and they plotted to escape together after the performance. They went through a charade of taking a change of evening clothes to the theatre, but, instead of joining the other dancers on the bus to the beachside restaurant, slipped through the auditorium and took a taxi to Copacabana Beach.

It was very dark and not very warm, but at least they were alone. As they faced the ocean, the sensation that there was nothing between them and the west coast of Africa lightened the claustrophobia of the constant attention they had been attracting. They passed a bottle of schnapps between them to keep out the cold as they watched the breakers in the moonlight and waited for as long as they could endure the cold to allow the busload of party-going dancers to drive by to their restaurant. It was well into the early hours when a local resident came down the beach to investigate the source of the chatter, ominously displaying a large hand-gun tucked into his belt; the couple decided it was high time they ate and dashed across the road to a restaurant. They carried on drinking with their meal and returned to the hotel about 4 a.m., very drunk and very happy.

Sleep seemed quite an inappropriate ending to what they felt was the most romantic night of their lives, and Mukhamedov spent the few remaining hours until morning with Masha in her room, just in case someone was camped outside his. When Ljuda telephoned as they breakfasted, Masha denied having seen him since the previous evening. They agreed that the sleep which, by now, they both desperately needed could only be guaranteed if they remained apart for a while, and Mukhamedov slipped back to his own room.

Just as she slid into oblivion, the ringing of her bedside phone dragged Masha back to consciousness. It was Mukhamedov. At first she thought her tired brain was simply refusing to function, for she could not understand a word he was saying. She soon realised, though, that the man was quite incoherent, and it was not just the alcohol. She tried to make sense of the jumble of words and sobs that came out of the telephone as he told her what a bastard he was, that he might kill himself, that she must never see him again, that he had betrayed her and himself. 'Come to me, Irek,' she said. 'Come here straight away and tell me what has happened.' A feeling of dread grew in Masha when he arrived and sat by her side, unable to look her in the eyes, and described what had happened.

Mukhamedov had gone to his room a happy man, still intoxicated by the schnapps, Copacabana Beach and Masha, and, neglecting to lock his door, stripped, fell into bed and went instantly to sleep. A movement by his bedside slowly woke him and he welcomed the woman climbing into his bed. With dawning horror, he realised it was not Masha, the only woman he wanted, but his wife, yet he was too drunk and too confused to resist. It was only later that the wave of self-revulsion hit him. He ordered Ljuda out of his room and sat for a moment, unable to understand or believe what he had done, before picking up the telephone and calling Masha.

He swore to her that he was revolted by what he had done and could never forgive himself. Masha was shocked and felt him slipping away from her, but she recognised that he must learn to take responsibility for his actions, that the time had now come when he must truly choose between them. She clung to her certainty that his protestations of love on Copacabana Beach were not all lies. Mukhamedov was shattered to learn of his propensity for betrayal, she knew, but how else at his age could he get in touch with his true feelings? How else could he discover what he really wanted out of life? Masha just held tight and hoped.

While no one could blame her for trying to regain her husband's affections, once again Ljuda had miscalculated. The next morning when Mukhamedov found his wife waiting outside his room to go with him to breakfast, he told her in brutally blunt words what to do and he and Masha ate together in the dining-room. Ljuda was treated to the same curt advice each time she tried to speak to either of them.

165

Masha was relieved that her lover had at last taken a tougher line in his personal conduct, yet she did not relax.

At twenty-nine Mukhamedov was a boy in a man's body. He had lived until then in a bubble of false security, channelling every ounce of physical and emotional energy into his work. He had complied absolutely with the dictum of his masters – don't talk, dance – from the age of ten. His recent discovery that men and women were more treacherous, loving, idealistic, cynical and infinitely more interesting off-stage than on shook him to his roots. He remembers how, after he and Masha started to live together in Brazil, he was startled to see enmity in the eyes of dancers to whom he had scarcely spoken for the past eight years, as strange to him as the warmth that greeted him from others. Mukhamedov blushes very easily and he recalls how he became fully aware of this when, after Masha had bought him some decent clothes, her girlfriends made it quite clear to the handsome and red-faced young man that he was good to look at. The fact that women all around the world had been languishing over him for years he found genuinely hard to believe.

Friends would ask Masha what on earth she found to talk about with Mukhamedov, who, for as long as they had known him, had seemed to epitomise the cliché that dancers keep their brains in their feet. As anyone friendly with him today will confirm, it is often difficult to get a word in during a conversation with Mukhamedov. Talking, even in a foreign language, is one of his favourite pastimes, and he fully appreciates the irony in the English sense of humour, so similar to the Russian. 'I saw his eyes,' says Masha, 'and knew that his brain made him the dancer he was, so why not the man?'

It would be easy to call this period of self-discovery with Masha a rebirth, but in truth so much of Mukhamedov had lain dormant for so long that to a great extent his personality was emerging for the first time. It was a revelation, for instance, to go shopping with Masha. She actually asked his advice, and he still remembers with what pleasure he heard her being complimented on a swimming costume he picked out for her. Having provided only the cash for Ljuda's shopping, never an opinion, this was quite a radical departure for him.

At the same time Mukhamedov began to re-evaluate his worth as a dancer. It had amazed him that the Bolshoi authorities – and that included Grigorovich – had not somehow censured him for the upset he had caused by openly leaving his wife and living with Masha without asking anyone's permission. In many ways they had tried to smooth his path where possible by making suitable accommodation or travel arrangements, and he had certainly not received the carpeting he fully expected for what he saw as his bad behaviour.

For some time he had been increasingly aware of how much the public perception of the Bolshoi Ballet centred around his performances: they always guaranteed full houses, there had been queues, he remembered, for returns for Irek Mukhamedov in New York and the press seemed to turn out in force only when he was dancing. So he experimented a little. He started to come and go as he pleased. He would say, for example, that he needed a car after the dancers' post-performance bus had left for the hotel, and would get it, or he would let it be known that he might be late for an official reception, and no one demurred. One day he and Masha ate lunch in the hotel's expensive restaurant, which was used only by the most senior figures in the company hierarchy. Galina Ulanova entered, and Mukhamedov was elated when she made a point of crossing the room and greeting them both. The fact that he was at that time as near the pinnacle of the Bolshoi's élite as Ulanova herself, or indeed any other dancer had ever been, took a long time to sink in.

As the Bolshoi Ballet continued its progress round Brazil, and Mukhamedov's confidence in himself and Masha grew, so Ljuda became more tormented. Her seduction had spectacularly backfired and, at a loss as to what to do next, she turned to Bessmertnova, asking her to speak to her husband, point out how cruel his behaviour was and advise him to return to her immediately. Bessmertnova, of course, would have nothing to do with it. Mukhamedov can remember how Ljuda hounded the couple as they travelled. In Belo Horizonte she tried to force her way into their car after a performance, then chased them through the hotel until they took refuge in their room. At parties she would insist on sitting at their table to make them feel uncomfortable and when they left each city's hotel, Mukhamedov would find her bar and other sundry bills credited to his room. 'In Russia we have a saying,' he says. 'If you don't want dirt to smell, don't stir it.' So he paid the bills.

But Ljuda's insistence on his always paying her debts led to her biggest mistake so far, revealing once again her total miscomprehension of the man she had married. During the company's return visit to São Paulo some friends invited Mukhamedov and Masha out to dinner one night. As they were dressing, Ljuda telephoned to say that the wallpaper for the new flat in Moscow had arrived, and could she have the money? Mukhamedov decided that he might as well hurry round and settle up with her right away to get her off their backs; Masha agreed and said she would be ready and waiting for him when he returned. Ljuda called out for him to enter when he knocked on her door, and after doing so he nearly passed out. His wife, he recalls, was wearing nothing but brief underwear and stockings, and made some observation that he had always pestered her to wear that sort of thing. Did he approve?

It was all starting again, he thought. Here was the woman to whom, in his youth, he had given his most solemn commitment yet again trying to please him. She was trying to convince him, even now, that she was willing to do as he wished to save their marriage, playing on his guilt, appealing to his childlike nature – that subservient state of mind he was so painfully struggling to leave behind. He attempted once more to make Ljuda face the truth, that he had changed, nothing was the same any more and their relationship would have been over whether he had met Masha or anybody else. It was a deeply upsetting confrontation for them both, and Ljuda realised she had overplayed her hand. Nevertheless, as Mukhamedov attempted to define his feelings about her and himself, a little of his own confusion dissolved. Time had raced by, however, and with a shock he saw that he had been absent from his room for nearly an hour.

Masha was frantic, and her friends kept ringing to find out what was causing the delay. She became sure that Mukhamedov had once again weakened in the face of his wife's blandishments. This is the finish, she thought. She could make excuses for one violation of their trust, but not two. She set out to look for him, and her heart sank even further when she saw her lover sitting at the end of the corridor, in tears. Mukhamedov tried to explain what an ordeal this latest confrontation had turned out to be, not because he had resisted temptation – there simply had not been any – but because he had been forced to face the truth in himself and knew that Ljuda would never understand. Knowing Masha would be thinking the worst only made him suffer more. Soon Masha too was in tears. Neither said much, but they realised that he had scored an important victory in his fight for a new life.

During these weeks in Brazil they spoke often of their future, of their shared desire for a family of their own. Both Mukhamedov and Masha felt that the emotional racking he had gone through had cleared his brain and strengthened his spirit enough for her to trust him. It was clear to them that, however messy it might turn out to be, they must divorce their respective partners as soon as they were back in Russia and then marry.

On the Bolshoi's last stop, in Recife, Masha telephoned Moscow and asked her mother to find them a flat to rent as neither of them could face sharing Aunt Lala's cramped accommodation, and Mukhamedov's premonition that he would never live in Third Tverskaya-Yamskaya Street with his wife became a certainty. They boarded the flight to Russia on 19 November. All three protagonists in the drama were dreading the landing at Sheremet'yevo airport the next day, aware that, once back in Moscow, their lives would change for ever.

Considerably fortified with drink, Mukhamedov and Masha lingered in customs in the hope that Ljuda would have gone by the time they eventually appeared to travel on to Aunt Lala's flat. She was waiting for them, of course, and, given the circumstances, it would have required a miracle to avoid a scene. Mukhamedov's Aunt Galina had arrived unexpectedly and was horrified to be told by Ljuda that her nephew had betrayed his wife and intended to run off with another woman. Ljuda's mother and father, there to greet their daughter and son-in-law, found that, instead of a respectable couple, they had an extremely distraught woman on their hands. Only Igor Yurlov, who had just returned from a tour of Britain with the Stars of the Bolshoi Ballet and was there to drive his friends into town, provided an oasis of calm in the echoing arrivals hall.

Masha muttered a quiet prayer as Ljuda rushed up to Mukhamedov, tearfully begged him to go home with her and said how much she loved him and needed him. Desperately trying to be firm and at the same time realising how cruel he must sound, Mukhamedov replied that he would never live with her again and that she must accept their life together was over. From now on his life was with Masha.

16

Divorce and Marriage

WHEN MUKHAMEDOV AND Masha landed in Moscow on 20 November 1989, they had just over six months left of their life in Russia. They immediately lost themselves in the delightful complexities of at last living together and the grim necessities of divorce and Bolshoi politics. As they struggled to get to grips with their change of circumstances in Moscow, they were in fact hurtling towards a solution of breathtaking simplicity.

The first priority was finding somewhere to live. A friend of a friend of Masha had returned to her parental home to have a baby, leaving her own flat empty. Masha and Mukhamedov could move in at once, she told them; it was fully furnished and the couple could stay there rent free. Their new home in Zheleznaya Doroga Street, off the Dimitrievskaya Chaussée and not that far from Aunt Galina, had been empty for some time. On the first morning after moving in Masha called on the services of a friend to help with the cleaning. Mukhamedov telephoned Ljuda and told her he would call round shortly to collect his things.

He knew it would not be an easy visit, but was nevertheless startled to see Ljuda's parents as well as his wife waiting for him when Ljuda opened the door. Ljuda said little, while her mother followed him and asked him if he would care for some coffee. When Mukhamedov joined her in the kitchen, she turned to him and asked why he had done this to her daughter. He was relieved that so far he had escaped the expected screaming attack from Ljuda and apologised to his mother-in-law. 'I'm to blame,' he said. 'I no longer love Ljuda and I am living with another girl. That's all there is to say.' He did not get out of the place without having to promise to help find, and pay for, some new furniture on the black market, but when he left with his suitcase, he was thankful to have got off so lightly. He should have known better. Masha told him that friends had telephoned to say that Ljuda was waving a calendar around the theatre that she had allegedly kept in Brazil; the crosses on it, she said, marked the dates when she and her husband had slept together. She was, she proudly claimed, very pregnant. A boast that only the passage of time could verify.

Mukhamedov found himself even more isolated in Moscow than he had been when living with Ljuda. He had never felt comfortable with her friends and had few of his own outside the company, and not many within it. Both he and Masha sensed the gathering enmity in the Bolshoi and began to withdraw from contact with the dancers, trusting only old established friendships such as that of Igor Yurlov and his family, who had proved exceptionally loyal throughout their stormy courtship. But one man to whom Mukhamedov could talk was Sergei Lavrov, a well-connected and wealthy businessman and entrepreneur he had met three years earlier when looking for a new car. Lavrov moved in social circles so removed from the Bolshoi and, indeed, the theatre that in his company Mukhamedov felt quite free from the ever tightening web of intrigue and trouble that was closing in on him at work. To Mukhamedov's relief, Lavrov was hugely delighted at his friend's romantic adventures. Lavrov had helped Mukhamedov with black-market purchases in the past, but when he was asked to find some furniture for Ljuda, he refused point blank. 'I never liked the woman from the moment I met her,' he said, and insisted the lovers come to eat with him and his wife, Natasha, and their new baby boy, Yegor, the following evening. It was the start of a short but fruitful closeness between the four of them, the extraordinary results of which were either purely random or cunningly planned. To this day Mukhamedov and Masha are still not sure which.

Life at the theatre was deteriorating daily for Masha. There were rows and tantrums night and day from Ljuda and, even though she moved dressing-rooms to get out of her way, she never seemed to be able to avoid her. Then, to make matters worse, when the schedule for the Bolshoi Ballet's tour of France in mid-December was posted, Masha's name was absent and Ljuda's was included. Mukhamedov went to Nikonov, an assistant director, and asked that Masha be added to the list. No, was the reply. Very well, remove Ljuda, he demanded. No, again. For the first time in eight years he delivered an ultimatum to the Bolshoi. 'If Ljuda goes to France, I will not,' he said as he left the office. Later that day Ljuda's name was erased from the notice-board. All hell broke loose, Masha remembers, when Ljuda realised she had been outmanoeuvred. Finally Masha had had enough.

Mukhamedov would be away from Moscow for nearly six weeks during December and January. First he was guesting again with the Royal Ballet of Flanders in Antwerp in *Don Quixote*, then, after a short three-day visit home, he would tour France with the Bolshoi; when the company returned to Moscow, he would remain to dance three performances of *The Sleeping Beauty* with the Paris Opéra Ballet at the invitation of Rudolf Nureyev. Masha knew that facing daily crises at the theatre alone was more than she could cope with, and decided she must persuade the company doctor that she was temporarily unfit to dance while Mukhamedov was away.

They were visiting the Lavrovs almost every day during this time. One evening in late November Sergei wondered if pregnancy might be the foolproof excuse Masha was looking for to absent herself from the theatre while Mukhamedov was out of Russia. They all laughed at this outrageous notion, but when they got home later that night, the idea somehow seemed very attractive to Mukhamedov. 'Shall we try?' he asked. Although he was convinced Masha had conceived on the first attempt, and that it would be a girl at that, they carried on trying for the next three days until he left for Antwerp, just in case.

Meanwhile, Masha convinced the doctor that her back needed rest, and on 30 November she danced the Spanish Princess in Act III of *Swan Lake* before starting her sick leave. For Masha at the time it was merely a temporary expediency, but fate had decreed that it was to be her last performance on the Bolshoi stage. In fact, it was to be the last time she was to wear a pair of pointe shoes in public for the next four years, until she appeared briefly at a small theatre in north London that she had never even heard of in November 1989.

During his week in Antwerp Mukhamedov called Masha every day and asked, 'Are you pregnant yet?' though he was certain that she was. On his return to Moscow he resumed his procreative endeavours. No sooner had Mukhamedov left for his tour of France with the Bolshoi on 15 December than Masha felt something happening, and the waistband of her skirt began to grow tighter.

According to Russian custom, women usually wait for six weeks before having a pregnancy test, but she told Mukhamedov, when he rang from Cannes late one night in the new year, that their efforts had brought the desired results. This was the most significant moment in Mukhamedov's life. Everything that had happened to him in the two years since meeting Masha again, everything he had lost and found, all the bad and the good he had discovered about himself suddenly gained perspective. At once everything was quite clear and it was at that point that their flight from Russia became inevitable. Although at the time the thought had never entered either of their heads, the events of the next three months seemed almost like a preordained timetable.

When they were together again in Moscow in the middle of January, they went immediately for a pregnancy test, which, as they expected, was positive. They agreed that Masha should not dance again until after the birth of what Mukhamedov was still convinced would be a daughter. The next stop was the Bolshoi to inform the authorities of Masha's decision. Marina Kondratieva, an assistant director, was delighted to see Masha back and immediately told her that she would be given many new ballets, such as Plisetskaya's *Carmen Suite*. When Masha told her the reason for her visit, however, Kondratieva misunderstood and advised that Masha have the baby aborted. Abortion is virtually a means of birth control in Russia – if you can afford a private doctor, the process takes about two hours – so there was nothing outrageous in the suggestion, but it was never an option for Masha. Both she and Mukhamedov wanted the child more than anything else, she explained. She was not prepared to take any risks with her pregnancy and had made up her mind to retire from the stage until the child was born.

The couple remember leaving the theatre after speaking to Kondratieva surprised and unsettled that no member of the company had exchanged a word with them.

By the end of January Masha was showing more and more and they decided that the next priority was to legalise the situation as quickly as possible. The first step was divorce, which in Russia can be simple: both parties agree to the process, appear in court and, after their internal passports are stamped accordingly, they are free of each other. If one partner objects, the proceedings can take up to three months, and the dissenting spouse may be summoned up to three times to appear before the court. Only after the third non-appearance is the divorce granted. Normally the matrimonial home stays in the possession of the partner in whose name it is registered. Both Masha and Mukhamedov were the title holders of their apartments.

Masha had spoken to her husband while Mukhamedov was in Paris, and he had agreed to a divorce without demur. He begged to be allowed to stay in the flat, though, since without the benefit of the Bolshoi Equity Committee it would be years before he qualified for one of his own. Masha took only her books and some tableware to supplement the meagre supplies in Zheleznaya Doroga Street and left Zubkov everything, except her car, wishing to bring no detritus from her past years to her new life with Mukhamedov. She collected the necessary papers and Zubkov signed. On Tuesday, 6 February, they both appeared before the local judge and it was all over. Ljuda, however, was quite a different matter.

Mukhamedov knew that it would take a miracle for her to agree to a divorce. Marriage meant present security and future prosperity to Ljuda, and he despaired of convincing her that she must no longer see him as her prop in life. He turned to Sergei Lavrov, a man who was as streetwise as any Muscovite and as hard as nails when he had to be. Lavrov readily agreed to back his friend, and Mukhamedov rang his wife to tell her they must meet to discuss divorce and arranged a date, but did not mention Lavrov.

Mukhamedov remembers the sinking feeling of *déjà vu* when Ljuda opened the door to his knock wearing only a negligée, and thanked God he had Lavrov by his side. Ljuda pulled on some warmer clothing and they sat down to talk. At first she flatly refused to co-operate; if he wanted a divorce, he must wait for it. Then Lavrov pointed out that the flat was in Mukhamedov's name and if she delayed she would lose everything. Mukhamedov stressed that she could keep it all, he only wanted his clothes. Everything else – the flat, furniture, her clothes, jewellery, even his prized Toyota car – was hers. 'If you want to live on the street, say no,' said Lavrov. 'If you want to go back to your parents with nothing, say no.' Lavrov's brutal candour seemed to carry the day, and the two men left with Ljuda's promise of co-operation. She subsequently signed the papers of divorce and the hearing was set for 4 March.

Ljuda recruited her old friend Svetlana Gromova as her second in the contest. Lavrov was with Mukhamedov, and the four of them met in an ante-room before entering the court to complete the formalities. In front of the two witnesses Mukhamedov repeated his promise to his wife that he would take all the blame for the breakdown of the marriage and give her everything. They sat in a row before the judge, who asked who took responsibility. Mukhamedov replied that he did. The judge turned to Ljuda and asked if she agreed to this divorce. Mukhamedov could scarcely believe what was happening when Ljuda answered that she loved him and needed him and did not want a divorce. It was one of the few occasions in his life on which he completely lost control of his temper. Lavrov had forcibly to pin him to his chair as the judge remarked that they clearly needed more time to consider their feelings on the matter and dismissed them.

Outside on the street Lavrov again had to restrain Mukhamedov, who was beside himself with fury as he screamed at his wife to take her belongings and her parents and get out of his flat before nightfall. Lavrov prevented Gromova from joining in, and when his friend had recovered control of himself sufficiently to be released, graphically detailed to both women what would happen if Ljuda played a similar trick again. At that point Mukhamedov was beyond reason, literally in a murderous rage, and he could not for a second have conceded that his wife's behaviour had any basis in affection, that perhaps on the verge of losing her husband of eight years she might conceivably have experienced some late surge of love that she had thought was dead and have felt compelled to draw back from giving him up for ever.

As Ljuda and Gromova got into their car – Mukhamedov's Toyota – he continued his tirade of threats and told them of his intention to fix another hearing as soon as possible. Lavrov pulled every string that he could reach in Moscow to eliminate any delay and on Tuesday, 13 March, they went through the performance all over again, this time with no last-minute changes to the scenario. The court retained their passports to stamp, and at last it was over.

Mukhamedov never set foot inside his flat again, and abandoned all he owned to Ljuda. He left the few personal knick-knacks he had collected on his travels around the world; other than the suitcase of belongings he had already taken, everything connected with that part of his life was left behind. As far as he knows, it is there still.

Mukhamedov and Masha were in a hurry. In addition to filming *Spartacus* (for the second time), *Ivan the Terrible* and *Legend of Love* at the Bolshoi for NHK, the state Japanese broadcasting company, during February, March and April, Mukhamedov had a busy summer scheduled. In May he was booked to perform in Austria with the Vienna Opera Ballet, dancing *Apollo*, his first Balanchine ballet, and in Spain with the Helsinki Ballet in the *Don Quixote* pas de deux. Then followed a tour of Italy in June and the United States in July and August with the Bolshoi Ballet. The couple reckoned that the baby was due in late August, so speed was of the essence if they were to marry, find an apartment of their own and settle Masha before he left, but they could do nothing until their passports, stamped with that magic 'Razvod' (Divorced), were returned from the court. Lavrov worked hard and the documents arrived later in the week, a remarkable achievement, but they still had to find a way around the statutory waiting time of three months between officially registering a wedding and the actual ceremony.

Three days later Lavrov accompanied the two of them to the local registry office, prepared to pay any price to sidestep the regulations, and they were armed with the usual gift for the registrar, a pair of free tickets to the Bolshoi to see Mukhamedov's *Romeo and Juliet*. Luck, though, was on their side, and Lavrov, ever the opportunist, clinched the matter for them. The couple in the queue before them had discreetly left their gift on the official's table, but so discreetly that the lady in charge had overlooked the little parcel. When she turned to Masha and Mukhamedov, Lavrov pushed the present towards her as if it came from him. It worked, together with the free Bolshoi seats, and they were given a blank slot at 11.30 a.m. on the same morning of that performance, Friday, 23 March.

The wedding day was hectic. As Mukhamedov was dancing Romeo that evening, class was essential, and after it he dashed from the theatre to the House of Weddings, pausing only to buy his new bride a bouquet of red roses. Masha and he had no supporters at the ceremony, but the registrar turned a blind eye to the lack of witnesses. So there were just the two of them, Masha in jumper and skirt and leather coat, Mukhamedov also casually dressed. They had not even bothered to buy rings. The official read out the formal declarations, the couple kissed, grabbed the certificate and ran.

In spite of having a pragmatic nature that is occasionally misconstrued as ruthless, Mukhamedov is a true romantic, and as he danced Romeo on his wedding night, he remembers, he saw not Natalia Bessmertnova's Juliet, but Masha. She was in the audience with Sergei and Natasha Lavrov and it was the start of a tradition: only illness prevents her from watching his every performance, and Masha is the first and only person from whom he accepts advice and comment on his work. That Friday night at the Bolshoi Mukhamedov's divided self, which as he now realised, had caused him so many years of unhappiness, began to heal.

The following day they took Masha's passport to have her name officially changed from Zubkova to Mukhamedova as they planned a short honeymoon by the Black Sea. Unless the hotel reception saw the right name on her passport when they registered, she would not be allowed to share a room with her new husband. Three days later it was done, and Mukhamedov told the Bolshoi administration that he was taking time off with Masha, having for almost nine years asked their permission to change his shirt.

They flew to Dagomys on the Black Sea, ironically in the same area where Masha had holidayed with Zubkov two years earlier immediately before the Bolshoi's tour of Italy and the rebirth of her romance with Mukhamedov. They stayed in a cottage in the grounds of the Dagomys Hotel complex and, although they both felt that their time in Brazil had been their true honeymoon, they returned to Moscow content with the world. They were greeted by another clog in the Soviet Union's bureaucratic machine.

During the breakneck bustle surrounding their divorces and wedding they had decided that Masha should accompany Mukhamedov on his visits to Austria and Spain. It would slightly lessen the time she would have to spend alone in Moscow, and as she would be five months pregnant by then, it would be perfectly safe for her to travel by air. They had telephoned the agent in Paris, Natasha Shabayev, who had prepared the engagements, to ask her to send an invitation to Masha, without which she could not be issued with an exit visa. To their consternation, when they arrived back from the Black Sea, there was no word from the agent. It was now mid-April and Mukhamedov was to fly out to Austria on 5 May. One evening at dinner with Sergei and Natasha Lavrov they were discussing the latest irritating hiccup in their plans. Lavrov tossed another apparently light-hearted notion into the conversation. 'Well, if you do take Masha with you,' he said jokingly, 'why don't you both stay in the West? Have you ever thought where you would like to settle outside the Soviet Union?'

Mukhamedov ridiculed the suggestion, reaffirming his dedication to his motherland. Regardless of how many inbred blind loyalties he had recently rejected, his patriotism was not negotiable; it was integral to every fibre of his being. After all, was it not Mukhamedov who played Russian music in foreign hotel bedrooms and longed to return to the rigours of his home climate and food queues? He knew he would gladly stand in line at six o'clock in the morning for powdered milk for his baby, having seen how difficult it was for other young fathers in the company to find supplies. And he was quite happy at the prospect of paying $20 for a packet of Pampers in a hard-currency shop. And yet . . . he had also seen with his own eyes how easy it was to walk into a shop on any street in, say, France or America and purchase these or any other commodity that a baby might need. Yes, he mused, it might be good to live like that, and choosing a favourite country, a favourite company, was a novel game to play, but it was not for him. Reality was here in Moscow with the Bolshoi and he intended his baby to be brought up a good little Russian in the country that had given him so much.

17

Flight

AT THIS STAGE in his life Mukhamedov was in a highly unstable state of flux, living proof that thirty is a dangerous age. He was experiencing the giddy afterglow of rejecting the many codes of conduct that had stifled him for so long. He had just married the woman he truly loved, the birth of the baby for which he longed was just a few months away – if anyone had convinced him of the rightness of flying to the moon, he would have launched himself into space without question. Only ballet rooted him in the past. He felt stronger than ever during the filming for Japanese television, more powerful, more true. So the shock when this last anchor was eventually destroyed did indeed send him into orbit.

One day, shortly after returning from their Black Sea honeymoon, Mukhamedov kissed his new wife goodbye and drove as usual to the theatre for his morning class. Masha cleared away the breakfast table, turned on the television set for company and put her feet up on the sofa to rest her back before facing the shopping queues. Dimly, strains of Khachaturian's score for *Spartacus* coming from the TV intruded on her dozing and when she at last opened her eyes, she saw her husband dancing on the screen. She vaguely heard the announcer's voice talking of a company and presumed it was a promotional advert for the Bolshoi Ballet. She thought no more about it. Five minutes later the telephone rang. It was Mukhamedov, clearly upset, ringing from the theatre, asking if she had seen the television ads for Grigorovich's new company. Masha told her husband that she was not at all sure what she had seen. 'I'm coming straight home,' he said.

Mukhamedov had arrived for class that morning and listened with disbelief to the dressing-room chit-chat about Grigorovich and a new company to be formed outside the Bolshoi. Then one of the dancers asked him if he had seen the advertisements, and he was

Top: Mukhamedov, Masha and Sasha in Earls Court Square.
Bottom: Mukhamedov and Sasha at home in Earls Court.

Top: With Lesley Collier in *La Fille mal gardée*, December 1991.

Bottom: With Vivian Durante in *Giselle*, January 1992.

Opposite top left: As Albrecht in *Giselle*.

Opposite top right: As the Foreman in Kenneth MacMillan's *Judas Tree*, March 1992.

Opposite bottom: In the 'Diana and Acteon' pas de deux, Irek Mukhamedov and Company, April 1992.

As Rudolf in Kenneth MacMillan's *Mayerling*, October 1992.

Hurrying home with Masha from the Royal Opera House after the death of Kenneth MacMillan.

With Lesley Collier in *The Sleeping Beauty*, February 1993.

In the title role of George Balanchine's *Apollo*, January 1993.

Top: In the title role of George Balanchine's *Prodigal Son*, June 1993.

Bottom: En famille in London, July 1992. *Left to right:* Masha, Sasha, Mukhamedov, Rasheda, Djavdat.

forced to admit he knew absolutely nothing about the whole affair. He had to get home as quickly as possible to find out for himself.

He and Masha sat together and watched as every hour a voice spoke, accompanied by Mukhamedov's film of *Spartacus*, inviting dancers between the ages of eighteen and twenty-five to audition for an exciting, dynamic new group being formed by Yuri Grigorovich, artistic director and chief choreographer of the Bolshoi Ballet, to be known as the Young Company. It was as if Mikhail Lavrovsky had walked into the room behind him and was repeating his prediction of twelve months ago that it would only be a matter of time before Grigorovich dismissed Mukhamedov as Mukhamedov had dismissed so many great dancers in that harrowing confrontation in the Beethoven Auditorium. Despite the shock of Grigorovich's growing disregard for him, Mukhamedov had remained deeply loyal to him. At that time, he says, he still saw Grigorovich as his father, his God, but listening to the plans for a new project of which he was completely ignorant, 'it was as though God had turned his head away'. He knew in an instant his time at the Bolshoi was over.

Why, he asked Masha, had Grigorovich not taken him aside and told him about the new project? Mukhamedov understood that he was probably too valuable to the Bolshoi to be sidetracked to a smaller company, and he would gladly have helped if he could. Had he not already been rehearsing a young dancer, Yuri Klevtsov, in some of his own roles? But he had been made to look a fool and, more dangerously, no longer Grigorovich's man.

Mukhamedov went to class the next day and for the first time since his school days hated every minute. He was depressed to find that not only had most of the dancers known of the project before him, but many had already been invited to join the new company. Nobody seemed to believe him when he told a few colleagues that he had had no prior knowledge of Grigorovich's plans. Luckily, he had no performances scheduled other than the filming, so he went through the motions in class and hurried home when he could, glad to be out of the place. The only exchange that took place between him and Grigorovich at that time, remembers Mukhamedov, was when one day in passing Grigorovich asked him to bring home some of Virsaladze's designs for *The Nutcracker* that were in Vienna. 'Of course, Yuri Nikolaievich,' he answered, knowing that he could never accede to another request from the man.

As the realisation of Grigorovich's very public rejection of him spread round the company, Mukhamedov became more and more isolated. The dancers were certain that the rebuff was a verdict not just on Mukhamedov's age and his future with the company, but on the sparks of independence he had been showing.

Mukhamedov had recently sensed in himself a vague disquiet about the limitations imposed on his artistic growth by his allotted roles in the Bolshoi repertoire, even though he had danced the title role in Mikhail Fokine's *Petrushka* at a Nijinsky Gala in late February. But it had been a single performance and he became aware of a need for something fresh. He might, he thought, have enjoyed working in the new company. He did not feel his career as a dancer was nearing an end – only, as he now realised, his usefulness to Grigorovich.

His depression deepened daily; every way he turned the problems became more insoluble. The euphoria of his wedding day and his new life with Masha and the expected baby was shattered. To begin with, he knew that it would be almost impossible for him to become eligible for a decent home for his family as both he and Masha were officially tenants of their own flats, even if neither lived in them, and, moreover, his was of the type reserved for the privileged few. It was extremely unlikely that he would be allowed the luxury of two homes. He also knew that his career at the Bolshoi was over. He might have another three to five years as a principal dancer, but then there would be nothing. When Masha returned to the company, the combination of her talent and his name would guarantee her promotion by the Bolshoi authorities to principal rank. That neither of them enjoyed Grigorovich's protection would be a signal for the jealousy of their combined enemies, of which there were an increasing number, to ensure his and Masha's ultimate professional demise.

Mukhamedov's breeding, his nature and the circumstances of his life had combined to produce a model Soviet citizen, but now he simply saw no point in abiding by the rules. He drove his car like a madman and when he was stopped by the notorious traffic police, instead of spending hours with official procedures, he just paid the fictitious fine like everybody else, and drove away. Standing in the

Moscow queues that he had patriotically justified as an essential part of the Russian way of life suddenly seemed babyish and he resorted more frequently to the black market for the day-to-day necessities. One day, Vladimir Nikonov, an assistant director, called him into his office at the Bolshoi and asked him to dance a performance of *The Nutcracker* at a few days' notice; the response was normally a foregone conclusion when it came to Mukhamedov and one of Grigorovich's ballets. 'Forget it,' he said to a startled Nikonov. 'I am not a little boy who will jump into somebody's place because you can think of no one else. I will dance only my own performances.'

Like most men who face professional ruin when they themselves feel at their peak, Mukhamedov was forced to take stock of himself and he was dismayed at what he found. He felt everything was slipping away: his career was crumbling and the security and well-being of his new family were threatened. Sergei Lavrov's off-the-cuff remark about a fresh start in the West suddenly seemed a realistic option. Lavrov had been right about the baby – why not this? Masha had anticipated his decision and the more they talked about the move between themselves and with the Lavrovs, the more inevitable it became.

A recurring blind spot in Mukhamedov's nature was, and to a lesser extent is today, a difficulty in assessing his own worth as a dancer. He knew he was good, but he did not use his talent as a bargaining factor as many in his position would have done. 'Would anyone in the West want me' was for him a real and haunting question. He had asked Natasha Shabayev to approach the Royal Ballet for guesting dates, but she had demurred, saying he was not sufficiently well known in the West and should aim for a smaller company like the English National Ballet. One evening at supper with the Lavrovs they pressed Mukhamedov to place himself in a world ranking of male dancers, and after much deliberation he said, 'Somewhere in the top ten.' That was enough for Lavrov, who knew his friend's modesty well enough to calculate that probably meant he was in the top two, if not the best in the world. 'Then there is no doubt,' he said, 'you must go.'

For both Mukhamedov and Masha, the unborn baby was of paramount importance. They could not put from their minds the plight of one young man in the company who had split from his mistress when his wife gave birth to their first child. The jilted girlfriend had bluffed her way into his flat and set it alight, killing the baby and seriously injuring the wife. No action had been taken by the police, and a suitable bribe would have taken care of the matter if it had. Then there were the rumours of new-born babies dying of Aids in Moscow hospitals after injections with infected needles. Rumours and hearsay perhaps, but both incidents summed up the gloom that they felt surrounded them. Mukhamedov knew that without the security of the Bolshoi, and Grigorovich, behind him, he would have to live like a criminal, as so many in the Soviet Union did, to provide for his family. Masha had faith in Mukhamedov and was content to take a chance with him.

The real problem was where to go. They both felt uncomfortable in America, preferring European cultures, and at that time the main US companies seemed to be stuffed with ex-patriot Russians. Mukhamedov had recently experienced first hand the insularity of the Paris Opéra Ballet; although he had never seen the Royal Ballet and had no idea of its repertoire, other than a video of Kenneth MacMillan's *Prince of the Pagodas* which he had been given, the desirable place to settle appeared to be London. Meanwhile, his situation at the Bolshoi continued to deteriorate. No one needed to put into words Mukhamedov's fall from grace – it enveloped him like a fog when he entered the theatre. Suddenly the issue of Masha's travel permit, now that Shabayev's invitation had arrived, assumed dramatic importance, for their rapidly forming plans to escape rested on that vital document. Mukhamedov knew that it would take only a word from Grigorovich to prevent either his freelance trip to Europe or Masha's permit, and they had already waited weeks for its issue.

They spoke to nobody of their plans. Not even Mukhamedov's parents or Masha's mother were taken into their confidence; only Lavrov and his wife knew. Once the unthinkable had been faced, there seemed little point in delay. Mukhamedov asked Sergei to use his contacts to sell everything they owned – dacha, car, television, video. And Masha's visa still did not arrive.

About this time the British ballet photographer Kristyna Kashvili, who is of Russian parentage, arrived in Moscow to add to her portfolio of pictures of Mukhamedov, recording him as one of the most popular male dancers the world had ever seen. She clearly remembers the disbelief with which she heard him contemptuously dismissed as an upstart who had had his day by acquaintances of hers in the Bolshoi administration. Mukhamedov was scheduled to dance *Spartacus* on Friday 20 April, but a hastily arranged official gala on that date to celebrate Lenin's birthday put the ballet back a day. On 21 April Kristyna shot happily away at the Bolshoi as Mukhamedov stunned the audience, as always, with his performance as the rebellious slave. She could not know that this would be the last time she or anyone else would see him dance Spartacus live on-stage, the role that had brought him such international renown.

Masha had already asked a friend she had made in London on their last visit to make an approach to the Royal Ballet on Mukhamedov's behalf, but time was rapidly slipping by – they were only two weeks away from their flight to Austria – and they decided to take Kristyna into their confidence. Having heard the talk around Moscow about him during the past few days, she was not totally surprised when he said, 'I think I am finished here. I would like to go to London. Will you help?' She returned to London on 23 April with a letter from Mukhamedov to Anthony Dowell, the artistic director of the Royal Ballet, outlining his proposals. He was careful to avoid any reference to his wish for a residency in the company, in case the letter was intercepted; he relied on Kristyna to relay that information by word of mouth if she felt it appropriate. But the tenor of the letter was quite simple to interpret: he needed a job.

With only days left before they flew out of Russia, perhaps for ever, there was one final duty Mukhamedov felt compelled to perform. His parents, he knew, would be aghast at his intention to abscond and he suspected that they would go to any lengths to stop him, but he thought a trip to Kazan to bid a silent farewell was the least he owed them. Even though he intended his child to be born thousands of miles from Kazan, it was comforting that Rasheda and Djavdat would feel their newest grandchild kicking.

They travelled by train to Kazan on Saturday, 28 April, still anxious that their passports had not yet been issued, and were met by an even more triumphant reception than when he had won the Grand Prix. A whole bus-load of Mukhamedovs was at the station and the couple all but vanished under a deluge of flowers. The party visited the local war memorial and solemnly laid a wreath, then Mukhamedov and Masha were greeted on the steps of the family apartment block with the traditional salt and bread. Rasheda and Djavdat were determined that their son and his new wife should be left in no doubt of his dignified standing in the town.

Masha remembers the sense of destiny with which Mukhamedov's parents viewed him. Rasheda asked her to keep a record, as she did, detailing how many curtain calls he received after each performance, what magazines or newspapers wrote about him, how many times Grigorovich shook his hand – it was all a matter of history, Rasheda explained. Mukhamedov had long ago accepted the somewhat impersonal relationship he had with his parents. His dancing was of prime importance to Aunt Galina too, and he had not been surprised when she had brought some apples to their flat in Moscow and forbidden pregnant Masha to eat them: they were vitamins for Mukhamedov! It was a happy time for them all. The family did not disguise the fact that Masha was infinitely preferable to Ljuda, even though she was a cosmopolitan sophisticate with her foreign clothes and Moscow accent, and they insisted that she sow some carrot seeds at the dacha as a sign of her acceptance into the clan.

Mukhamedov spent a good deal of time walking in the evenings with his mother, father and brother, explaining some of the problems in his life, his feelings about his baby, the Bolshoi and his relationship with Grigorovich. He hoped that they would remember what he had said when he left his homeland and understand some of his motives. He felt no guilt at not taking them into his confidence – nothing must jeopardise the future of his unborn baby. On 3 May, carrying in their suitcase a book of Tartar names for them to choose from and a hand-embroidered Tubetieka hat to remind Mukhamedov of his roots, he and Masha journeyed back to Moscow. To their infinite relief, their travel documents had been issued. They collected them the next day and at 7 a.m. on Saturday, 5 May, boarded the flight for Vienna.

The sale of their joint worldly goods in Russia had netted a grand total of $10,000; they declared half of it on the airport customs form, and strapped the remainder round Masha's waist, already a considerable size at five months pregnant. They had just two suitcases in the aircraft's hold, one containing Mukhamedov's practice clothes and the other a few of Masha's belongings. They had no idea if Mukhamedov had a job either in London or anywhere else, but they knew a return to Moscow would see a speedy end to his career and future prosperity. Mukhamedov took a colossal gamble that morning, but he was a desperate man.

Thus Irek Mukhamedov, who epitomised to the world Russian ballet and the Soviet way of life, turned his back on it all.

18

London

MUKHAMEDOV AND MASHA landed in Austria in a dream. The relief of leaving behind the unpleasantness that threatened them in Moscow was overwhelming. They felt human again; suddenly there were topics to talk about other than the Bolshoi Ballet and the impossibility of their situation. Mukhamedov was earning $4,500 for each of his three performances with the Vienna Opera Ballet, so they decided money was no object and went shopping for clothes for Masha – but not for the baby, as in Russia it is considered bad luck to do so before the last week of pregnancy. They ate at the best restaurants, found being unable to read the menus hysterically funny and discovered again how much they enjoyed each other's company. Like most fathers to be, Mukhamedov found nothing too much trouble to keep Masha happy, and she was blooming.

Motherhood already clearly suited Masha; morning sickness had passed after the first two or three weeks and her appetite was splendid. She particularly relished the Viennese maternity-wear shops where she could buy clothes designed for pregnancy, instead of the merely outsize dresses that were the only choice in Moscow. It was the first time that she and Mukhamedov had travelled abroad together without her working, and the experience was a delight.

Needless to say, their troubles in Moscow continued to simmer in their absence. Masha was startled out of her euphoria a few days after their arrival when Mukhamedov answered the phone and heard, 'This is Yuri Nikolaievich. I wish to speak to you, Irek.' Rumours that the couple had left Russia for good had swept through the Bolshoi the day they flew to Austria, and Grigorovich was naturally anxious to know whether or not he would have a leading dancer to take on his company's summer tours. 'I hear you are defecting,' he said. 'Is it true?' 'No,' lied Mukhamedov. 'The impresarios are worried about Italy. Will you be there?' asked Grigorovich. 'Yes,' came the same lie. They heard later in London from friends that Grigorovich had called a company meeting and told the assembled dancers that he had spoken to Mukhamedov, that the stories of his defection were false and that he would be dancing with the Bolshoi in Italy and America.

Mukhamedov had still received no definite news from the Royal Ballet, but fervently hoped he would be dancing in London.

Meanwhile, he was in Vienna to dance one of George Balanchine's most famous one-act ballets, *Apollo*. It was Mukhamedov's first experience of western modern choreography, apart from his unhappy involvement with Roland Petit's *Cyrano de Bergerac* in 1988. Balanchine choreography was a very different challenge. 'I had to learn how to dance with turned-in legs,' he recalls, 'and to keep my knees stretched and my feet pointed.' Strangest of all for the dancer who had made his reputation sweeping through epic dramas, there was no story to speak of. But Mukhamedov enjoyed working with American dancer Richard Tanner from the Balanchine Foundation and would happily have danced on his head at this time in his life. To add an extra frisson to his performances, Kristyna Kashvili arrived at last with return air tickets and an invitation from the Royal Ballet to travel to London for discussions concerning the possibility of his engagement by the company as a guest artist.

As the idyllic interlude in Vienna drew to a close, he and Masha prepared themselves to go on to Helsinki, where Mukhamedov would rehearse the *Don Quixote* pas de deux which he was to dance with the Finnish Company in Madrid. Mukhamedov's hold on his finances was rocked when he came to reckon up his profits and pay the hotel bill, which he had agreed to do in order that Masha could accompany him. Natasha Shabayev had omitted to tell him that he would be liable for tax, which meant a loss of $1,500 per performance in Vienna; instead of $1,000 for each performance in Madrid, he would receive only $100 after deducting tax, agent's fees and hotel expenses. Shabayev had brought to Vienna the $6,000 he had earned at the Paris Opéra in 1989, but he still had to find the air fare for Masha's round trip. Compared with the risk of their plans not working out, money problems were a minor irritation, particularly as the likelihood of a return to Moscow receded. What did worry the couple as they flitted around Europe for the next three weeks like refugees with just their two rather battered suitcases were the airports.

Mukhamedov had often met the KGB general socially in Moscow, for he was a friend of the top Bolshoi administration; and although Gorbachev's glasnost was in full swing in his homeland, no Soviet citizen in his right mind yet trusted the alleged new-found freedoms. He knew as well as anyone else that the old apparatus was still firmly in place. It would be all too easy for the Russian authorities to 'find' drugs in his luggage at any of the customs posts through which they had to pass, or to discover the smuggled dollars on their persons or simply to withdraw their passports. So they spoke to no one, except Kristyna and Masha's friend in London, both of whom were liaising with the Royal Ballet on their behalf. As far as the Bolshoi was aware, Mukhamedov was busy fulfilling his commitments in Europe and would return to Moscow in time to rejoin the company for its tour of Italy on 10 June. But, as any Soviet citizen would know, anything is possible.

So, half elated, half apprehensive, they flew to Helsinki and then on to Madrid, finding the presence of the Royal Ballet air tickets in their pockets an enormous comfort. As Masha's pregnancy progressed, she felt healthier by the day, and Mukhamedov had not been so relaxed and at ease with himself for months. All they had to do was behave themselves and all would be well. Mukhamedov's release from the tensions of the past twelve months and the good food and wines he had enjoyed in Europe had all resulted in a weight gain by the time he reached Madrid. Nevertheless, the Finnish National Ballet's season was a success, as was Mukhamedov. Finally the day arrived when they were to catch their flight to London. They knew that once they landed in Heathrow under the official aegis of the Royal Ballet, they would be safe from any interference from the Soviet authorities, for a time at least, but there was still the obvious possibility that they might meet with some trouble at Madrid airport. Some discreet but determined presence might be waiting to make quite certain that they boarded the Moscow flight. Dora Laine, the director of the Finnish Ballet, insisted that she should accompany them to the airport and see them aboard their flight, and arranged to meet them early in the morning in the hotel lobby.

As the London-bound flight left Madrid shortly after 9 a.m., just after the plane to Moscow took off, the timing of their arrival at the airport and their movements thereafter would be crucial. First they had to miss the well-meaning Dora Laine and her farewells, which meant checking out of the hotel an hour before their agreed rendezvous with her. They took a taxi to Barajas airport and hovered between the two departure gates labelled Heathrow and Sheremet' yevo, nervously hoping that Dora would not have followed them. Delaying entering the departure lounge for Heathrow until the last possible minute, they heard the announced departure of the plane to Moscow and watched in silence by a window as the Aeroflot plane took off without them. They boarded the London flight and Mukhamedov settled Masha in her seat. As their plane rose above Madrid and turned west towards England, they knew they would never return to Russia.

They landed at Heathrow at 11.50 a.m., twenty minutes late, on 1 June, 'the first day of our English life', as they remember it. Their money problems had been solved and Masha's money belt now held $16,000, thanks to the fees they had managed to accumulate in Europe – still hardly a fortune on which to build a future from scratch. Kristyna was waiting for them and as the tired couple pushed the trolley carrying their scanty luggage across the arrivals hall towards her, she vividly recollects how shocked she was by the enormity of the task that lay before them. She did not tell them that two other Bolshoi dancers, Nina Ananiashvili and Alexei Fadeyechev, who were booked for guest performances with the Royal Ballet, had landed from Moscow at precisely the same time at terminal 1 and, unless they were very lucky, they would all meet in the taxi queue.

A friend of Kristyna had offered to rent them a flat in Beaumont Crescent, West Kensington, and they knew they were in a new land when they compared the place with the accommodation they were used to in Moscow: an unheard of two bedrooms, a connecting sitting- and dining-room, a combined kitchen and breakfast area and a bathroom as well as a separate shower.

Kristyna took them straight away to Earls Court police station to register as foreign aliens and she had a first-hand taste of Mukhamedov's effect on British women. Word apparently spread round the station that a hunk of a Russian ballet dancer was there on business, and a surprising numbers of WPCs just happened to walk past the sergeant's desk where Mukhamedov and Masha were struggling with their official forms. They left to a feminine chorus of good wishes.

A little later in the afternoon Anthony Russell-Roberts, administrative director of the Royal Ballet, arrived with a star-sized bouquet of lilies for Masha, champagne for Mukhamedov – and a draft contract.

As Russell-Roberts himself puts it, the whispers running round the international ballet world that Mukhamedov intended to leave Russia had reached a climax when the dancer and his new and very pregnant wife had arrived in Austria. He and Anthony Dowell were anxious to put the Royal Ballet in the position of being the first company to welcome Mukhamedov before he went to the United States, where he would most certainly be snapped up. And coincidentally, without yet knowing Mukhamedov's wishes, they were interested only in offering a resident contract, not in recruiting another permanent guest. Neither had met him personally, yet both Russell-Roberts and Dowell suspected from watching his performances that he was an artist who would prefer to contribute more to the company than just a few dazzling appearances.

'Although he was a star,' says Russell-Roberts, 'one felt he was absolutely committed to his art. And more than almost any other dancer in recent years, he was very much a *man* dancing.

'We felt that he was a very sensitive interpretive artist and a consummate actor, and therefore he was somebody that would adapt and would drink up the chance of working in a new field.'

Russell-Roberts was at once struck by Mukhamedov's frankness. There were no formal handshakes; he was immediately embraced in a Russian bear-hug and made to feel as if they had all known each other for years. And, like Kristyna at the airport, he was taken aback by the paucity of their personal belongings. 'I expected a star's paraphernalia – cases and hatboxes,' he remembers. 'But there seemed to be just one suitcase.' As they talked, Mukhamedov and Masha unpacked what they had, including the traditional Tartar hat given to him by his parents on their last visit to Kazan – 'in case it is a son' – and his Hans Christian Andersen Prize, 'For the World's Best

Dancer' which he placed on the mantelpiece next to Masha's china model of a seated ballerina given to her by her mother when she was a child. These solitary souvenirs are still displayed in their house in west London, but are today surrounded by more obvious signs of success. Although the topic was not mentioned, Russell-Roberts was in absolutely no doubt that the Mukhamedovs would never return to Russia.

Russell-Roberts was treading a delicate path: he wished to demonstrate the Royal Ballet's genuine intentions and at the same time avoid appearing to rush a man so obviously in crisis. Through an interpreter he outlined the terms of the draft contract. He then added that Mukhamedov and Masha should forget all about business until the dancer had met Anthony Dowell the following week, and join him and his family for a weekend in the country.

The Stars of the Bolshoi Ballet were touring Britain when Mukhamedov and Masha landed in the country, headed by Natalia Bessmertnova; among them was Ljuda, his ex-wife. It was a potentially disastrous piece of timing that Mukhamedov had been unable to prevent. His departure from Russia had been inextricably linked to his guest appearances with the Vienna Opera Ballet and the Helsinki Ballet in Madrid, about which he could do nothing without the risk of arousing suspicion in Moscow. However much faith Masha had in her husband's decision to move to London, she needed a familiar face and language, and telephoned Marina Filippova, the one friend in the Stars company whom she knew she could trust implicitly, and invited her round for supper. Masha enthusiastically set about cooking her first meal in their new country, chicken and fried potatoes, with which Kristyna had previously stocked the fridge. It was a disaster. The cooker was strange and out of Masha's control, she was tired and nervous, the English butter burned too quickly and the chicken was charred, but they washed it down with good Russian vodka and later slept soundly.

The next day Russell-Roberts drove the couple down to join his wife, Anne, and two young daughters, Tabitha and Juliet, for a taste of country living at Chandos Lodge, a rambling six-bedroomed house in Suffolk he had inherited from his uncle, the late Sir Frederick Ashton. The first thing the Russian émigrés learned about an English summer weekend was how to enjoy it despite the weather. No sooner had they arrived than the heavens opened with a downpour that persisted unabated until they returned to London three days later. They met Tamara Finch, widow of Australian actor Peter Finch, for the first time that weekend. Tamara, a former dancer, is of Russian parentage, but was brought up in Paris, and she is frequently used by the Royal Ballet to translate for its Russian guests. It was the beginning of a close friendship that continues today.

The Mukhamedovs were impressed on arrival at Chandos Lodge when the car crunched round the gravelled drive and they saw the high stone walls and the ornamental lake complete with Japanese bridge in front of the old building. They were fascinated to watch from their bedroom window the early morning menagerie of rabbits and hedgehogs that gathered on the front lawn, only realising a few years later that they had probably spied on the descendants of Peter Rabbit and Mrs Tiggywinkle, the source of Ashton's inspiration for the choreography for his ballet *The Tales of Beatrix Potter*.

They swam in the indoor pool, learned to play croquet, weather permitting – Masha discovered she was a mean hand with a mallet – and were full of admiration when Russell-Roberts emerged from the kitchen bearing an artistically decorated whole poached salmon. Mukhamedov and Masha soundly trounced Russell-Roberts and his wife at backgammon, drank Pimm's, visited Ashton's tomb at nearby Yaxley graveyard and were thoroughly soaked every time they ventured outside. In short, it was a very English weekend. 'They were like carefree children,' says Tamara Finch, 'enjoying their sudden liberty.' But they were not, they were adults in the real world, and a strange one at that, and serious decisions were facing the man splashing about in the pool singing, 'We all live in a yellow submarine', or teasing his host in his broken English.

Four years after that country weekend Mukhamedov tried to define how he had felt. 'I was tired of being a Soviet hero, of supporting Grigorovich, the state, Communism. If I found roubles in the street, I would always try to find who lost them, or give them to the police. People of my generation, born in the sixties, were all the same. You either lived by the system or went to prison or became a criminal. I had seen through it all and woken up – maybe late, but not too late – and I feel no guilt about thinking about myself.

'It was time I took responsibility for myself and Masha and the baby. I did not look far into the future, anticipating disaster or success. I just did what any man would do for his family.

'I knew I had a talent, but never thought of it as something to sell. That would be awful. But I trusted that I would receive the sort of money I was worth.'

It was Mukhamedov's obvious trust in the unknown that Russell-Roberts noticed particularly. 'What struck me,' he recalls, 'was how centred he was as a person. How calm he was. He was clearly aware that it was a momentous time in his life, yet he was full of a quiet power. It was very moving how trusting he was. He's a very strong, very exceptional personality.'

Kristyna Kashvili remembers how amazed she was at Masha's peace of mind. 'Masha was deeply content expecting her first child,' she says, 'and the only other thing that mattered in her life was being with the man she loved.'

Russell-Roberts returned to his office at the Royal Opera House on Monday morning, leaving his house-guests to travel back by train to London, only to find himself embroiled in what threatened to become a diplomatic incident. As far as he recalls, the Home Office, the Foreign Office and the Immigration Department all telephoned him during the course of that day to express concern for the well-being of Mukhamedov and his pregnant wife, particularly in the light of Margaret Thatcher's imminent meeting with Mikhail Gorbachev in Moscow. The diplomatic world, like Mukhamedov, was apparently aware of the continuance of old practices in the new Soviet order, and they wished to put the couple beyond the scandalous possibility of 'taxi-loads of counsellors from the Embassy' turning up on their front door and causing a scene. A blanket press embargo was imposed by the Opera House, and all requests for interviews with Mukhamedov were refused. Russell-Roberts suggested that they return to Chandos Lodge with Kristyna, to extend their holiday for another ten days or so, which they were quite happy to do. But first it was time for Mukhamedov to meet Anthony Dowell, to make a final decision about the contract on offer and his future with the Royal Ballet.

They met in the Poule au Pot restaurant in Ebury Street, Victoria. Although Dowell had already made up his mind to bring Mukhamedov into the company, it was important, he felt, to become acquainted before making a final commitment. 'I had seen his performances, of course,' says Dowell, 'and I was impressed by the incredible power. He was very vital and alive and terribly committed.

'I was told at the time by someone close to him that he wanted to live in London, and wanted to be part of the company. I thought it was wonderful.

'I liked him immediately,' says Dowell of their first meeting over lunch. 'it's a wonderful face to sit opposite, and though it was difficult through an interpreter, I could sense the humour in the man, which is one of the first things I search for.

'I saw Irek as another creative force that would excite the company. I remember when I grew up with people like Erik Bruhn and Nureyev around, it puts a zing in the air, and that's what I wanted.

'And it has worked.'

Mukhamedov and Masha observed Dowell's modest demeanour, as well as the variety of jewels on his fingers, and liked him at once. They knew of his reputation as a great British dancer, but had no idea how a British director would conduct himself. The friendly bantering over the lunch table delighted them and gave them heart for the future.

The following day the two Anthonys and Tamara Finch met Mukhamedov at his flat to finalise the terms of the agreement between them; it offered a five-year residency, the opportunity to guest elsewhere if he chose, Royal Ballet commitments permitting, and a salary that made Tamara's eyes bulge, he remembers. Then he, Masha and Kristyna boarded the train back to Suffolk. They were puzzled to see Kristyna collect bills and ask for receipts from taxi-drivers, and when she explained it was for her accountant, they were even more perplexed. Kristyna began gently to reveal to the Russian ex-patriots the financial complexities of living and working in a capitalist society.

Anthony Russell-Roberts was convinced that a further period of enforced idleness would be not merely a wise diplomatic manoeuvre, but a necessity, allowing Mukhamedov and Masha to marshal their resources after the events of the past six weeks, and he was right.

The weather had improved, but not much, and they again spent most of their time around the swimming pool. Kristyna marvelled not only at the Mukhamedov physique, but also at his lung capacity; she watched with awe as he effortlessly swam three lengths of the pool under water on one breath. Masha had registered with the Hammersmith Hospital at Tamara's insistence, but felt confident and well, and happily gave in to a growing craving for bananas. Kristyna did the cooking, though Mukhamedov was known occasionally to throw together his breakfast speciality, Armenian scrambled eggs – a rather haphazard assembly of tomatoes, eggs and anything else that might be at hand – and it was shopping for food that provided the best recreation.

Masha ate her first Cornetto and although they had both travelled extensively with the Bolshoi Ballet and had visited supermarkets in Europe and America, the range of foods available even in a small village like Eye constantly surprised them. One day Masha decided to cook bortsch, and needed a marrow bone for the stock. Kristyna clearly remembers the three of them calling at a local butcher and being invited to choose the joint they wanted from the carcass hanging in the back room. With eyes popping out of their heads at the sight, the Mukhamedovs could only observe that in Moscow such an invitation would have provoked riots.

Kristyna discovered that Mukhamedov hated spinach and loved MacMillan's *Manon* after they had watched a video of the ballet she had brought from London. They talked endlessly of ballet, and Mukhamedov could not disguise his anxiety about Grigorovich. 'What will Yuri Nikolaievich think when I do not turn up?' was his constant worry. And he steeled himself to deal with Yuri Nikolaievich as their tranquil pastorale drew rapidly to a close.

19

The Royal Ballet and Kenneth MacMillan

NINE YEARS, ALMOST to the day, after being recruited by Yuri Grigorovich as principal male dancer of the Bolshoi Ballet in Moscow Irek Mukhamedov was introduced at the same rank by Anthony Dowell to the Royal Ballet in London. On 18 June 1990 he and Masha walked the short distance from their flat in West Kensington to the company rehearsal rooms in Barons Court to meet the dancers in class. It was a hot day and Mukhamedov was worried that the heat might prove too much for his wife, but Masha was glad of the walk.

Mukhamedov was nervous, not from any doubts about the rightness of his situation, but because in the two and a half weeks since their arrival he had been putting off dealing with the uncomfortable consequences of his actions, such as the response to Grigorovich and his parents and the demands of his new company. Now he had to face it all; he had rested long enough absorbing the shock, and now it was time to tell the world that he was here. Everyone had assumed he would do the class that morning, but Mukhamedov thought that it would be better to ease himself more gently into his new life. Besides, he felt enormous after the weeks of idling round the Lodge's swimming pool eating all those delicious new foods.

Both Anthony Russell-Roberts and Anthony Dowell were waiting to welcome him and Masha. Together they went to the Covent Garden studio, where, after a brief introduction from Dowell and a polite round of applause in greeting from the dancers, they sat to watch their first class in Mukhamedov's new company, taken by a former Royal Ballet dancer, the late Brian Shaw. When the dancers left the barre and started the centre work, Mukhamedov could not understand why the principals stood at the back instead of in the front row, and both he and Masha were astonished to see some of the dancers leaving before the class was over. He had yet to learn of the exacting rehearsal schedules that were common in the UK, let alone the democratic principles that are so dear to the British. It was the first of many inevitable differences between the Bolshoi and the Royal Ballet with which he had to cope, as puzzling at first as a two-bedroomed flat and British butchers.

The next day Mukhamedov joined in the class, starting with only barre work but immediately establishing an intensity in the class-room that was to become legendary. He knew what everyone was waiting to see, however: Spartacus. Gradually he worked his muscles into some sort of shape, and after about a week he felt ready to define his territory. One day he finished off an enchainement with a blistering series of turning jumps that earned satisfying gasps of astonishment and applause from his classmates. Mukhamedov had arrived.

Now that he had returned to the most vital of his realities, ballet, it was time to address other issues pressing for attention. Mukhame-dov knew that his parents must be devastated at his actions, and managed to put through a call to Kazan. He was right – they were appalled. 'How can you live without Grigorovich and the Bolshoi?' they demanded. Although he felt no guilt, he carefully composed a long letter to his parents, trying to help Rasheda and Djavdat understand his motives. He told them that he felt the current situation at the Bolshoi was critical, and that if and when the company collapsed, he did not wish to be buried under the debris. Then he explained the extent of the medical care available to Masha in London, and the wonderful support she and the new-born baby would receive, hoping that his mother, at least, would appreciate such benefits. He made it quite clear that they would always be welcome in his home in London, as soon as he got one of his own.

The next duty he could no longer delay was to face up to Grigorovich, the man who, no matter how betrayed and manipu-lated Mukhamedov might feel, still represented in his heart his true spiritual and artistic father. As soon as his position at the Royal Ballet had been formalised and the contract signed, Mukhamedov sent a fax through the company office to the Bolshoi administration, but he knew the only honourable course of action was to speak directly to the man himself. The Bolshoi was by now on its tour of Italy, and

Mukhamedov, only too familiar with the hotel in Rome in which Grigorovich would stay, telephoned him there.

It was not a comfortable conversation, but neither was it acrimonious. Mukhamedov's feelings were ambivalent and he blamed no one, restricting himself to telling his former master that he wanted Yuri Nikolaievich to hear from himself that he thought it was time for a change in his life, he had signed a five-year contract with the Royal Ballet and would not be returning to the Bolshoi. Grigorovich, he remembers, replied that as he had done Mukhamedov no harm, he could not understand his reasons. Why had he caused such problems for him in Italy and the USA? The conversation was brief, and Mukhamedov replaced the receiver with relief, hoping it had laid their relationship to rest.

The Bolshoi Ballet was due to commence its tour of America in three weeks' time and the promoters, the Entertainment Corporation, had spent a great deal of money on an advance advertising campaign strongly featuring Mukhamedov, who had been such a success on previous visits. The corporation's joint chairmen, Victoria Charlton and Peter Brightman, were anxious to persuade him to make an appearance in the States, however limited. Anthony Russell-Roberts recalls 'receiving a bit of a battering from the Entertainment Corporation' at the time, but he made it clear to Charlton and Brightman, and to Mukhamedov, that the Royal Ballet would have no objection to his appearing with the Bolshoi in America. It was far too soon, however, for Mukhamedov to take a backward step, and he steadfastly declined. Reports filtered back to London alleging that ticket sales were poor and that patrons were demanding their money back when they learned that they would not see Mukhamedov. Peter Brightman says, 'It was the first time that a Bolshoi Ballet tour lost money.'

Meanwhile, as Mukhamedov's class work honed his figure to performance fitness, Masha continued to expand, and she gave in to Tamara's insistence that she have a medical check-up. She duly visited a doctor, the first she had seen since her pregnancy test in Moscow in January, and, as she had known it would, the examination found both her and the baby fit and well. Masha tried to go with her husband to watch class every day, as at that time she intended to resume classes again herself once the baby was born. One day a tall, stooping man with grey close-cropped hair sat next to her. And when the class was over, she and Mukhamedov were introduced to Sir Kenneth MacMillan.

The press, the public and the Opera House management were earnestly hoping that Mukhamedov would develop a 'dream partnership' with a Royal Ballet ballerina, as Rudolf Nureyev had with Margot Fonteyn, but the true fusion of Russian soul and British talent in fact took place between these two men, Mukhamedov and MacMillan. The possibility of this artistic harmony had been part of the calculated gamble that Anthony Dowell had taken in bringing Mukhamedov to Britain, but he had had no idea how fruitful it would be. Sir Kenneth's widow, the artist Deborah MacMillan, remembers the excitement her husband felt at the time. 'Kenneth was very impressed that Irek, a great international star, made it quite clear that he wanted to be part of the company and the rep, not just the first nights and then buzzing off abroad,' she says. 'He also found Irek exceptionally musical. I mean exceptionally. He was surprised at how quickly he grasped Western music that perhaps he hadn't heard a lot of before.

'And he realised straight away that Irek was a mature, responsible person. He had made a grown-up decision to leave Russia, and Kenneth liked that in a dancer. He felt there was a really intelligent mind at work.'

MacMillan, who thought he had been neglected at the Opera House during the previous decade, had found a fresh creative impetus by 1990. The première of his latest three-act work, *The Prince of the Pagodas*, the previous December had featured twenty-year-old Darcey Bussell, and the germ of an idea based on Chekhov's play *The Three Sisters*, which had been fermenting at the back of his mind for years, now began to mature. The first stage in his as yet undefined project would be a pas de deux for the two new stars, and rehearsals started at once.

Mukhamedov was amazed at the speed of events. Only one role, Boris in *The Golden Age*, had ever been created on him, and that process eight years ago had been very different from the one that now unfolded as MacMillan made steps for Mukhamedov's particular abilities. Everyone was nervous at the first rehearsal, but none as much as Masha. Before they left Russia, she and Mukhamedov had not defined his future career beyond finding a job as a dancer. Although she had been impressed by a video of his *Sleeping Beauty* in Austria, she knew his years with the Bolshoi had ill prepared him for such a classically based company as the Royal. And she was immediately worried by Bussell's height.

MacMillan's method of working was a revelation to the Russians. He neither sat back and expected his dancers to show him steps that he could choose nor came prepared with an inflexible picture of what he wanted to do. He came into the studio with a head full of ideas and carefully translated them into movement on and through the bodies in front of him. And, strangest of all to Mukhamedov, he kept on saying thank you. This process of mutual creativity and appreciation was more than Mukhamedov had dreamed of, and as the rehearsals progressed, he absorbed the new language that MacMillan's choreography created for him like a sponge. The steps flowed like a conversation, he remembers; they were difficult at first, but time and practice made them seem simple and light. He had to learn all over again how to express himself through his legs and feet. The breadth of movement as he opened his shoulders so expansively as Spartacus and the athletic stretch of his back and arms as Boris in *The Golden Age* were now augmented by a control and precision in his legs that spoke just as eloquently. It was by no means an easy task, even though MacMillan was careful at first not to make the change too extreme. But MacMillan at once saw the possibilities of Mukhamedov in *Mayerling*, which had last been revived in 1986, *My Brother, My Sisters* and *Orpheus*, all of which featured strongly dramatic male leads and required virtuoso techniques.

When the rehearsal was over, Mukhamedov thanked his partner and the choreographer in the usual way, and was taken aback when MacMillan made a point of saying, 'No, thank *you*!' It would be taken as a normal politeness by the average Briton, but to Mukhamedov it was an extraordinary acknowledgement of his presence as a human being, not merely a ballet machine, and it was a courtesy that made a deep impression in that early, difficult time of adjustment.

Mukhamedov and Bussell first performed the 'Farewell' pas de deux from *Winter Dreams* during a gala to celebrate the Queen Mother's ninetieth birthday at the London Palladium on 19 July in the company of Cliff Richard, Sarah Brightman, Kiri Te Kanawa and Placido Domingo. He remembers how nervous they both were – Bussell got a fit of the giggles as the curtain went up – but it went well and he was thrilled to meet the royal family on-stage after the performance and to be told by the Queen Mother how pleased she was to have him in the country. His only disappointment was not being allowed to kiss her hand.

To Mukhamedov's amazement, life in London was working out more smoothly than he had ever dared to hope: his working relationship with MacMillan promised an artistic future that he had never imagined, the Royal Ballet dancers did not just accept his presence among them but seemed to go out of their way to welcome and help him, and Masha's pregnancy was progressing healthily. Their stay at the flat in West Kensington was drawing to an end; they had to vacate the premises by the end of August, a move that Masha particularly welcomed as she found the area dusty and noisy and the four flights of stairs increasingly burdensome. She did not relish bringing a new-born baby into such a home. With the assistance of friends they found a three-bedroomed flat in Earls Court Square that was spacious and quiet, and, they were assured, a reasonable buy at £210,000.

The Opera House had announced Mukhamedov's début in Makarova's staging of *La Bayadère* in November at the beginning of the 1990–91 season, but decided to introduce him to London audiences as soon as possible and slipped the 'Farewell' pas de deux into the middle of the performance on 1 August in which David Bintley's new ballet, *The Planets*, was to receive its première. Mukhamedov was acutely aware that the entire British ballet world had assembled at Covent Garden, for what was his real début with the Royal Ballet in its home theatre. They were there to see not only Bintley's long-awaited new work, but also the première of William Tuckett's *Enclosure*. How would the audience react to a short, seven-minute duet after all that, he wondered. Masha was in the orchestra stalls, naturally, where she was to become a regular and well-known face whenever her husband danced.

There was an extraordinary feeling of welcome in the theatre that night, which is unusual for ballet audiences, who are not normally noted for their charity. Everyone seemed anxious to demonstrate to the self-exiled Russian star that they were glad he had chosen London as his new home. Even a forty-minute delay when Ralph Koltai's monumental set for *The Planets* choked on its own hydraulics failed to dampen the house's enthusiasm when the curtain finally rose to reveal a bare stage, a grand piano, Darcey Bussell – and Irek Mukhamedov. The pas de deux passed in a flash of power and energy, but fulfilled everyone's feeling of rightness about him and his future in the Royal Ballet.

Kathrine Sorley Walker, dance critic of the *Daily Telegraph*, wrote of the 'Farewell' pas de deux: 'This introduced the Royal Ballet's exciting acquisition, Irek Mukhamedov, as a regular member of the company. MacMillan's eloquent and tender choreography showed the former Bolshoi Ballet virtuoso in a new light, deploying his technical prowess with sensitivity.' 'An auspicious beginning to a new era,' wrote John Percival the next day in *The Times*, a sentiment both true then and prophetic.

The contracts for the new flat were exchanged in the second week of August, a couple of weeks before the baby was due. Although they were unable to move in before the beginning of September, with the first flush of home-making that overtakes most first-time fathers Mukhamedov set about decorating the only home he and Masha had ever really owned. Masha chose the décor while Mukhamedov wielded the paintbrush, and, despite Masha's changing her mind about the wallpaper, they made good progress. At about ten o'clock on the evening of 21 August Mukhamedov and a friend were enjoying a tea-break in the kitchen when Masha, who had carried on hanging the bedroom wallpaper, felt the first serious stirrings of the birth. She quickly showered, and Mukhamedov drove her home and telephoned the hospital.

Tamara had carefully rehearsed him in the intricacies of how to describe the contraction intervals in English, and they were told to wait and keep timing them for a little longer. Mukhamedov went to bed and Masha sat in front of the television with her watch in her hand. Mukhamedov had resolved not to be present at the birth as, if anything went wrong, he was sure he would kill the doctor, but when Masha called out at midnight that at last it was time, he accompanied her in the ambulance. Tamara joined them and was also present for the delivery.

Few first babies enter the world in an atmosphere of quiet dignity, and baby Sasha's arrival was a fairly normal and noisy affair. Towards mid-day on Wednesday 22 August, she made her intentions clear to her by now exhausted mother, and a chorus of 'push' in at least three languages filled the delivery room. Mukhamedov held Masha's hand and shouted at her to stop shouting, while the doctor shouted at him to stop shouting at his wife. At 12.26 p.m. Alexandra Chulpan Mukhamedova, to be known as Sasha, was born. Tamara had to show the new-born infant to Mukhamedov to prove that it was the girl he had always wanted, and he and Masha were entranced by their offspring, who had blue eyes, brown hair and a dark complexion – a true Tartar!

Tamara was more tired than any of them and she left the three Mukhamedovs to make their own way back to the general ward, where, contrary to Russian practice, not only did Sasha lie with her mother immediately, she also suckled straight away. More than anything it had been the prospective birth of their daughter that had given the couple the strength to flee their homeland, and as they rested together, they knew beyond any doubt that they had done the right thing. They could scarcely believe the ease and comfort that surrounded them, and they continually compared the flower-filled ward, with its ultra-modern amenities, to what would have been available to Masha and her new baby in Moscow. At that moment in the Hammersmith Hospital, scarcely four months after flying out of Russia, Mukhamedov became irrevocably locked into his new life.

While Masha telephoned her astonished mother in Moscow to give her the details of her granddaughter, Mukhamedov went home to rest. Igor Yurlov, who was still in Britain with the Stars of the Bolshoi Ballet, telephoned him, anxious to know of any developments. 'Where have you been all night?' he demanded, and went wild at the news of baby Sasha's arrival. Yurlov immediately told the Bolshoi dancers, only one of whom was not equally overwhelmed with joy. A short time later Mukhamedov, having finished rehearsal at the Opera House, was on his way out for lunch when he was informed at the stage door that a slightly built female Russian dancer who spoke no English had been asking for him and had been sent up to the rehearsal room he had just left. Mukhamedov knew at once that it was Ljuda. As he slowly climbed back up the stairs, he prayed to God that somehow he could avoid her. He did not exactly hurry, and when he eventually reached the studio, it was empty. By the time he had completed his equally slow descent he was told that the lady had left. It was the nearest he was ever to come to seeing his ex-wife again.

Masha left hospital on Saturday and returned to West Kensington, where the family stayed for a further week before moving to Earls Court Square. Sasha took up residence in the cradle sent by Lady Anya Sainsbury in the newly decorated room her parents had meticulously prepared. She was immediately surrounded by flowers and toys as the news spread around the Mukhamedovs' small but growing circle of friends. Sasha still enjoys this happy position, as gifts constantly arrive from her father's admirers in London and all around the world.

20

Manon, *The Judas Tree* and a Home of Their Own

THE ROYAL BALLET reassembled after the summer break shortly following Sasha's birth, and Mukhamedov started rehearsals for Natalia Makarova's staging of Petipa's three-act classic of 1877, *La Bayadère*, which the company had taken into its repertoire the previous May. At once the shift of emphasis in his career was apparent, for the three roles in which Mukhamedov had been cast for his first season in London as a resident dancer were all classically orientated: Solor in *La Bayadère*, Jean de Brienne in *Raymonda* and the Prince in *The Nutcracker*. The days of Soviet heroics were over, both personally and professionally.

It was ironic, Mukhamedov remembers thinking, that, although *Bayadère* is a staple of the Bolshoi's repertoire, he was never cast in the ballet during the nine years he led the company, and here he was making his début as Solor in his first full-length work with the Royal Ballet. His Nikiya was Lesley Collier, at that time the Royal's principal ballerina; considered to be one of the finest exponents of the English style, she had been dancing better than ever since the birth of her twins in January 1989. Mukhamedov was delighted at Collier's obvious pleasure in dancing with him, an element that had always seemed lacking in his partnerships at the Bolshoi. The opening performance of *La Bayadère* on 7 November 1990 was nerve-racking for Mukhamedov. He felt that on that night, of all nights, he must prove to everyone – the company, the press, the audience and, above all, himself – that his acceptance into the Royal Ballet had not been a hideous mistake.

The evening was a huge success, and for the first time in his life Mukhamedov took a solo curtain call. The idea was so foreign to him that Keith Gray, the stage manager, had to manhandle him through the gap in the curtain. When he eventually stood there alone, the audience's reaction left him in no doubt of his welcome. Lesley

Collier introduced him to another British stage tradition when she presented him with a single bloom from her bouquet. Mukhamedov was momentarily confused; the men in Russia gave their partners their flowers, not the other way round, and at first he tried to give it back. It took a little longer, though, to fathom some of the British dance world's other little quirks. 'In Russia,' he says, 'if you have a success, everyone comes and hugs you. Here it is different. If you do a good performance, no one comes near you, but if it is bad, they come and say, "Darling it was brilliant!"'

Collier again partnered Mukhamedov in *The Nutcracker* a month later, and Anthony Dowell, fully aware that his new dancer possessed neither the reputation nor the conventional image of a classical dancer, felt the performance fully vindicated his decision to place Mukhamedov immediately in the classical repertoire. 'It was the solo variation that he did, that was very correct, very classical and very schooled,' he says. 'It was a different side of him, but it wasn't that we'd said to him, "Do it right" – that was how Irek approached that role.'

Bayadère had been an easy initiation. The ballet was, after all, in both style and choreography part of the tradition in which he had been reared. He had yet to prove himself in the British repertoire, and he started rehearsals for Des Grieux, the principal male role in MacMillan's *Manon*, with some trepidation. In preliminary discussions about the ballet with Dowell and MacMillan Mukhamedov had been taken aback at the suggestion that he should learn both the leading and the secondary male roles, the poet Des Grieux and Manon's drunken brother, Lescaut. It was not that he baulked at the workload – the dramatic challenges were irresistible – but in the Russian system it would be unthinkable for a leading dancer to appear in a supporting part. As Spartacus, for instance, he would never be allowed to dance Crassus, the Roman general. Being one of the Bolshoi Ballet's great Romeos, it had taken him eight years to persuade Grigorovich to allow him to tackle Tybalt, a highly unusual privilege.

MacMillan created Des Grieux in 1974 for Anthony Dowell, when Dowell was at the height of his technical and artistic prowess. Dowell's technique was rooted in the British tradition of precision and purity, with high extensions and superb control, and MacMillan, seizing on these gifts, created passages of male dancing quite alien to Mukhamedov's schooling. A piqué turn is a pirouette taken in any position by stepping on to a fully stretched leg, women on pointe, men on half pointe, instead of taking off from a plié, the more usual preparation for a man, which enables him to utilise his strength to increase the number of turns. It is a small variation that to a virtuoso technique such as Mukhamedov's is of little consequence, but when incorporated into steps at a slow tempo, it demands an earthbound control quite at odds with Mukhamedov's natural style of high-speed performance, usually in flight.

In Julia Matheson's BBC TV *Omnibus* programme he described some of the difficulties: 'I remember my first rehearsal, the solo from *Manon*. I said, "I think I must refuse", because absolutely nothing was working. I could not do anything. I could not understand it.

'At first I got cramps in my calves because I was not ready for such changes, such exact and clean execution. It was very hard work.'

Dowell rehearsed Mukhamedov during the preparations for *Manon*, at a time, he recalls, when Mukhamedov must have felt as though the carpet was being pulled from under him. 'Here was a great bravura dancer dancing something that was all line and lyricism and adagio. It was two opposites meeting,' he says. 'It was wonderful working with him.'

Darcey Bussell was cast as Mukhamedov's Manon, but as rehearsals progressed, it became obvious to all concerned that while the combination had worked smoothly enough in the 'Farewell' pas de deux, *Manon*, built around a continuous series of pas de deux for the two leading characters, was quite a different proposition. The disparity in height between Mukhamedov and Bussell – she is half a head taller than he when she stands on pointe – made MacMillan's complex choreography physically impossible. During the final dress rehearsals, a week before the opening night, Bussell was withdrawn and Viviana Durante took over the role. Durante said then, 'We just whizzed through rehearsals for a couple of hours, and everything worked perfectly. It was amazing.' Durante's previous experience in the role and the fact that Mukhamedov is one of the best partners of his generation overcame any last-minute panic, though much was made in the press of the 'battling ballerinas'. It was claimed that

Bussell's career lay in ruins, that Durante had been chosen as the next Margot Fonteyn – and it was all arrant nonsense, of course. Life in a ballet company is more mundane than the world of newspaper headlines might suggest. Dancers must deal with the practicalities of overhead lifts and thrown jetés to earn their living, not daydreams.

Mukhamedov's first performance in a new work is quite often his least satisfying; although in rehearsal he digs into the character he is portraying both physically and emotionally to a phenomenal degree, it is always on-stage that his performance matures. But in his début in *Manon* on 16 January 1991, as Mukhamedov went from lovesick boy to ardent lover and finished, as the curtain fell, a broken man cradling the corpse of his mistress, it was clear to all that here was an artist with something very special to offer to the Royal Ballet repertoire.

Judith Mackrell wrote in the *Independent*: 'It was humbling . . . to see just how hard Mukhamedov had worked to adapt himself to this role – how much longer and leaner his line already looked, what reserves of control he was finding within himself . . . In Des Grieux's first smitten solo the slow reach of an arm, the magnetised turning of his head, the sudden lavish arch of his back registered with shocking acuteness the hesitant churning of the lover's stomach, the hectic racing of his pulse.'

His interpretation of Lescaut three weeks later was no less impressive, and it was already obvious not only that the Royal Ballet had an undisputed star and an actor of consummate skill in its midst, but that Mukhamedov had struck a rich creative vein in the works of Kenneth MacMillan. It was precisely the challenge he needed at this precarious time in his life. He had put down roots in a strange country, invested in property and he had a new-born daughter. To cap it all, as he approached his thirty-first birthday, he had found the impetus he had longed for to give his career a new dimension.

It was not just working with MacMillan that deepened Mukhamedov's understanding of his interpretive powers. The new choreography that he now craved came thick and fast. MacMillan created his new one-act ballet *Winter Dreams* around the 'Farewell' pas de deux danced by Mukhamedov and Bussell in January 1991; in May he was the second cast in David Bintley's *Cyrano*; and a month later he made his début as the Andantino Boy in Bronislava Nijinska's

1924 comedy of manners, *Les Biches*. Fascinating as it was to watch Mukhamedov gradually add a smooth refinement to his daring technique and ease himself into the English style, *Les Biches* disclosed yet another facet of his astonishing talent, which was to prove a danger to unwary choreographers. No matter how meticulously he re-creates the steps of any ballet, the depth of Mukhamedov's interpretation illuminates them afresh and often reveals their inherent failings; Mukhamedov's performance in *Les Biches* was a vivid example of this. He also outraged a number of purists by pirouetting to the left when the rest of the stage turned to the right.

The most English of all choreographers was Frederick Ashton, and in December 1991 Mukhamedov danced Colas in Ashton's *La Fille mal gardée*, one of the cornerstones of the Royal Ballet's repertoire. It is the most lively and romantic of bucolic romps, with maypoles, clog dances and ribbons aplenty – a sentimental Victorian dream of an agricultural idyll. Mukhamedov's partner was again Lesley Collier, the finest interpreter of the role of Lise since it had been created for Nadia Nerina in 1960. They made a remarkable partnership, she small-boned and blond, he dark and passionate, and both with the lightest of comedy touches. It was an entrancing clash of cultures, but sadly one unlikely to be repeated following Lesley Collier's retirement from the Royal Ballet and her pursuit of a freelance career.

The press's and the public's increasing desire to match Mukhamedov with a 'dream partner' was raised to fever pitch on 18 January 1992 when both he and Viviana Durante made their débuts together in *Giselle* at Covent Garden. But the truth began to dawn that perhaps Mukhamedov possessed gifts that rose above such limitations. John Percival wrote in *The Times*: 'with which of the ballerinas does he find the "special chemistry" people have hoped for ever since the days of the Fonteyn–Nureyev partnership in the sixties? The answer, I think, is all – or none.

'Mukhamedov is such a committed man of the theatre, giving himself to each role he plays and everybody on-stage around him, that he almost manages to look ideally suited to whomever he dances with.'

Clement Crisp says of Mukhamedov's Albrecht in *Giselle*, 'He is one of the greatest Albrechts I have ever seen . . . and I have seen some very great Albrechts – *none* has quite the touch of Mukhamedov in the first act. Mukhamedov *absolutely* understands it and gets right to the romantic core of the ballet.'

It was with Kenneth MacMillan that Mukhamedov found true artistic satisfaction. His arrival in London coincided with the emergence of a strong contingent of male dancers within the Royal Ballet (Bruce Sansom, Stuart Cassidy, Michael Nunn, Sergiu Pobereznic, Errol Pickford), and MacMillan had embarked on a project that had fascinated him since the horrific scenes of official treachery and massacre witnessed on television in Tiananmen Square in Peking in 1989, the result of which was to be a pivotal work of twentieth-century choreography. The subject was betrayal, the central character was a Judas figure called the Foreman, the ballet was titled *The Judas Tree*. In the leading role Mukhamedov faced the biggest challenge of his career.

The action takes place at night in designer Jock McFadyen's dismal evocation of urban dereliction and decay, and is set to a commissioned score by Brian Elias. There is gang rape, murder and suicide. The only female is a Mary Magdalene enigma of prostitute and virgin; the Foreman brutalises, dominates and destroys all that he touches, including himself. It is a work of resonances, not facts, of the dread of the unspeakable, not the obvious, and Mukhamedov powered through it like a whirlwind. The ballet's setting is figurative and its essence abstract; by catching and then reflecting every nuance of music and movement Mukhamedov truly broke with his heroic heritage and proved himself not merely an international star, but a world-class artist of rare gifts indeed.

Deborah MacMillan sums up a quality her late husband saw, and utilised, in Mukhamedov: 'Kenneth felt in Irek the thing he feels happens in great male dancers – a great element of danger. There is this man doing things that could be beautiful, even soppy, but it's not . . . You have a marriage of power and poetry, softness, hardness and strength – a poetic, exquisitely soft, wonderfully tender brute force.

'It's the absolute antithesis of anything feminine . . . Call it sexual or whatever, but the hair on the back of your neck stands up. It involves a response from the audience that is quite terrifyingly exciting and thrilling . . . You're so close to the wind, both in the idea and the physicality of the idea, that it puts you on the edge of your seat.' *The Judas Tree*, with Mukhamedov as the Foreman, was premièred on 19 March 1992, just a month after an important move in his private life.

At the end of the previous year the Mukhamedovs had become thoroughly disillusioned by the burdens of leaseholding. They felt they had been badly advised at the time of their purchase of the Earls Court flat; Masha remembers wondering about the small print at the bottom of the deeds at the time of the purchase and being told not to worry about it. Those undeciphered lines had cost them, in scarcely twelve months, more than £20,000, the charge for repairs to the communal areas of their building, and astronomical estimates for replacing the lifts had then arrived. The last straw for Mukhamedov came when he realised that he was not allowed to install a satellite television dish without permission from all the building's other residents, an infringement of his personal liberty that smacked too familiarly of life in the Soviet Union. They resolved to buy a house of their own.

Tamara Finch mobilised help for them from within London's Russian community as Mukhamedov's English was still meagre and Masha's virtually non-existent, and they soon had a shortlist of houses to view to the west and south of the capital. One of the properties recommended to Mukhamedov and Masha was in a broad, affluent street in south-west London. They were given the number of the house, but were not told that there was only a name on the gate. When they eventually worked out that the house in question was in fact the detached converted stable block behind high courtyard walls and lofty gates past which they had walked at least four times, they were at once captivated. Masha looked through the window and fell in love. After five minutes inside Mukhamedov said, 'I'll buy it', instinctively knowing that he and his family had truly arrived home.

Mukhamedov is fond of describing his life in entomological, if scientifically shaky, terms – egg, caterpillar and butterfly. The start of the new year certainly saw him spread his wings. As he and Masha waited for the purchase of their new home to be completed at the end of February, not only were rehearsals for *The Judas Tree* racing towards its première in March, but preparations were well under way for the first appearance of his own group, Irek Mukhamedov and Company, on 14 April at the Derngate Theatre, Northampton, the scene of the fracas with his erstwhile colleague, Yuri Smirnov, which now seemed a lifetime ago. Mukhamedov's natural instinct for hard work, coupled with his years of summer holiday touring with the Bolshoi – and a revived urge to test the limits of his own resources – had led Mukhamedov to persuade a few of his friends in the Royal Ballet to put together an evening of divertissements and new choreography during the company's annual break. Mukhamedov had established a solid working relationship with Julia Matheson during the filming of the *Omnibus* programme and asked her to join him in setting up a short, three-venue tour of England. The new group would provide Mukhamedov with an outlet for his surplus energy and Masha with an opportunity to coach and produce items from the Bolshoi repertoire for the girls; it would also give her a chance to use her considerable skills in costume design.

It was both a critical and popular success, particularly in Northampton, though a failure to publicise it adequately meant that audiences in Oxford and Bradford were below expectations. This resulted in a personal financial loss for Mukhamedov, not the enormous gains that were rumoured at the time. But so spectacular was Mukhamedov's performance with Viviana Durante in Vaganova's 'Diana and Acteon' pas de deux that the Royal Ballet asked him, with Masha to assist him, to re-create it for its own repertoire, and he and Durante danced it in May during the company's tour of Japan.

Mukhamedov continued to inject new life into MacMillan revivals, and none more spectacularly than *Romeo and Juliet*. When he made his début in the ballet on 21 July 1992, with Viviana Durante as Juliet, Mukhamedov was thirty-two years old, yet as Romeo he seemed no more than a boy. There was no cute artifice; he shed the years through his total conviction and sincere sympathy with the character. For many in the audience that night, thanks to Mukhamedov's illuminating performance, it was the first time that the ballet truly made sense.

His working life was a frantic flurry of activity, but at least he now had his own refuge to go home to at night. Mukhamedov, like many married men, considers himself an equal partner when it comes to looking after the home and baby, and he is certainly the most paternal of men. Nothing is too much for Sasha. In the early days he vowed that nappy-changing was as much a pleasurable duty for him as for his wife. Masha, though, remembers things a little differently, just as she remembers the many decorating projects he instigated around the house that she found herself finishing, and still does today. Mukhamedov, however, will point with pride to the bookshelves in the breakfast room, one job he did see through, while pretending to ignore their pronounced slant.

The house itself, though apparently small from the outside, is large and has been converted from a stable block with considerable discretion. The main living area is spacious and airy; the original byre, still intact, is used for dining, and what was the hayloft is now the guest room. Sasha's domestic requirements are apparently quite demanding. She occupies a room decorated by her parents with animal-covered wallpaper and a full-sized bed, and has an overspill next door for toys. In fact, Sasha's toys are an integral feature of the Mukhamedov household's décor. The only land that went with the house was the front cobbled courtyard, but Mukhamedov quickly discovered that gardening, on whatever scale, was an essential ingredient of the British way of life, and had raised flower-beds installed, which he tends himself. Soon a Wendy house appeared, then a pergola over the small patio, followed by the inevitable barbecue. When Sasha grew and began to play outside, the Honda Civic was banished to the street and the courtyard paving was replaced by grass. The suburban image was complete.

Mukhamedov bought his little family Honda saloon in 1992 and passed his driving test on his second attempt in April 1993. He has survived various brushes with British traffic regulations and systems, such as one-way streets, by brandishing his Russian licence at bemused policemen and claiming in thickly accented tones that he speaks no English. He loves the way the English act on the roads. 'Everyone pretends they are a gentleman,' he says, 'waving graciously to one another while behaving disgracefully. It is a game I enjoy.'

For Masha the process of acclimatisation to a foreign country was not so easy as for her husband. She missed Moscow deeply at first – and ballet. When they first arrived in Britain, Masha had no intention of giving up her career and hoped to join the Royal Ballet with Mukhamedov, as is the normal procedure in Russia, particularly if one of the partners is a leading dancer. As soon as she could after Sasha was born, she began classes at the Royal Ballet School to get back into practice. It soon became clear, however, that it was not to be, following a misunderstanding between the Mukhamedovs and the Royal Ballet administration, and in March 1991 Masha dropped all ideas of instantly resuming her dancing.

It was probably the worst way for a dancer to give up her art. Facing the ageing process is painful enough and even a voluntary retirement can be a traumatic experience, but to feel that the decision is forced on one is almost unbearable. Masha suffered. 'It was like a knife in my heart,' says Mukhamedov, 'when Masha cried about her dancing.' Masha is a very strong young woman, however, and is ferociously devoted to her child and husband. If life at the moment dictates that she fulfil the role of wife and mother, so be it; she will cope with the boredom until some other area of activity presents itself.

As Mukhamedov says, 'Life is not easy, but we didn't come here for an easy life. We came here to be together.'

21

Mayerling, and the Final Link is Severed

In July of 1992 Rasheda and Djavdat made their first journey outside Russia to visit their son and daughter-in-law in London and to see their latest grandchild. Although Mukhamedov was naturally glad to see them, he realised that they would no more be able to understand his life in London than they had appreciated his difficulties in the Bolshoi. When his horrified parents had learned of their son's departure from Russia, they talked to a distinguished local sculptor, the Aga Urmanchi, a very old man but a radical free-thinker. He was convinced that Mukhamedov had done the sensible thing in leaving Russia for the sake of his family in the light of the country's worsening political climate. Urmanchi persuaded Rasheda and Djavdat of the rightness of their son's decision, so there were no recriminations to endure nor was there a need for lengthy justifications. Nevertheless, a gap remained. Rasheda and Djavdat appeared daunted by life in London, and relied on the company of Mukhamedov and Masha to venture outdoors; they got hopelessly lost on at least two occasions when they went out walking on their own. And they refused to call the baby by any name other than the Tartar one, Chulpan. Even so, Mukhamedov considered that he had done his duty.

As soon as his parents had returned to Kazan, Mukhamedov started rehearsals in earnest for what he still believes is the biggest challenge and most successful role he has yet danced in Britain: Crown Prince Rudolf in MacMillan's *Mayerling*. When the ballet was created in 1978, Rudolf was performed by David Wall, one of the most remarkably gifted actor-dancers the Royal Ballet has produced during the past three decades, including Christopher Gable, Wayne Eagling and Stephen Jefferies. The story – as in many of MacMillan's works, a dark one – is an examination of Rudolf, the heir to the Habsburg empire. Driven to the point of madness through syphilis and cocaine, he makes a suicide pact with his mistress, the teenaged baroness Mary Vetsera. Rudolf's self-inflicted death at the age of thirty in 1889 contributed to the instability in Europe that led eventually to World War I.

Mukhamedov at first felt hampered by his inability to read English, since studying books had always been his first task when creating historical figures, such as Spartacus and Ivan the Terrible, and he could not but reflect that he had had four months of preparation for *Spartacus* and only six weeks for *Mayerling*. Although Mukhamedov's spoken English was improving day by day, he and MacMillan had developed an almost telepathic working relationship. If a nuance escaped him, MacMillan elaborated on the character's motives almost before Mukhamedov asked, and if MacMillan thought that the dancer had not grasped a point sufficiently, he would ask Mukhamedov to explain it to him, instead of the other way round, and make Mukhamedov explore the characterisation himself. It is essential to Mukhamedov that his every move and reaction is crystal clear to him before he ventures on-stage. Otherwise, he feels, what chance does the audience have of understanding him?

Rudolf, more than any other character he had yet portrayed, even the mad Ivan, had violent mood swings and a progress through the ballet of such deepening negativity that the dénouement risked leaving the audience admiring Mukhamedov's skill but alienated by Rudolf's callous selfishness. The problem was further compounded by Mukhamedov's natural strength of personality on-stage. How could he persuade the audience that the powerhouse they knew as Mukhamedov had transformed itself into the spineless, vicious wreck that was Rudolf? Part of his solution was mentally to write his own book of the story and put a dialogue under the steps. Mukhamedov explained to himself as he went along the motives that fired each arbitrary tangent the character followed. And the irresistible magnetism of his own personality came into play as it had in *The Judas Tree* when he danced the Foreman, the wretch for whom the audience felt sympathy even as he finally reaped his just deserts and swung from a noose.

If there had been any doubts about Mukhamedov's perfectionism in rehearsals before *Mayerling*, none remained after them. A Russian convention dictates that dancers will stop in rehearsals until they think they have got everything right, while in the Royal Ballet, particularly during stage rehearsals, dancers must continue come hell or high water. Mukhamedov stopped until every finger, turn of the head or pirouette was to his liking. His first working rule is that only by killing yourself in the studio will the audience understand what you do on-stage.

The anticipation before Mukhamedov's début in *Mayerling* was almost more intense than it had been before his first appearance with the Royal Ballet two years previously. All his performances sell out immediately, yet there was an extra frisson in the packed Opera House on 20 October 1992. Masha was in her usual seat in the stalls and Kenneth and Deborah MacMillan were, of course, also in the audience, sitting in the circle. As the performance progressed, it became increasingly obvious that MacMillan had found a great Rudolf in Mukhamedov.

During the second interval MacMillan told his wife he was going backstage for a moment. It was quite common for him to wander about the theatre during performances, but when the last act began and he did not reappear to watch it, Deborah became concerned. She followed her husband to the dressing-rooms, where she learned that he had collapsed shortly before she had arrived and died of a heart attack. He was sixty-three.

Mukhamedov was not told what had happened until after his own death as Rudolf in the ballet. As he prepared for his curtain calls during the epilogue, a deeply distressed Keith Gray took him to a nearby room, sat him down and gave him the dreadful news. Mukhamedov felt that a switch had been thrown and a light had gone out. He was speechless. As he later took his calls in front of a rapturous house, Masha wondered why he was so clearly upset, while the audience assumed he was still portraying the anguish of Rudolf. Jeremy Isaacs's announcement a few moments later of the loss of Kenneth MacMillan, 'one of the very greatest figures in the history of ballet', explained everything.

Masha rushed backstage to comfort her husband, and they both hurried from the theatre, too shocked to think of anything but returning home to Sasha.

Deborah MacMillan was as aware as anyone of how intensely Mukhamedov had enjoyed working with her husband: 'That's what was so sad, because Kenneth was enjoying it too. It probably hastened his death, because he was really working too hard – he was very excited, and he wasn't supposed to get excited. But I'm glad it happened, because he had a very happy last four years, the last two thanks to Irek.

'I'm absolutely certain Kenneth knew the days were very, very limited and I think Irek knew it too and he never mucked up, never wasted time. Kenneth appreciated that. There was never any time wasted, just this constant focused attention.

'My personal feeling is that I am very grateful to Irek that he saw someone that he could really work with. And it's tragic that it's over, because I think the two of them might have done extraordinary things together – a lot of extraordinary things.'

Mukhamedov was deeply depressed following the death of MacMillan, the man with whom he had discovered a creative force more fulfilling than he had ever imagined possible. He felt empty and could no longer see a future. 'Kenneth was a genius,' he said, 'and I will miss working with him for many, many years.' He was worried then that he would not find another choreographer as inspiring as MacMillan, and he is still worried today.

However shocked and thrown off course he felt following MacMillan's death, Mukhamedov had to make his first appearance as Siegfried in the Royal Ballet's *Swan Lake* just over a week later, on 6 November. This was the role that he had never once been allowed to dance in Moscow during his nine years with the Bolshoi, the ballet that had his colleagues rolling about with laughter in the wings when he first appeared with Ljudmilla Semenyaka in Act II in Mexico City in 1984. The phrase 'cardboard prince' was probably coined for this particular character, but Mukhamedov destroyed that misconception at a stroke. His Siegfried, a flesh and blood man, was genuinely heartbroken when he discovered his betrayal of Odette. His final, anguished crawl across the stage to join her in death probed the tragedy of the character with a truth rarely seen in the classical repertoire. Unfortunately, his pairing with Viviana Durante as Odette/Odile was the least successful of their partnership. Her approach to classicism seemed so remote as to render her invisible, while his humanity riveted the eye, creating an imbalance that the ballet could not sustain.

The two and a half years since his arrival in Britain had seen a dazzling series of professional successes for Mukhamedov. His association with Kenneth MacMillan had ended abruptly, but the choreographer had left him two ballets made especially for him, and with him Mukhamedov had discovered creative powers in himself that gave his work a quite new dimension. Equally as important to Mukhamedov as his life in ballet was the fulfilment of the resolve made in Russia to provide a decent lifestyle for his family. They already had a beautiful home and Sasha's name was down at the local school; she was now attending kindergarten and learning English more rapidly than her parents. Masha was achieving an equilibrium, compensating for her disappointed career by her involvement with her husband's and Irek Mukhamedov and Company. She was enjoying slowly decorating their home and developing into a wise and caring mother. But one link with the past remained that was yet to be broken.

The Bolshoi Ballet came to Britain in January 1993, and clearly it would have been childish for Mukhamedov to avoid contact either with the company with which he had won international status or with Yuri Grigorovich. He had never breathed a word of criticism of the company or its director, saying only that that episode of his life was past and buried. But now the past was coming to find him in his new homeland, and he wondered how to handle himself without appearing apologetic or defiant. Grigorovich saw him only as a pliant and willing son, not as an independent artist responsible for his own way of life. Mukhamedov recognised that he had to face up to Grigorovich once and for all in order to truly become his own man. At first he decided he would throw a party for the company at his home and invite Grigorovich, thus demonstrating his new life to them all. Then he changed his mind, deciding that that course of action could be too easily misconstrued as self-justification.

Just a few weeks earlier, in late December, Mukhamedov had spoken to Grigorovich for only the second time since leaving Moscow. He had had last-minute problems finding a partner to appear with him in a performance in Rome, where he was to receive the Gino Tani Award for Dance. The Bolshoi, he discovered, would be in Italy at the same time, and he telephoned Inna Petrova in Genoa, a young principal dancer with the Bolshoi, to ask her to dance the Act

II Adagio from *Giselle* with him at the Teatro Sistina the following week, on Monday 22 December. She was delighted to accept. As they had danced *Giselle* often together during his years with the company, only the minimum of rehearsal would be necessary.

Mukhamedov asked Julia Matheson, then acting as his manager in Britain, to inform the organisers in Rome, and they assumed the formalities with the Bolshoi administration would be completed. Mukhamedov was dancing *Swan Lake* at the Royal Opera House, Covent Garden, on the evening of Saturday 20 December. During final rehearsals Julia told him that she had had a panic-stricken message from Rome saying that Grigorovich wanted to speak to him urgently from his hotel in Genoa. He dashed home and telephoned Italy.

There followed a fairly testy exchange between the two of them, the outcome of which was, as Mukhamedov recalls, that he could not have Petrova in Rome – unless he appeared with the Bolshoi in London. Mukhamedov was furious. His flight was booked to Italy for the following morning, the awards ceremony and gala were only forty-eight hours away and he had no partner. As a result of yet more frantic telephoning, Marion Tait, the leading ballerina of Birmingham Royal Ballet, dashed down to London that night and danced *Giselle* with Mukhamedov in Rome.

Shortly after this skirmish between the two, I interviewed Yuri Grigorovich in Moscow, on the eve of the Bolshoi Ballet's visit to London. With little prompting on my part, he spent some time talking about Mukhamedov and his departure, entirely without rancour. Grigorovich said, 'I could understand him, but it's a pity. It was a difficult time for the theatre . . . and all the time he supported me. He never fought against me. He was always with me – thankful and loyal.

'We never had an open quarrel. I'd like to talk together and sit together. I would see him with pleasure when I am in London.'

There was intense speculation in London at the time as to whether or not Mukhamedov would be asked to dance with his old company during the season, particularly as rumour had it that ticket sales were not as healthy as they should have been. On 9 January, the Bolshoi opened at the Albert Hall and Mukhamedov was still uncertain. The following afternoon Masha telephoned their friend Tamara Finch, as she does nearly every day, and was amazed when Tamara said, 'I've just been talking about you. Yuri Nikolaievich is here . . . '

Luckily, Masha's mother was staying with them, and they were able to leave Sasha in her care and drive the short distance to Tamara's house in Kensington. Mukhamedov remembers Grigorovich's first words as they met: 'Now I will kick somebody's bottom!' 'Why do you say that, Yuri Nikolaievich?' Mukhamedov replied. 'I am not a child.' And the unspoken boundaries were drawn. Everybody hugged everyone else and Mukhamedov's cheeks were soundly pinched. The more Grigorovich told him how much he loved him, the more uncomfortable Mukhamedov felt. Could the man not see that he was no longer the impressionable youth who had fallen under his spell more than a decade ago in Moscow and been flattered and pleased when Grigorovich praised him? He parried Grigorovich's offer to dance with either the Bolshoi or his new group with vague evasions, carefully evaluating everything he said. Eventually Grigorovich asked him why has was so suspicious of him. 'It is my own words that I am checking, not yours,' Mukhamedov answered.

Grigorovich invited the couple to that evening's performance of the Bolshoi Ballet and a few of their former friends were quite openly delighted to see them when they went backstage at the Albert Hall. Mukhamedov and Masha were polite to Grigorovich and Vladimir Kokonin, the general director, but made it clear to everyone that they were there because they wanted to be, not merely at Grigorovich's bidding. There was one awkward moment when, after Mukhamedov had refused a Russian television camera man's request for an interview, he was manoeuvred to stand next to Grigorovich. He saw the Russian filming them both and heard him referring to Mukhamedov as the prodigal son.

Although Mukhamedov was busy preparing for his début in Balanchine's *Apollo* at the Opera House on 21 January, he and Masha attended two performances of the Bolshoi during its London season. They were saddened by the clear evidence they saw of the social and economic collapse in Russia, which was affecting the whole of that country's culture, and now, sadly, the Bolshoi. It seemed to them that the dancers were weighed down with material problems and, instead of feeling free to express the joy of dancing, were concentrating only on the steps while ignoring the spirit. Mukhamedov felt nothing touch his soul. As he watched his former company, with all its echoes of his spectacular professional success and bitter personal failure, guilt and foolishness, he realised that, even if asked again to do so, he could never dance with the Bolshoi. Too much had happened in his life to make such a step back in time anything but meaningless; there had been too much hurt, too much growing away. He knew he was a different creature and also realised that Grigorovich, like his parents, would never see it. He finally accepted this painful reality as the price for taking his own place in the world, and a great weight lifted from his shoulders.

Ironically, while the Bolshoi was at the Albert hall, Mukhamedov danced his first Prince Florimund in *The Sleeping Beauty* at Covent Garden, a part in which he had never appeared in his native Russia. John Percival in *The Times* found a further irony: 'Why is it that Irek Mukhamedov, born and brought up in the USSR, looks entirely at home . . . in *The Sleeping Beauty*, whereas many of the Royal Ballet's men, educated under royal patronage in a monarchy, seem either uncomfortable or too casual [in] this grandest of Imperial Russian creations?' But since the days of Margot Fonteyn that spirit had not been better evoked than in the partnership of Mukhamedov's Prince and Lesley Collier's Aurora. For him it is a tragedy that the age difference between the two of them is too great. Otherwise, they would probably have made that dream partnership so passionately desired by so many.

As the Bolshoi left London in February, Irek Mukhamedov and Company travelled to Bilbao in Spain for a two-night appearance. Mukhamedov finished the 1992–3 season at Covent Garden with his first experience of Baryshnikov's staging of *Don Quixote*, dancing Basilio with Viviana Durante as Kitri. He then performed in two more ballets that were new to him: in the title role of Balanchine's *Prodigal Son* and, opening the new season in October, as Woyzeck in MacMillan's *Different Drummer*.

Mukhamedov is as concerned as everyone else about the drop in the number of his scheduled performances since his arrival in London four years ago, but accepts the reality of the trap that is currently gripping the Royal Opera House. The much publicised financial strictures have forced both a cutback in the number of ballet performances at Covent Garden recently and a reduction in the number of programmes presented annually by the Royal Ballet from twelve or thirteen to eight. A preponderance of the works on view have been the standard classics instead of the newer dramatic works for which the company is so highly regarded and at which Mukhamedov excels. On the other hand, it would hardly seem good business sense not to present a star attraction whenever possible if his name on a poster guarantees a full house. But it is a situation that the Royal Ballet hopes may come to an end as their finances become, if not more healthy, at least less critical.

Both Anthony Dowell and Anthony Russell-Roberts see the next four years of Mukhamedov's presence within the company as as important a chapter in the life of the Royal Ballet as the last. Not only is he a performer of rare power and depth, but his bravura approach to the repertoire has given a much needed competitive edge to the company. And his example as an indefatigable and strictly discip-lined perfectionist in the studio, as well as his down-to-earth manner off the stage, has given a lead to the younger dancers that Dowell feels has been lacking for some time. 'I threw Irek into the company like a spanner in the works,' he says, 'and it has been a success.'

It would be simplistic to say that Mukhamedov's move to Britain has been an easy transition, even for one as adaptable as he, because, although he left Russia behind, he brought his Russianness with him. It is this very quality that makes his appeal so unique, yet occasionally prevents him from fitting as snugly as he would wish into the company – in itself, perhaps, an important element of his contribution to it.

Mukhamedov is probably the last product of the now defunct Soviet system that was theoretically geared to bringing out the best in all its citizens yet, in reality, thrived on privilege and personal preferment. His early development was not constrained by financial burdens, and when he joined the Bolshoi Ballet, it was as Yuri Grigorovich's protégé. He was cradled in the special world that surrounded the powerful director, free to think only of his art, and there were thus no demands on him to be anything but himself. An ideal candidate for a western ballet company – a star without a star complex! But there is a rigid hierarchy in a Russian company that is accepted as a fact of life, and in which Mukhamedov's position at the top was never questioned. Without that support, Mukhamedov sometimes still feels lost.

Today, with the traumas of his early life purged from his system, he can look back with an objective eye on his years in Russia, and can easily acknowledge his gratitude both to Yuri Grigorovich and to the Bolshoi Ballet for all the benefits he gained. But on balance he is in no doubt that he made the correct decision in joining the Royal Ballet, even though his crucial and largely unexpected association with MacMillan ended so prematurely. The richness of its repertoire is a constant source of inspiration to him. He is relieved that he is no longer treated like a little boy; his opinions are sought and listened to by the company's administration. His inclusion in the classical repertoire, he feels, has extended his scope and proved to himself – and the world – that his strict classification as a demi–character dancer from his first days in the Moscow Ballet School was unjustified.

Mukhamedov's insatiable thirst for more and new work has remained undiminished by the years. On 9 February 1994, a month before his thirty-fourth birthday, Irek Mukhamedov and Company made its first London appearance at Sadler's Wells Theatre, in a collaboration with Danish choreographer Kim Brandstrup's Arc Dance Company. Brandstrup created a one-act work, *Othello*, for Mukhamedov, a part that had always attracted him. It was his first foray into modern dance. The season was sold out, but Brandstrup's understated, though beautifully crafted, style did not explore the depth and power of Mukhamedov's talents, and the experiment was not considered the success everybody had hoped for; it was the second half of the programme, a selection of divertissements, that almost inevitably proved the most popular. Due to last-minute cast changes Masha was called upon to perform a Goleizovsky Russian dance and a tango with her husband created for them by Juan Carlos Copes in Argentina, one of that country's leading exponents of the tango. It was the first time she had danced in public since her last appearance at the Bolshoi in Moscow in November 1989.

This is where the future probably lies for Mukhamedov. He relishes the responsibility of pulling together a group of dancers and assembling a programme in which his experience and authority are required to range over wider demands than his individual role in a performance.

Mukhamedov has now conquered two cultures, and his vast knowledge of his art makes it certain that his contribution to the future of ballet will be as broad and significant as that of Nureyev, Baryshnikov or Dowell.

Wherever his professional future may lie, his personal life still roots Mukhamedov in London. He and Masha have made the city their home; they feel comfortable with the place and the people. Sasha's name is now down for a well-known public school, and she is firmly established on the nursery school party circuit. Perhaps the most positive guarantee for her future happiness is not just her parents' devotion to her, but their love for each other. It is scarcely six years since they met again on the beach in Crete, and the tortuous course of their relationship is a best forgotten memory. After years of allowing himself to be dominated by women, Mukhamedov has found trust in Masha. 'With Masha,' he says, 'it is a continuing romance.'

Mukhamedov enjoys being a star in the West, though he considers it a tempting and dangerously sweet fruit for a former Soviet citizen who has been forbidden to taste that success for so long. He is determined that Masha, and particularly Sasha, remember him as a loving husband and father, not as a star.

He has discovered much in the process of examining his life, motives and aspirations for this book and feels that, with Masha's help, he has pinpointed an objective. Ignoring it brought him to the brink of losing everything in Russia, and he must now remain faithful to it for the sake of all their futures – to be honest with himself.

Chronology of Roles and Awards

Irek Mukhamedov's Roles with Moscow Classical Ballet (1978–81)

Ensemble, *Creation of the World*
The Venetian, 'Carnival in Venice' pas de deux from *Saturnilla*
Shepherd, *The Rite of Spring*
Basilio, *Don Quixote* pas de deux
Tybalt, *Romeo and Juliet*
Ali, *Le Corsaire* pas de deux
Romeo, *Romeo and Juliet*
The Wise Man, *Memolyotnosti*
Armen, *Gayaneh*
Acteon, 'Diana and Acteon' pas de deux from *Esmeralda*

Irek Mukhademov's Débuts in Roles with the Bolshoi Ballet in Moscow (1981–90)

4.12.81	Spartacus, *Spartacus*
20.6.82	Basilio, *Don Quixote*
4.11.83	Boris, *The Golden Age*
25.2.83	Ivan, *Ivan The Terrible*
21.4.84	Romeo, *Romeo and Juliet*
30.6.84	Jean de Brienne, *Raymonda*
24.9.86	Albrecht, *Giselle*
31.12.87	The Prince, *The Nutcracker*
25.3.88	Cyrano, *Cyrano de Bergerac*
21.12.88	Lucian, *Paquita Grand Pas*
14.3.89	Ferkhad, *Legend of Love*
13.5.89	Tybalt, *Romeo and Juliet*
28.2.90	Petrushka, *Petrushka*

Irek Mukhamedov's Tours with the Bolshoi Ballet

1981	Turkey	1986	Austria
			Argentina
1982	Czechoslovakia		Brazil
	Poland		England
	Italy		Ireland
			France
1983	Germany		The Netherlands
	Austria	1987	India
			Nepal
1984	Mexico	1988	Italy
	India		Greece
1985	Germany (March)	1989	China
	Poland		France (Paris Opera)
	Germany (May)		Austria (Mukhamedov
	Australia		appeared with the Vienna
	New Zealand		Opera Ballet for the first
	Hungary		time in *Sleeping Beauty*)
	Czechoslovakia	1989/90	France

Irek Mukhamedov's Débuts in Roles with the Royal Ballet (1990–)

1.8.90	'Farewell' pas de deux from *Winter Dreams*
7.11.90	Solor, *La Bayadère*
29.11.90	Jean de Brienne, *Raymonda*
19.12.90	The Prince, *The Nutcracker*
16.1.91	Des Grieux, *Manon*
6.2.91	Lescaut, *Manon*
7.2.91	Vershinin, *Winter Dreams* (première)
6.5.91	Cyrano, *Cyrano*
5.6.91	Andantino Boy, *Les Biches*

24.7.91 Siegfried, *Swan Lake* (Miami)
10.12.91 Colas, *La Fille Mal Gardée*
18.1.92 Albrecht, *Giselle*
19.3.92 The Foreman, *The Judas Tree* (première)
21.7.92 Romeo, *Romeo and Juliet*
24.5.92 Actaeon, 'Diana and Actaeon' (Yokohama)
29.10.92 Rudolf, *Mayerling*
6.11.92 Siegfried, *Swan Lake* (ROH)
21.1.93 Apollo, *Apollo*
1.2.93 The Prince, *Sleeping Beauty*
7.4.93 Basilio, *Don Quixote*
4.6.93 *The Prodigal Son*
23.10.93 Woyzeck, *A Different Drummer*
18.6.94 *Fearful Symmetries*

Guest Appearances by Irek Mukhamedov Since Leaving Russia

1991
April   Hamburg, gala with Darcey Bussell
July   Istanbul/Athens, *Don Quixote* with Royal Ballet of Flanders
            Tokyo, galas with Lyudmilla Semenyaka
October   Oslo, galas with Viviana Durante
November   Paris, gala with Lyudmilla Semenyaka

1993
March   Milan, galas with Alessandra Ferri
March   Australia, *Don Quixote* with Australian Ballet
May   Clermont Ferrand, galas with Isabelle Guerin
August   Buenos Aires, galas with Eleonora Cassano
December   Tokyo, galas with Asya Verzhbinsky
            Sweden, Royal Swedish Ballet

1994
January   Turin, *La Fille Mal Gardée* with Birmingham Royal Ballet

Irek Mukhamedov & Company

First tour 1992

14 April	Derngate Theatre, Northampton
15 April	Apollo Theatre, Oxford
18 April	Alhambra Theatre, Bradford

Second tour 1993

19/20 February	Arriaga Theatre, Bilbao, Spain

Third tour 1994

9–12 February	Sadler's Wells Theatre, London

Awards

1981	Grand Prix, Moscow International Ballet Competition
1985	Honoured Artist of the Russian Federation
1988	Hans Christian Andersen Prize 'For the World's Best Dancer'
1992	*London Evening Standard* Award for Ballet
1993	*Dance and Dancers Magazine* Best Male Dancer
1993	Gino Tani Award for Dance

Index